I0453011

Colonies
in Ruins

EAST ASIA WIT

CHINA

BURMA

LAOS

HAINAN

*S
C*

SIAM

INDOCHINA

CAMBODIA

*ANDAMAN
SEA*

*GULF OF
THAILAND*

Acheh (Atjeh)

MALAYA

Malacca

Sarawak

o *Singapore*

Dutc

SUMATRA

Pladjoe o

DUTCH EAST INDIES

J

Soenda o o *Soebang*
Batavia (Djakarta) o o
8 *Tjiater Pass*
Bandoeng o **JAVA** o *S*
Tjilatjap

KOREA *JAPAN*

MAP AREA

o *Lourenço
Marques*

OLDER NAMES

FORMOSA

H
A

PHILIPPINES

Jesselton
h North Borneo

CELEBES
SEA

neo

o *Celebes*

Hollandia o

DUTCH NEW GUINEA

baja

| 0 | | 500 Miles |

| 0 | | 500 KM |

BY THE SAME AUTHOR

Paradise in Ruins: A Novel (View) of the Pacific War
(historical novel, Author Reputation Press 2019, 376 pages)

Colonies *in* Ruins

Transformed by the Pacific War

ANTYWN PRICE

ARPress
ILLUMINATING IDEAS,
EMPOWERING VOICES

Copyright © 2019 by Antywn Price.

All rights reserved. No part of this publication may be reproduced, distributed, or transmitted in any form or by any means, including photocopying, recording, or other electronic or mechanical methods, without the prior written permission of the copyright owner and the publisher, except in the case of brief quotations embodied in critical reviews and certain other noncommercial uses permitted by copyright law. For permission requests, write to the publisher, addressed "Attention: Permissions Coordinator," at the address below.

ARPress
45 Dan Road Suite 5
Canton MA 02021
Hotline: 1(888) 821-0229
Fax: 1(508) 545-7580

Ordering Information:
Quantity sales. Special discounts are available on quantity purchases by corporations, associations, and others. For details, contact the publisher at the address above.

Printed in the United States of America.

ISBN-13:	Softcover	979-8-89330-292-9
	eBook	979-8-89330-291-2

Library of Congress Control Number: 2024901459

CONTENTS

DEDICATION

This work is dedicated to the gallant soldiers, sailors, and airmen of the multinational American-British-Dutch-Australian (ABDA) Command who, together with civilian Home Guard detachments of the Dutch East Indies, did their very best to defend Java from Japanese invasion forces in early 1942.

Hastily assembled from the remnants of colonial militias, naval, and aviation units; short of supplies and key personnel; unpracticed in joint exercises; many of these brave men and women of ABDACOM lost their lives for a cause made hopeless by the lack of preparedness and political will in their home countries during prior decades.

Stranger, go tell the Spartans
We died here obedient to their commands.
Inscription at Thermopylae

Linger not, stranger; shed no tear;
Go back to those who sent us here.
We are the young they drafted out
To wars their folly brought about.
Go tell those old men, safe in bed,
We took their orders and are dead.

Inscription for a War, by A. D. Hope,
courtesy of the Australian Poetry Library

A SPECIAL NOTE TO
THE READER

Thank you for purchasing *Colonies in Ruins*, a collection of short stories based on historical events that took place in the Asia-Pacific Region before, during, and after World War Two. I hope you find the stories interesting, and that you will be kind enough to leave a review on Amazon to share with others.

However, reading stories full of unfamiliar foreign names is a serious challenge for anybody! It is tempting to simply jump over those names or try to ignore them, but to do so is to deny oneself an understanding of history and geography. A suggestion from someone who has often struggled with this problem, is to pause briefly at each unfamiliar name and break it into syllables, then read it again before proceeding. I sincerely hope that this technique will help clarify these stories about a bygone age and faraway places.

Cordially,

The Author

INTRODUCTION

"If a civilian's house gets blown up in a war, who's to help him rebuild it? Probably not the warring parties."

Peter Perry, *Paradise in Ruins*

Colonies in Ruins: Transformed by the Pacific War is a collection of short stories from here and there, depicting tumultuous events that took place among the prewar colonies of the Asia-Pacific region during their transition through the Second World War to—*Merdeka!*—Independence. While the stories do not include a detailed chronology of the Pacific War battles themselves (although there is a summary of the battles following the End Notes), some of the important actions are discussed in terms of their effect upon individual colonies during the postwar period.

Each major European or American colony had its own unique story to tell, but their many similarities—including social discrimination and denial of individual freedom to the indigenous people—led the author to visualize their prewar histories as if they were scenes from a one-act stage play. This is because the British, French, Dutch and American colonial masters were all trying—feebly and unsuccessfully—to achieve the same goal, the pacification of Japanese aggression.

Similarly, after surviving the war, the indigenous people of each colony were aiming for the same goal—independence!—but with various degrees of success and without much mutual teamwork. Those individual national struggles against fading colonial powers gave rise to another collection of stories, and scenes for a second one-act play. So this is how *Colonies in Ruins* is structured: <u>five prewar scenes, an intermission, and five postwar scenes</u>.

It is ironic that Japan's *Greater East Asia Co-Prosperity Sphere*, a widely promoted scheme intended to liberate all Asian people from foreign colonialism (and in turn subject them to Japanese control), became the spark that eventually brought about true independence for all concerned. Although the Americans had already agreed to grant Independence to the Philippines, the British and French and Dutch fully intended to return to their Asia-Pacific colonies and carry on as if the horrendous war with Japan had not really taken place.

Colonies in Ruins is also a companion to the author's earlier work, *Paradise in Ruins: A Novel (View) of the Pacific War*, a historical novel that dealt with the wider conflict between Allied forces and the Empire of Japan, as experienced by native people and expatriate civilians who were caught up in the mighty naval, land, and air battles that eventually convinced Japan to surrender.

Although Japan was thereby subdued, and peace returned to the Asia-Pacific region in August 1945, it was only a temporary peace. This book, *Colonies in Ruins,* looks at postwar upheavals in the British, French, and Dutch colonies of SE Asia that began soon after the American warriors— apart from garrisons in Japan, Guam and the Philippines—went back home to their families.

This early postwar period also saw the rise of Communism in Asia, a rival force that likewise aimed to banish European colonialism but was determined to plant Communist governments in their place. Nationalist China, a WWII ally of the European powers, fought against Communism but eventually lost in 1949 to the Peoples Republic of China. Similar Communist threats appeared in Malaya, Indonesia, the Philippines, Korea, and Indochina, some of which succeeded.

The author was a boy growing up in Singapore, Java, Canada, and Australia as the gathering war clouds burst forth. Some of this book's material is gleaned from his own recollections, while other pieces of the fascinating puzzle were gathered from prewar residents of the region through their published memoirs or by personal interviews. Additional sources were business acquaintances in the Asia-Pacific region as time went on, or people who had been refugees during the war. A recent addition came from the daughters of a Dutch plantation manager who had worked for the same organization in Java as the author's English father, P&T Lands. Another recent source was an English friend whose parents formed the basis of JJ and Janice Howell's adventures in Scene I.

Very little of this lost colonial history is generally known in the United States, so hopefully US readers will find *Colonies in Ruins* to be fresh and intriguing material. To assist with geography, some historical maps and photos are provided throughout the book, and custom-designed reference maps of the Pacific Region can be found at the very beginning and the very end of the book, the former using prewar names for the countries and cities, and the latter using modern names. By means of these maps, the author hopes that geography may become a favorite subject for at least some of the readers.

Following this **Introduction** there is a **Prologue** that examines the curious rise of twentieth-century Japanese militarism and Japan's self-imposed isolation from Western nations. The Prologue is followed by **Ten Main Scenes** (chapters) divided by a somewhat fanciful **Intermission.** Some fictional stories in these scenes are based upon actual historical happenings, while other stories are historically accurate as stated.

Each of the first five (prewar) scenes and the Intermission begin with a brief historical preface, upon which their ongoing stories are based. The beginning and end of each preface is identified by the *Yin-Yang* symbol shown below. If historical background is of interest to the reader, those short prefaces will provide useful information to help interpret the ongoing stories, but if the reader is more interested in the human dimension, then the prefaces could be omitted without a significant impact on the stories themselves.

PROLOGUE

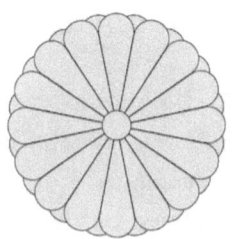

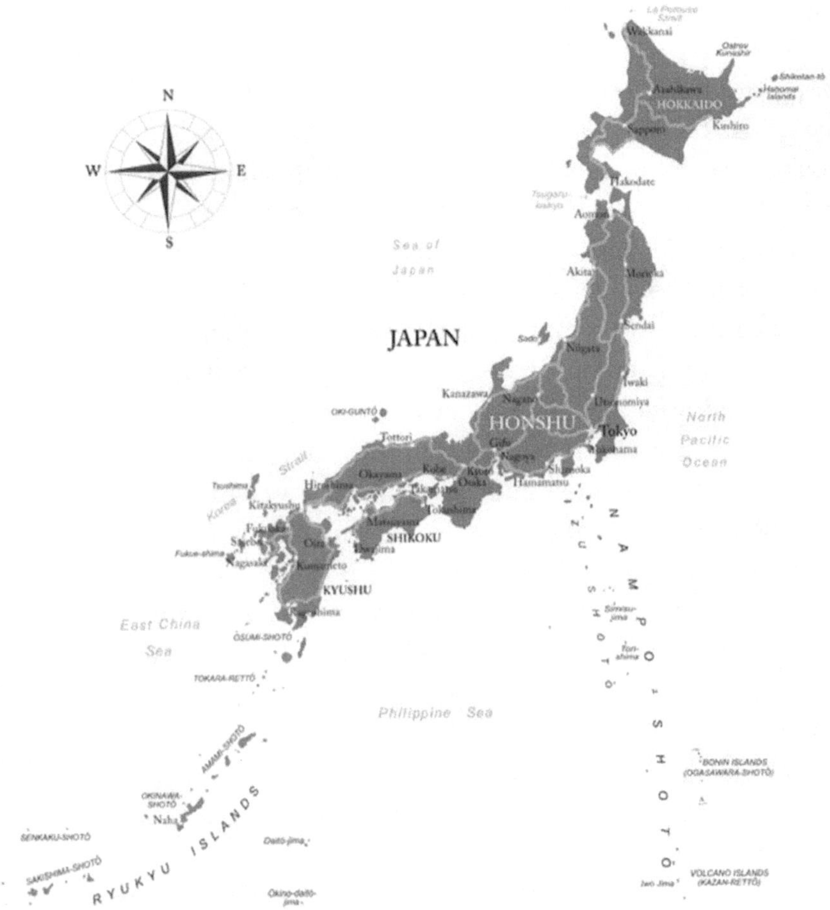
N
W
E
S
Sea of Japan
JAPAN
HOKKAIDO
Asahikawa
Sapporo
Kushiro
Hakodate
Akita
Sendai
Sado
Kanazawa
HONSHU
Tokyo
Iwaki
North Pacific Ocean
OKI-GUNTŌ
Tottori
Okayama
Kobe
Nagoya
Hamamatsu
SHIKOKU
KYUSHU
Tsushima
Korea Strait
Fukue-shima
East China Sea
ŌSUMI-SHOTŌ
TOKARA-RETTŌ
Philippine Sea
AMAMI-SHOTŌ
OKINAWA-SHOTŌ
Naha
SENKAKU-SHOTŌ
SAKISHIMA-SHOTŌ
RYUKYU ISLANDS
Daitō-jima
Okino-daitō-jima
NAMPO-SHOTŌ
IZU-SHOTŌ
BONIN ISLANDS (OGASAWARA-SHOTŌ)
VOLCANO ISLANDS (KAZAN-RETTŌ)
Iwo Jima

*** *THE MIKADO* ***

At the time of young Emperor Hirohito's ascendency to the Chrysanthemum Throne in December 1926, it was still the Japanese people's belief that his imperial household was descended from heaven and that individual emperors were personally anointed by the gods upon their ascension to the throne.

Perhaps the long succession of ancestral emperors also believed this about themselves, but in case they did not they were schooled throughout their youth in all manner of Japanese customs, rules, and protocols, so that they could unflinchingly deal with any crisis or calamity with an appropriate and expected response.

Prince Hirohito (1901-1989) was the first such heir to the throne who was permitted to leave Japan and go abroad to politely observe firsthand the goings-on of European leaders during a 1921 tour. This tour was no doubt inspired by the noble cause of Peace that followed the Great War of 1914-18, a universal yearning for which had resulted in the formation of the League of Nations, to which Japan became a member.

Upon his return home, the twenty-year-old Royal Prince was thoroughly debriefed, and—in case he had become intrigued by any peculiar Western ideas—he was firmly reminded of the comparative disadvantage that all other world leaders faced without access to the stabilizing platform of Japanese history and tradition, a platform that stretched back in time for at least two thousand five hundred years, so it was surmised.

But it remained quite difficult for ordinary Japanese citizens, and for nearly all foreign observers—however skillful—to discern whether Japanese Emperors, with the power of all heaven reportedly at their disposal, were indeed the nation's ultimate rulers, or merely a series of programmed automatons, bedecked in the musty trappings and speech patterns of antiquity.

Would the Emperor control his ministers, or would the ministers control the Emperor? This was the question which other nations inevitably pondered.

Tenno (Son of Heaven) was the usual title used by Japanese to refer to their emperors, but an alternate name was *Mikado,* meaning 'Occupant of the Royal Palace,' i.e. the Royal Incumbent. For the young, confident, and newly installed Emperor Hirohito a few years after his return from Europe, who had already served two years as regent for his ailing father Yoshihito, there could surely have been no doubt in his mind about who was in charge, when at every snap of his fingers there was someone at hand to do his bidding. From 1926, when his reign was given the designation Showa (Bright Peace), Japanese calendars began to count the years accordingly: Showa-1 was 1926, Showa-2 was 1927, and so on. The new Mikado must have been supremely confident in his authority at that time.

To many outside observers—even among the English, who liked to belittle empires smaller than their own—there had been serious doubts in the 1930s about who controlled Japan, considering its persistent aggression in China and Korea. English newspaper readers—influenced, no doubt, by the amusing and hugely popular Gilbert and Sullivan operetta *The Mikado*—may have assumed that Japan was led by a quaint Imperial Paradox who was probably harmless, but the more astute among them felt that the truth lay otherwise.

China and Korea certainly knew otherwise, and there were even graver doubts in Russia, whose naval fleet had been defeated by the Japanese in 1905 at the Battle of Tsushima during the reign of Japan's Meiji Emperor, grandfather of the new Showa incumbent. This shocking defeat of a European power by an Asian nation is considered by some to be the spark that lit the fire of revolution in Russia, and generated a similar yearning for independence among the Asia-Pacific colonies.

After defeating the Russian fleet, Japan abruptly took control of the railway linking Russia and China and began stationing troops in those parts of China's Manchuria region over which the expensive steel tracks lay. The troops were there ostensibly to provide railway security, but they were also the genesis of a formidable Japanese military machine—the Kwantung Army, as it came to be called—that soon set about making war with China.

In 1917, Russia experienced a great social upheaval—including the crude execution of the Czar and his entire family—and began exporting the ideologies of Communism and World Revolution. The new Bolshevik leaders allowed Japan to continue running the Russian end of the railway, but also held grave doubts about Japan's long-term intentions.

At the other end of the line, China's own doubts about Japan were, of course well founded. In 1895, Japan had coerced the Empress Dowager of China into ceding them the large Chinese-and-Malay-populated island of Taiwan (known in the west as Formosa), as payment for damages allegedly suffered by Japan during the First Sino-Japanese War of 1894-5 (that had actually been instigated by Japan).

In 1910, a short-lived Empire of Korea—which Japan had been trying for some time to control as a protectorate—lost any doubts about Japanese intentions when the Mikado's troops forcibly took over the entire Korean peninsula. Was this the Meiji Emperor at work, or an even more sinister force, the Koreans wondered? The northern border of Korea was conjoined at the Yalu River with Manchuria, a neighboring territory that had conquered China centuries before to establish China's final imperial lineage, the Manchu—or *Qing (Ch'ing)*—Dynasty that lasted until the Republic of China was formed in 1912.

In 1931, early in Japan's Showa regime, renegade Japanese troops of the Kwantung Army in Manchuria staged an incident designed to appear as though Chinese bandits had attacked the railway, causing Japanese troops to dutifully respond. The world readership saw Japanese reaction to the Mukden Incident, as it was known, blossoming rapidly into a takeover of the entire Manchurian territory. Japan soon declared the occupied region to be an independent nation called Manchukuo, separate from China and, of course, under Japanese protection. To give this puppet state a veil of legitimacy, Japan installed former imperial Manchu heir Pu-Yi, the Last Emperor of China—who had been out of a job since the Chinese revolution of 1911—as titular head of government for Manchukuo.

Was Showa content to have this fellow emperor become the public face of Manchukuo? Almost certainly.

Korea and Manchukuo thus became unwitting Japanese colonies—joining Formosa that Japan had coerced from China in 1895. All this conflict, in the opening half of the twentieth century, brought about the first real test of the League of Nations since its formation after the Great War. Upon careful investigation by its representatives, the League ruled in favor of China and against Japan's intrusion into Manchuria. Japan's angry response was to withdraw from the League in 1933—and to retain control of Manchukuo.

The United States of America, whose audacious Commodore Matthew Perry had been responsible for opening Japan to Western trade in 1854, became concerned about Japan's withdrawal from the League of Nations, and by Japan's rumored militarization of former German island-territories in the Pacific Ocean. Oversight of those islands had been awarded to Japan by a League of Nations mandate after Germany's defeat in the Great War. The collection included the Marianas (less Guam), the Carolines, the Marshalls, and the Palaus. What was one to make of all this erratic and aggressive behavior by Japan, the State Department wondered?

And what was the *Greater East Asia Co-Prosperity Sphere* all about? News had filtered back to the US that this new Japanese concept and organization had been founded by an anti-war philosopher named Miki Kiyoshi, yet other sources said the Co-Prosperity Sphere was being promoted by militant Japanese ministers like Tojo Hideki, and actively touted in Japanese-controlled places like Korea and Manchukuo by the army itself. What a confusing situation!

It was even said that the Japanese Emperor himself was quite enthralled by the Co-Prosperity concept and had appointed several young army officers as his personal emissaries to the peoples of East Asia. Did that mean the Emperor was a militant leader and empire builder, or just an idealist who wanted to free Asia from colonial domination by the West?

Stay tuned: these stories will explain what happened.

ACT I

The Status Quo

Scene One

British Malaya And Singapore

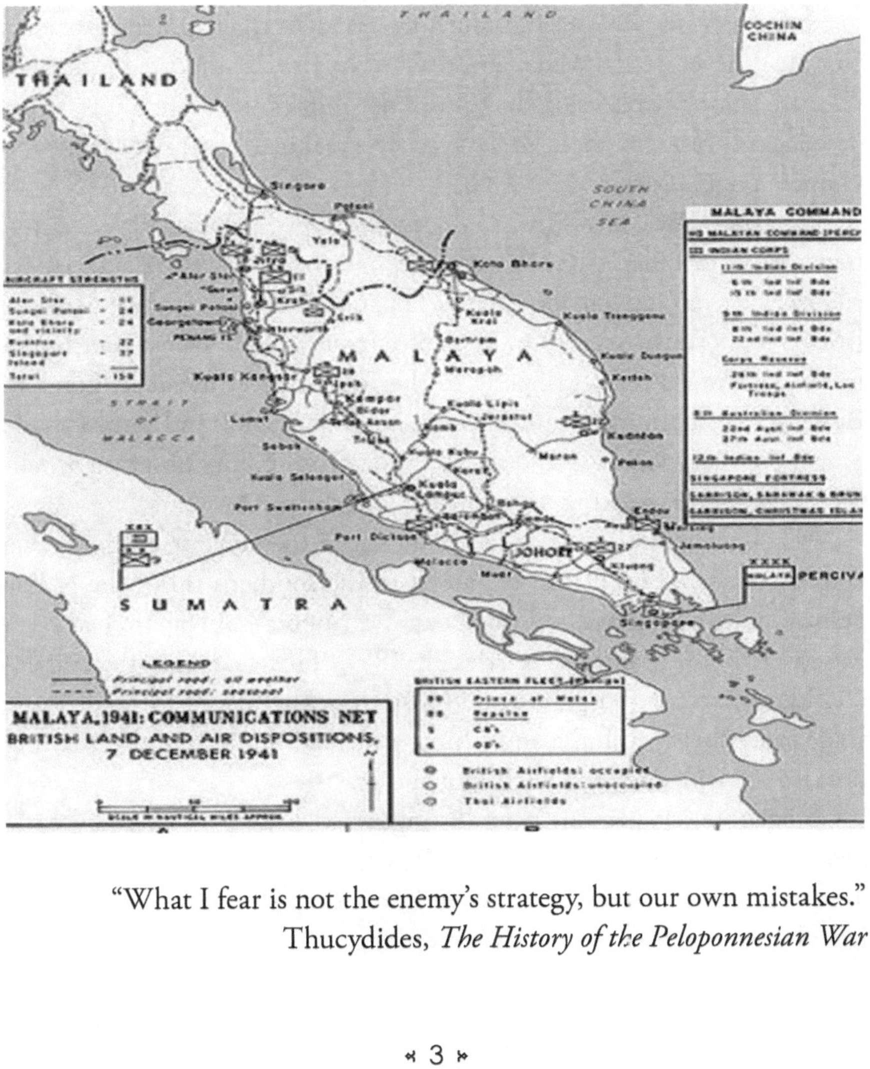

"What I fear is not the enemy's strategy, but our own mistakes."
Thucydides, *The History of the Peloponnesian War*

 Malaya was not considered (by the British at least) to be a colony, but a protectorate instead (there's that term again). Individual states on the Malay Peninsula were classified as Federated or Unfederated and both were nominally ruled by sultans who had authority over matters of Malay or Islamic custom. Malaya was a large Muslim region like much of that part of the world, the result of Arab traders, centuries before, whose proselytizing had supplanted the earlier Hindu and Buddhist beliefs.

Each Federated Malay State had a British Resident who was theoretically an assistant to the Sultan, but had centralized control over export commodities, chiefly tin and rubber. The Unfederated States chose to have just a few British advisors and much less modern development. Arduous work had never been a Malay priority, so the British imported legions of Chinese laborers to develop the various new mines and plantations. Their descendants brought about today's nearly equal mix of ethnic Malay and Chinese populations.

Singapore, by contrast, was a highly developed colonial city-state and port which, together with Malaya's offshore island of Penang and coastal city of Malacca (and less-important Labuan in N. Borneo), comprised the British Straits Settlements, an opulent Crown Colony whose Singapore-based governor reported directly to the British government in London. Branches of many powerful London trading houses and banks made Singapore their domicile, and the expatriate community observed a well-established social pecking order throughout the prewar years.

A balmy island just thirty miles north of the equator, being in due course connected by British engineers to the southern tip of the Malay Peninsula by a road and rail causeway (next photo), Singapore had been 'discovered' by Stamford Raffles in 1819. This feat brought Raffles considerable fame and gave Britain a strategically placed toehold in the trade routes between India and China, a toehold that was also a listening post on the fringe of the Dutch East Indies.

Singapore island's one-time distinguished history in the very early centuries of the Common Era (CE), when the island was known as Temasek, had somehow transitioned into a deep sleep under the care of Malay custodians, until Raffles came along.

During the years that followed the Great War—or the First World War as it was later known—the British Straits Settlements brought unparalleled prosperity to its local and expatriate residents, and to its offshore investors. Penang, Malacca, and Singapore were all free ports without inward or outward tariffs, thereby attracting many shipping lines and banks to set up their Pacific regional headquarters. This successful duty-free model was also used for establishing the British Crown Colony of Hong Kong on the Chinese mainland, some three decades later.

Prosperity brought about a steady enhancement in civil infrastructure for Singapore, and a burgeoning population growth in skilled labor and management. During the 1920s and '30s, the docks and roads were in good order, the tap water was drinkable, and the entertainment was plentiful and varied. It was a prestigious job posting for adventurous families from Britain, who brought along with them their cherished customs and traditions—and prejudices.

Enjoying competitive sports was one facet of British expatriate life that quite often left the local population puzzled and amused. Living near the equator all their lives, most locals tended to conserve energy and seek shade from the tropical sun wherever possible. Not so the Europeans who were put in charge of things. Brought up in the competitive British or Continental

European school systems and social orders, newly-arrived expatriate managers and engineers invariably sought out—or formed—sporting clubs

Rowers at St Andrew's Cathedral, 1933 – Doris Pickering photo

that were also social venues. Thus, the Royal Singapore Yacht Club, for example, would hold monthly dances, and maintain an open bar and eatery during the week with formal dining on weekends and holidays, providing billiards and other table games to its members and their families—all this in addition to the core business of racing or cruising various classes of yachts.

There were likewise rugby and cricket clubs, bowling clubs, rowing clubs, tennis clubs, horse racing clubs, and so on, to keep their members entertained and fit. Seldom were local people invited to join these clubs, however, although the racial barriers were beginning to fall shortly before the Second World War began.

Some other colonial clubs were mainly social and not sports-centric, such as the exclusive Tanglin Club in Singapore which top government and business leaders were invited to join. These 'posh' clubs were not open to local people even after the war had ended, and it is said that Lee Kwan Yew, the Republic of Singapore's first prime minister after post-war independence, had been denied membership in the Tanglin Club, much to the club's later shame and sorrow.

*** SIGNS OF WAR ON THE HORIZON ***

Although the 1929 US stock market crash had caused economic chaos for most of the world, the Far East colonies for the most part were not greatly affected during the 1930s. The regional prosperity of the East tended to insulate colonial governments and businesses from the friction and stress in Europe and elsewhere. This was the *status quo* that was soon to be undone.

The stage was being set in Germany for events that would soon erupt into a holocaust and engulf the African and Asian colonies as well. An obscure veteran of the Great War, Adolf Hitler, after a decade of political agitation and manipulation, was appointed Chancellor in 1933 in an effort by German industrialists to appease his militant Nazi Party. Instead of Hitler's expected cooperation, however, the Nazi Party continued its civil disobedience and disruption of German politics, until it eventually removed all traces of democracy in Germany. Its Trump Card was the so-called 'Crystal Night' rampage in Berlin by mobs of Nazi supporters bent on riot and destruction.

Upon the death of President Hindenburg in 1934, Hitler assumed the full powers of a dictator and began to take revenge on the forces that he had constantly blamed for Germany's—and his own—post-war humiliation. A main target for Hitler's wrath was the Treaty of Versailles, which had forced Germany to pay reparations to countries damaged by German wartime aggression. His other main target was the entrenched Jewish population, which he loathed and intended to systematically exterminate.

By 1935, signs of hostilities in Europe had begun to concern the British government, resulting in a gradual militarization of Singapore and Malaya to defend against German 'Commerce Raider' warships that were preying on the maritime commercial shipping routes of the Pacific region. When on 30 August 1939 Germany invaded Poland and war broke out between Europe's various military alliances, the arming of Singapore was stepped up to include large-caliber coastal guns for the navy.

After Germany, Italy, and Japan signed their Tripartite Pact in September 1940, alarm finally began to register in Singapore and other allied colonies, but further efforts at militarization were to prove too little, too late.

*** *AN EXPATRIATE FAMILY* ***

Living with his family in a comfortable two-story home at the shore of MacRitchie Reservoir, English civil engineer Peter Perry was a middle-management expatriate who had gone out to Singapore in 1928 as a bachelor. He returned in 1931 after his first six-month home leave, newly married to Wendy Joules of Jersey. Their son John was born in Singapore a few years later and was their only child, the worldwide depression of the 1930s having discouraged larger families.

Close to six feet in height and smooth-shaven, brown-haired Peter Perry was trim and athletic and quite competent at rowing and rugby football, having been the captain of both sports for the Monmouth School in Wales in his younger days. Wendy, by contrast, was not much interested in competitive sports, although she occasionally had a go at tennis with some of the other wives among their circle of Singapore friends, and she grew to love their little sailing dinghy named *Sloopy* that was stored in a shed with other small boats at the RSYC—the Royal Singapore Yacht Club off Trafalgar Street.

What had most attracted Peter to Wendy—apart from her green eyes and ready smile—was her wide knowledge of things international, which came from an upbringing in the Channel Islands of Jersey, Guernsey, and Sark. Peter was intrigued that she and her family were equally comfortable with the lifestyle and customs of France and England, whereas his own view of the world was largely the product of a Welsh border town and the industrial city of Manchester.

Wendy's sophisticated conversation skills lent her a certain mystique that fascinated Peter, who would otherwise have been quite content with the companionship of fellow engineers and sportsmen. Peter represented for Wendy an escape from the tedium of her recently-acquired teaching job at Ipswich in England—which had in turn been an escape from the nuns at the Catholic boarding school on Jersey where her socially-active parents had placed her (Wendy's mother, nicknamed 'Gypsy', was a strikingly beautiful socialite on the quest for eternal youth, who on occasion would introduce Wendy as her sister rather than her daughter).

Wendy also saw in Peter the chance to experience an even wider world than that of Europe, albeit from the comfort of a colonial lifestyle that took the raw edge off the Mysterious Orient. She fell in love with Singapore at once and was thrilled with their first city home in the Tanglin district, where she and Peter would live for several years in blissful harmony. When an eventual pregnancy began to curtail her activities, Wendy was evermore grateful for her expatriate support system, and had an easy time of the delivery at Cairnholm Private Hospital where John was born in 1935.

A year later, the Municipality of Singapore awarded Peter a larger home for both his expanded family and his elevated engineering responsibilities. The new residence at the edge of Singapore's main reservoir, was located near the village of Bukit Timah.

By 1940, the Perry household included a *syce* (driver), a cook, an *amah* (to watch over John), and a married couple who cleaned house and cared for the ample grounds that sloped down a gentle hill to the chain-and-post shore of the reservoir. Staff members lived in a one-story row of rooms attached perpendicularly to the main house, that included the household kitchen. All but the Malay *syce* were straits-born Peranakan Chinese who preferred—male and female—to wear Malay sarongs for working, which were much cooler than typical Chinese or Western attire.

The Perry automobile, a sporty two-seater Morris roadster (into which young John was squeezed when the family went touring by themselves on weekends), was normally parked at the main entrance to the home beneath its *porte-cochère*. The *syce* would drive Peter to the office on weekday mornings, then return to the residence in case Wendy had appointments with her friends or wished to go shopping.

By late afternoon, Wendy having returned home, the *syce* would be off again to retrieve Peter from his office, or from a job site such as another reservoir or water treatment plant, for Peter was—with twelve years on the job—the chief water engineer for Singapore, having replaced the former incumbent Alan Rees, who had resigned and gone to Java two years previously for a similar but more lucrative position in that Dutch colony.

Peter was thereby responsible for the equipment and infrastructure that provided Singapore households with potable water and the treatment of household waste. He was also responsible for the three reservoirs and their catchment areas that were, by 1941, scarcely able to supply the island with enough water for a steadily growing population, especially during the dry season.

Alan Rees, like Peter Perry, had been worried about the water shortage problem and had proposed to the governor that Singapore should consider sourcing water from the neighboring Malay state of Johore, where larger catchment areas could be developed. As 1941 unfolded and Alan had left for Java, nothing had been done in that regard, mostly due to a lack of government-approved investment funds.

The Perry family named their new Singapore home *The Lake*, it being the custom in England and Wales to bestow names rather than numbers on semi-rural dwellings. *The Lake* on MacRitchie Reservoir was several miles away from the City Center, the principal business district where he worked. Peter found that he was having to leave home earlier and earlier as time went on, due to increased road traffic between Bukit Timah township and the City. At times he longed for their first bungalow that was a mere half mile from his office on the Padang, but the peace and solitude of *The Lake* on weekends lulled him into agreement with Wendy that their present situation was a better one overall.

"The Lake" Singapore 1935 – photo H. Price

Peter's city office was in the Municipal Building at the inland side of a rectangular, evergreen, and carefully tended field known as the Padang, which was (and still is) the main assembly and sports field for Singapore. The Municipal Building (today's City Hall) was in turn flanked by the colony's elegant Supreme Court. At the shorter ends of the Padang rectangle, the Cricket and Tennis Clubs faced one another, and not far away from the latter stood Saint Andrew's Cathedral, built in 1856 by convict labor, where members of the expatriate community gathered on Sundays to thank their Anglican God in Heaven for His bountiful munificence.

At the seaward side of the Padang, opposite the Municipal Building and Supreme Court, there were no buildings at all. Instead, a thoroughfare called Beach Road ran along a somewhat sandy shore. Another five hundred yards down the road from the Padang, beyond the Cathedral, stood a comfortable three-story lodging called the Raffles Hotel, which boasted a lovely Palm Court for lunching and an amazingly long and very popular inside bar that could, from time to time, quench a thirsty horde of Padang-event spectators seeking relief in a Gimlet or Gin Sling. The Long Bar, as it was known far and wide, could also enliven weekend dances held at the hotel ballroom. Founded in 1887 by Armenian investors, the Raffles Hotel was a world-famous Singapore watering hole in pre-war colonial days and has been ever since (despite modernization).

*** *P&T LANDS* ***

Back at the MacRitchie Reservoir, roughly two hundred yards away from *The Lake* stood another vintage residence of similar proportions that had previously been the residence of the Rees family before they left for Java, both homes having been built in the heyday of the late 1880s. The other home's more recent—but temporary—occupants, a Dutch family from Java, had been the Perry's neighbors for nearly a year, having been sent from Java to Singapore by Alan Rees. Their amazingly bilingual little blond-haired son Bart was a bit older than John Perry, and the families often got together for walks around the reservoir or horseback rides, for both homes possessed stables and a pair of thoroughbred geldings.

The Dutch family, surnamed Van Noorden, was in Singapore to learn how the island's excellent water treatment and purification systems were designed, maintained, and operated, so as to duplicate them in a certain region of Dutch Java. Their fact-finding presence in Singapore was funded by a large British-owned plantation complex on Java called P&T Lands that dated back to the early 1800s when Stamford Raffles was Lieutenant Governor of Java under British custodianship during the Napoleonic Wars of Europe.

Ronald van Noorden had been born in Java, but after secondary school he was educated in the Netherlands at the highly respected University of Leiden. There he met and married his pretty wife Corrie after a whirlwind courtship that was amply stimulated by Corrie's flirtatious manner. Her father was a Dutch colonel of cavalry, who not long before Ron and Corrie's 1933 wedding, had retired the regiment's beloved horses to green pasture and adopted a clanking array of light tanks in their place. It was perhaps in subliminal imitation of her father's aggressive nature that Corrie developed a tendency to charge after every goal that caught her attention. The pursuit of Ron van Noorden was but her latest foray into military tactics once she had recognized that the tall colonial engineering student with his dry sense of humor and international background was just the mate she had been waiting for. With her father's blessing after a man-to-man evening of brandy and soda, she and Ron were married in the military chapel at his regimental post.

Unlike Wendy, who had delayed motherhood for several years after marrying Peter in 1931, Corrie—the youngest of three sisters—was eager to present her father with a male heir, which her siblings had been unable to do. Accordingly, she managed to get pregnant—and quite ill—during the ocean voyage from Rotterdam to Batavia, thereby developing a strong dislike for passenger ships as a form of transportation. It was a huge relief to Corrie when Bart was born in the Soebang hospital just three months after Ron had taken a job with P&T Lands that he had found while they were staying in Batavia with his parents.

P&T Lands included twenty or more large plantation estates—some run by English managers, others by Dutchmen—producing indigo, cacao, rubber, sugar, coffee, tea, pineapples, and many other such valuable market commodities. Each individual estate had developed its own rudimentary water system over the years, some using Jewell Filters for partial purification but most others being more basic. The P&T directors, at the urging of Alan Rees, had agreed to modernize and centralize all their water production, distribution, and treatment, with Singapore's help. Considering that the area of the combined P&T estates on Java was about the same as the entire island of Singapore, but with more complex terrain, this was likely to be a formidable task.

Ron Van Noorden would eventually be returned from Singapore as the P&T water engineer for their planned centralized network of reservoirs, pumping stations and sewage plants, where Alan Rees—with nearly a decade of former experience in Singapore—was now the company's head engineer. Alan and his wife resided in Soebang, the company headquarters town, as did P&T Managing Director Charles Jackson with his wife Daphne. Soebang is where the Van Noordens would be stationed as well, when they returned to Java in 1942.

Peter had learned from Alan that the holding company for P&T Lands—whose directors resided not in Soebang, but in Batavia and London—was called Anglo-Dutch Plantations of Java Ltd. It seemed to Peter a much more dignified and international name than P&T Lands.

*** A NEW ASSIGNMENT ***

News of the war in Europe was becoming worse and worse, thought Peter Perry's wife Wendy, as June 1941 arrived. She was quite worried for her parents, who had been living under German occupation in the Channel Islands since July of 1940. Although the occasional reassuring letter did manage to reach Wendy in Singapore via an unpredictable network of neutral countries, she knew that the regular inhabitants of those little islands must be feeling hardships.

And now Peter had come home from the office with what sounded to Wendy like more upsetting news. He had been appointed by Singapore's governor to assist the American army at a remote Pacific island called Canton, and what was worse, he was not permitted to bring his wife and son with him on the new assignment.

"Darling, it will just be for a few months, they say, and you'll be much more comfortable here at home than you will with me in some fly-ridden tent or one of those American Quonset huts."

Wendy was not convinced. "Peter, I won't mind the flies as long as we can be together with John as we always have been. Besides, you know that I love being on passenger ships, and perhaps we'll stop at some other islands along the way."

"Ha, well I doubt you'll enjoy being up in the air! I'm not going there by ship; y'see; there aren't any that go from here to there. No, I'll be flying on one of those Pan American seaplanes that have been coming here over the past year—thankfully we won't be paying for it! —and I'll come back here the same way, which will make my absence all that much shorter. They want me to install and test a desalination and purification system for the Pan Am station and a few soldiers, which should take three months at most. I've installed several of those small systems in Malaya already, just without the 'de-sal' module that the Americans require for converting saltwater into fresh. It should be a snap to do this on tiny Canton Island, Wendy, with lots of help available."

Wendy was still doubtful but tried not to interrupt Peter, occasionally dabbing her eyes with a crumpled handkerchief.

"Now please don't fuss about it, dear," Peter continued, "I really don't have a choice in the matter. I'll ask Ron and Corrie to keep a Dutch eye on you and John, and everything will be all right—you know that. Besides, I won't be leaving until early August and that's still a long way off. We'll definitely have time for our little driving trip and holiday in Malacca."

"Yes, I suppose you're right as always," Wendy conceded with a long sigh, "but what about the war situation? What if it spreads out here to the Pacific while we're separated? We both know that our army friends are worried about Japan these days and are bringing in more soldiers and guns and things."

"That's true, they are," Peter answered, giving Wendy a kiss, "but that's just to convince the Japs not to try anything silly over here. They'd have a huge mess on their hands if they tried to take on our Singapore and Malayan forces, plus the Americans, the Australians, and the Dutch. I believe the Japs are smarter than that, don't you? Come, let's drop in on the Van Noordens and see if they'd like to take a walk around the reservoir with us this lovely evening. Bart has a new dog of some sort that John has been wanting to see. Hmm, I can't really pronounce it, but the breed is spelled 'k-o-o-i-k-e-r-h-o-n-d-j-e', according to Ron. He showed me a photo, and the dog looks something like a Spaniel, brown and white. Gad, whoever invented Dutch spelling must have been drunk!"

"Now, now, Peter, that's not at all nice," Wendy laughed. "All right, let's take John to meet Mr. Dutch Spaniel."

When August came, after a fascinating visit to the ancient city of Malacca on the wide waterway that separated Malaya from Dutch

Sumatra—where the Perrys learned that Malacca had been a Chinese city in ancient times, then Portuguese in the fifteenth century, Dutch in the sixteenth, and finally British in the eighteenth—the day that Wendy had been dreading finally arrived. Peter would depart for Canton Island on August 10th.

Watching tearfully as Peter's huge Pan American seaplane departed eastward from Keppel Harbor with the great roar of four powerful engines amid a mass of frothy water, bound for Manila in the Philippines, Wendy was afterwards surprised to learn that his flight would eventually end up in Hawaii following more refueling stops at Guam and Midway islands, places that she had never even heard of.

She had certainly heard of Hawaii, though, and envisioned Peter enjoying himself with a troupe of hula dancers or carousing with American tourists. Although she was told by the ticket office that he would board another Pan Am flight westbound from Hawaii to Canton Island, she had forgotten to ask how soon it would be before that second flight left Hawaii: a day? a week?

It wasn't fair that some faceless American bureaucrat could press a button and take away her husband just like that, with the connivance of Singapore's governor, Sir Shenton Thomas. Wendy had a good mind to telephone Lady Thomas and complain but thought better of it after another glass of sherry. Instead, she went to John's room to read him a book, which ironically was about the Boy Scouts in places like America and Canada.

The following days became weeks and then months. Wendy and Peter wrote to each other regularly as it became clear that Peter would not be back home by December, which Wendy had feared all along. Meanwhile Singapore's peaceful way of life faded away as more and more military and naval uniforms were seen on the streets and at social events. Japan was spoken of more often and with heightened apprehension, especially after Singapore's Japanese residents gradually disappeared.

*** *CONFUSION IN SINGAPORE* ***

Placed on full alert in Singapore and Malaya after an RAAF Lockheed Hudson had reported a large Japanese fleet at sea in the Gulf of Siam on

December 6, the British high command was reviewing its options for the second day in a row.

In charge of Allied ground forces was Lt. General Arthur Percival, while the air force and overall military was commanded by Air Chief Marshal Robert Brooke-Popham, who was quite close to retirement and known to doze off occasionally in meetings, which he showed signs of doing at the precise moment that General Percival was again addressing the group of a dozen officers:

"Because a state of war with Japan has not actually been declared," the general intoned, "we commanders have no authority over the civilian population of Singapore, which is free to pursue its usual activities at night, such as attending a film or enjoying itself at the outdoor food courts and dance clubs. Is that understood?"

Everyone nodded drowsily, for the evening meeting had gone on for three hours already, and it was well known by everyone present that Singapore town was lit up like daylight during those pleasant December evenings. Moreover, the colonial governor and his wife, Sir Shenton and Lady Marguerite Thomas, felt it their duty to appear as often as possible at public functions, to dispel doubts on the part of the populace that Singapore might soon be under threat. These activities by the governor rather annoyed General Percival, who was quite certain that Singapore was soon to be under quite serious threat, but in matters to do with the civilian population the governor was clearly within his rights to act calmly and carry on.

"On the positive side, Admiral Tom Phillips has recently arrived in Singapore," General Percival informed the staff, "with a pair of Royal Navy warships—HMS *Prince of Wales*, a new battleship, and HMS *Repulse*, an older battlecruiser—and their escorting destroyers."

At this announcement, there were mutterings of "jolly good show" and "hear-hear" from around the table.

"But unfortunately," the general continued, "the admiral could not attend our meetings these days because he went off by plane straight away, to confer with General MacArthur and the American admiral Thomas Hart in Manila."

It was probably clear to everyone that this fact rather annoyed the general, who doubtless felt that the Navy's top priority should be the

British garrison of Singapore, and not some rowdy Americans in the Philippine Islands.

In those days, however, Singapore was felt to be well defended from attack by air and sea, although woefully unprepared to resist a land invasion from the north, through Malaya, which—despite the supposedly impenetrable Malayan jungle and limited roads—is what the Japanese seemed likely to attempt, considering the location and course of their recently-discovered war fleet.

That likelihood, in turn, created another problem in the minds of senior British military functionaries, which was how to deal with Siam, Malaya's immediate neighbor to the north. General Percival pondered this problem aloud:

"Some of you gentlemen have probably surmised that Japan may land troops on Siam and then cross the border into Malaya. I too feel that this could happen and that we should therefore execute our *Operation Matador* to confront the Japanese while they are still bottled up in Siam, as it is unclear whether the Siamese government will, or can, prevent the Japanese from landing on their many long sandy beaches. On the other hand, Britain and Siam signed a mutual defense treaty just last year, and we are legally bound by the treaty. Without an official state of war, we cannot rush into Siam ahead of the Japanese without risking retaliation by our treaty partners themselves. Bit of a 'sticky wicket', what?"

After someone nudged the Air Chief Marshal, whom General Percival had just asked for an opinion on the course of action to be taken, 'Old Brookers' suggested that they adjourn and get some sleep, then see how things looked on the morning of the 8th, adding that "my man Howell is patrolling the Malayan border up north and will certainly let us know if anything appears to be amiss." Unfortunately for Singapore, the Air Chief Marshal's suggestion was taken, and the meeting was adjourned until the following morning.

The Japanese had no such inhibitions regarding Siam, as it turned out. They informed that nation's Prime Minister that they did not wish to fight with Siam, only to cross through it to attack the British colonies of Burma to the west and Malaya and Singapore to the south, but they were prepared to fight if Siam would not willingly allow them the right of transit. And they gave the Prime Minister just two hours to respond, before the early morning landings were to commence.

Old Brooker's 'man Howell'—Squadron Leader Jason. J. Howell of Fighter Squadron 453—had been detached from RAF Sembawang in Singapore the previous day to RAAF Bomber Squadron 1 stationed at Kota Bahru on the northeast coast of Malaya, with confidential instructions to have the Australians double-up their patrols of the Malaya-Siam border with their Lockheed Hudson bombers as far west as the RAF base at Butterworth near the island of Penang. Upon landing at Kota Bahru in his Brewster Buffalo fighter plane, Howell learned to his surprise that a Hudson patrol bomber had just reported a Japanese fleet at sea in the Gulf of Siam. The resident Australian squadron leader was still awaiting telephone instructions from Sembawang naval base in Singapore, when he greeted Howell and asked him to join in the plotting room.

An hour later, the telephone rang from Sembawang to say that the Air Chief Marshal's orders were to avoid attacking the convoy, since a state of war did not exist between the Allies and Japan. Instead, an RAF Catalina, with its longer patrolling range, had already been dispatched from Butterworth to take over tracking of the Japanese fleet the following morning.

"Cripes, that sounds like unwelcome news," the Australian said to Howell. "Let's go to my office and have a tot. You'd better stay here for the night and we'll see what develops tomorrow. We're refueling your wretched bird meanwhile." The universal Australian disdain for the plodding Brewster Buffalo was well known throughout the Far East Air Services, but the Air Chief Marshal seemed to harbor a nostalgic liking for his collection of the old American machines, having flown one himself in recent memory.

Howell nodded his thanks with a slight grin and tossed a package of cigarettes to the duty staff as he followed his Australian host to the door.

"By the way, JJ, I remember the last time we met," the Aussie continued, "you told me your wife was a pilot also, with her own plane no less, and was often away to Saigon on weekends. I hope that's not the case just now."

"No fear," Howell replied, "She hasn't been up there for a month, but does enjoy the francophone environment very much since she's a French-speaker herself."

"And enjoys the food too, I shouldn't wonder. Yes, I remember your saying that she worked at the old French consulate in Singapore. It's a shame that job ended when the Vichy became allied with Hitler. What sort of bird does she fly, then?"

"It's a Lockheed Electra, like the one Amelia Earhart had before she disappeared. In fact, it was Amelia who convinced Janice to lease one of those American machines when they met in London five years ago, when Janice was first learning to fly. Now she won't let me near it but insists it's a better machine than either you or I have available!"

"Ha! That's a truism if ever there was. But JJ, isn't Indochina under Vichy control now? How is Janice, being a Brit, able to fly in and out with ease?"

"Well, I don't really know," JJ replied thoughtfully. "I always assumed she had a special pass from the old French consulate here, but that doesn't make much sense now, does it? Hmm, I'll have to ask. Is it time for that drink?"

*** NUMBER 8 GOODWOOD HILL ***

The days and weeks had dragged slowly by for Wendy after Peter Perry left for Canton Island, even though she saw the Van Noorden neighbors from time to time and some English friends as well. Although Peter and Wendy wrote often to each other, Wendy was still depressed by her lonely new routine. Peter's engineering colleagues and their wives were very kind to her, but she soon tired of the repetitive parties that seemed to have no real purpose, and instead spent more and more time at *The Lake* with John—and her supply of sherry.

On September 1st, Wendy had been shocked to receive a telephone call from someone at Peter's Singapore office, saying that Alan Rees had died in an accident in Java and would she be so kind as to inform her husband. She was torn between anger (at the silliness of the request, since they could send Peter an official teletype message that would reach Canton Island far faster than any letter she could write) and despair (for the sad news about Alan and wondering what would happen to Maggie Rees). She decided to write Maggie first, with an offer to help if she could get back to Singapore.

Eventually December 1941 arrived, and Wendy forced herself to join other mothers at John's school to prepare for the Christmas season—which of course would be nothing like the frosty winter of England even though the ladies tried hard to remind their children of various icons like Father Christmas and his merry elves. Peter's project on Canton Island had already been extended twice, just as Wendy had feared all along, so she prepared herself to grin and bear it until February which was the newly announced month for his return.

On December 7th, Wendy and the other mothers held a rehearsal of the Christmas pantomime that they would be performing for the youngest children at the Tanglin Infant School, and when she got back to *The Lake* she was completely worn out. She told the staff that she would sleep late the next morning and asked them to relax and not worry about her breakfast. She took a sleeping pill and collapsed into oblivion.

Being sound asleep several miles out from the city, Wendy failed to hear the Japanese planes that roared in to bomb Singapore at 4am. When John's *amah* got up the courage to awaken her at 8, Wendy was shocked almost senseless at the news for she had dreamed of this scenario many times, even before Peter had left her for Canton Island. Wendy never told Peter about this dream, being afraid he would make fun of her. And now the wireless was also talking breathlessly about a huge Japanese raid on Pearl Harbor Hawaii, at which Wendy gulped again, worried about Peter's return flight to Singapore. *Would Pan American Airways still be flying commercial planes?* she asked herself in a panic.

Ron Van Noorden, who had been assigned as an auxiliary fireman during his time in Singapore, did hear the bombs and drove hastily into the city to his muster station at the Goodwood Park Hotel on Scotts Road. He returned to MacRitchie Reservoir in the afternoon, after helping put out several fires along a circular road called Goodwood Hill that was near to the hotel. It was on Goodwood Hill Road that some of the poshest homes on the island were located. One of those mansions, Number 8, had been nearly demolished by Japanese bombs and its occupants all killed, he told Corrie and Wendy who were together at the Perry home

"It appears that the United States of America are officially at war with Japan," said Ron to the ladies, "and so are Singapore and Malaya. I suppose my Dutch islands will soon be at war also. I'm sorry I could not return to

Java when Maggie's dear husband was still alive," he added, "but my final tasks here were not complete. Now Corrie and I must try to get back to Java with Bart and his puppy, who will both miss playing with John, but I'm afraid we must get away as soon as possible." Wendy nodded absent-mindedly, being lost in thought over the whole upsetting state of affairs.

"It also looks like we water engineers are lucky to live out here by the reservoirs," Ron told Wendy and Corrie in all seriousness. "There were many other homes destroyed in the Tanglin district besides Number 8 Goodwood Hill, I suppose because Tanglin is so near to Army headquarters."

*** THE DEMISE OF FORCE Z ***

"It was a hell of a fight!" said Captain William Tennant of HMS *Repulse* to Singapore-stationed Rear Admiral Arthur Palliser, former chief of staff for the late Vice Admiral Tom Phillips who had been lost at sea when his battered flagship *Prince of Wales* slid under the waves off the coast of Malaya.

"To answer your question, sir," the captain continued, "we detached the destroyers so that we would have ample room to maneuver the capital ships individually and fight off the Jap planes. Thank goodness we did, or those old escorts would probably have been lost too, instead of being able to help collect survivors, and I wouldn't be here to tell you this sad tale."

"But thank goodness you *are* here, Captain," Admiral Palliser said. "I'd like you to join me, please, in telling young Midshipman Leach that your old friend and colleague Captain Leach—his dear papá—was unfortunately not amongst the *Prince of Wales* survivors. Afterwards you can tell me about the battle, unofficially at this point, and how Force Z came to be near Kuantan rather than north of Kota Bahru where we thought you were."

"Yes, of course, sir. But I didn't realize the lad was here in Singapore. What a sad coincidence."

"Quite so. He just arrived to join his recently repaired ship for its movement to Ceylon, and I've had him wait for us at the duty officer's quarters. It appears that Admiral Phillips did not give Captain Leach permission to personally abandon ship, until it was too late for the two of them to get away safely. As you said, Captain, thank goodness for the destroyers or we would have lost far more than eight hundred unfortunate souls."

A few minutes later, Midshipman Henry Leach was told officially of his father's death by drowning, although it appeared that one of the survivors had just informed him as well. Clearly shaken by the news but honored to be among the first to learn the details of the tragedy, the young man remained silent as Admiral Palliser extracted the story from Captain William Tennant of HMS *Repulse*.

"We turned back after dark on the 9th, you see, having lost the element of surprise when the enemy learned of our approach to Singora, but Admiral Phillips didn't advise you because he was probably worried about giving away our new position if we broke radio silence."

"That course change was unknown to us," Admiral Palliser confirmed, "so I continued sending Force Z information that related to Singora where we assumed you were heading. What happened next?"

"Shortly before midnight we received your message about a Japanese landing at Kuantan, so the admiral decided we should attempt to intercept those ships on the way back to Singapore. Apparently, we were spotted again—probably by another Jap submarine—and when we found no landing in progress at Kuantan after all, suddenly at dawn on the 10th we were under attack from torpedo planes and bombers that must have somehow known our position in advance."

"You managed to bag some of the planes, so we've been told. Was it the torpedoes that did you in?"

"Yes, sir, it was the torps. Those Jap pilots were very clever. They went after the battleship first, smashing her port side hard and causing a serious list, after which they managed to lay a couple more into her starboard quarter and she began sinking."

"So, then it was your turn. Didn't *Repulse* have protective torpedo pods installed?"

"We did indeed, sir, and they certainly must have helped quite a bit. We managed to dodge the first lot of bombs and torps, but on our last evasive turn another sortie suddenly appeared on the opposite side and hit us with at least four more torps before we could straighten out to dodge them. The sky was full of planes."

"Damned shame we couldn't have gotten air cover for you," said the admiral.

"Yes, it was," the captain glowered. "Those Jap bombers were unescorted—their fighters didn't have the range, apparently—so even a couple of dozen Brewster Buffaloes from Singapore might perhaps have saved the ships—and this fine boy's father."

At the mention of Captain Leach's son, Admiral Palliser seemed to jump back to reality:

"Oh, I am sorry, young Henry Leach, I should have let you go back to your ship. HMS *Mauritius,* isn't it? Come, let me escort you aboard; I'd like to give my regards to your captain.

"And thank you very much for *your* time, Captain Tennant," the admiral continued. "I regret keeping you away from dealing with the survivors. We'll get together again soon for a more official interview. This informal chat is off the record, but I should think we three have a healthier respect now for our Japanese adversaries."

*** *NEW AIRCRAFT AT LAST* ***

Newly promoted RAF Wing Commander Jason J. Howell—known simply to one and all as JJ—had been back in Singapore for two weeks from a special assignment at RAF Butterworth, striving without much sleep to cope with the gradual attrition of his squadron of obsolete Brewster Buffaloes after the fall of nearby Penang on 17 December, and losses of a squadron each of Blenheim and Hudson bombers as well. Air Chief Marshal Brooke-Popham had recently been recalled into retirement, leaving Lt. General Percival in overall command of the Malaya and Singapore defenses. Percival urged the remaining RAF leaders to do their utmost to reverse Japan's present air superiority over Singapore, and rewarded JJ with the temporary rank of Wing Commander to help him succeed.

The only bright spot in JJ's day was the arrival of some four-dozen crated Hawker Hurricane fighter planes from Britain via Australia by cargo vessel on January 13th, with two dozen veteran pilots. The Hurricane was an acclaimed fighter plane that had distinguished itself in the Battle of Britain against the Luftwaffe's deadly ME-109. If these new planes could become airborne, the RAF just might achieve General Percival's air superiority goal after all.

But it was not to be.

With herculean efforts by the maintenance crews, the new planes were assembled within 48 hours and half of them were made airworthy three days later. In their first encounters with Japanese attackers, roughly half the dueling aircraft were lost on both sides, which was better than the Buffalos were ever able to achieve but it was still a bitter disappointment. Some modifications were made to the remaining Hurricanes to reduce weight and improve their rate of climb, but the high losses continued even though that was also true for opposing Japanese planes. The air war over Singapore was becoming a battle of attrition, which the Japanese would surely win.

At the end of January another four dozen Hurricanes reached Singapore aboard aircraft carrier HMS *Indomitable* but were flown off to a Dutch airfield near Palembang Sumatra to help defend the crucial oil fields. Unfortunately, thirty of those planes were soon destroyed on the ground in a single Japanese raid. After Japanese troops succeeded in crossing to Singapore from Johore on 7 February, the remainder of Singapore's Hurricanes and Buffaloes were flown or transported by ship to Sumatra, together with Wing Commander Howell and the ground crews, to form RAF Fighter Group 226.

*** SUMATRA BOUND ***

JJ had been pleading with his wife Janice for weeks to leave Singapore herself. Unable to face a separation with JJ by leaving him in advance, yet also unable to join him aboard the commandeered ship due to RAF regulations, poor Janice ended up demolishing her beloved twin-engined Electra to keep the plane out of Japanese hands, since no aviation fuel was available to civilians because of wartime restrictions and a genuine overall scarcity. After seeing JJ off at the port and promising to find him in Sumatra somehow, a fiercely anti-Japanese Janice rolled her sporty MG into Singapore harbor the next day from one of the piers. Producing a ticket that she had stood in line for nearly thirty hours to obtain—Janice joined a small Sumatra-bound Dutch merchant ship that was already loaded with other Europeans fleeing from doomed Singapore.

Carefully threading its way from Keppel Harbor at sundown on 9 February, the little diesel-fueled ship managed to weave its way through the string of Riau Islands south of Singapore, to eventually deposit its twenty-four seasick and hungry passengers at Bangka Island, which was separated from East Sumatra by a wide waterway known as the Bangka Passage, or Bangka Strait.

It was then that the Dutch captain told the passengers that Palembang appeared to be under virtual siege from daily air attacks, and that there was not enough fuel remaining on board to take them through the Soenda Strait to a safe port such as Padang on Sumatra's south coast. Instead, he and the officers had decided to scuttle the ship off Bangka Island and use the four lifeboats to cross over to Sumatra the following evening, 12 February. This was apparently a safer bet than trying to sink or beach the vessel off the coast of Sumatra because of the daily Japanese air patrols. Each lifeboat would hold six of the twenty-four passengers, plus one officer and four crew members. The little boats would navigate at night under sail, with oars for backup.

*** DIFFICULT DECISIONS ***

Two days later, at secret inland base P2 near Palembang, JJ Howell received an alert from Singapore that a large formation of Japanese bombers was headed toward Bangka and East Sumatra, escorted by at least 50 Nakajima 'Oscar' fighter planes. Rather than sending his eighteen remaining Hurricanes to certain oblivion by intercepting the Japanese air armada, JJ decided to detach them to the ABDA—American, British, Dutch, Australian—force that was building up near Soebang Java, some 400 miles away, where they might be put to better use. He had been given permission to do this at whatever point he deemed it necessary. Into two remaining Hudson bombers he packed as many ground crew and crucial spare parts as possible and sent them away with the Hurricanes. JJ then mustered the remaining ground crew and stray Allied soldiers to man defensive antiaircraft weaponry against the Japanese bombers that were sure to attack the lonesome Dutch airbase. The only planes left at P2 were a few Dutch observers.

Janice and her shipmates heard and saw the Japanese planes cross overhead in the direction of Palembang that lay some five miles inland from the Sumatra coast. It was mid-morning on 13 February and the four lifeboats had managed to stay together despite considerable tacking with the sails during the night. The ship's officers had been very careful with their signaling lamps in order not to attract attention from the approaching shore. They reached the Sumatra coast soon after sunup as planned, and the four little boats were carefully hidden inside the mouth of a small river—just in case of future need.

Their next problems were how to get some food, apart from the meager lifeboat rations, and how to reach Palembang, although the latter task was beginning to seem impractical in view of a major air raid that by then must have been in process.

*** PULLING IN TWO DIRECTIONS ***

With broad brush strokes the Allies had decided early in the campaign to divide the Dutch East Indies between two different Allied commands. Java would become part of the ABDA Theater, whereas Sumatra would be joined to the CBI—China, Burma, India—Theater. In a sense Sumatra, with its huge oil fields, became orphaned by this decision, and deprived of a focused proactive Allied defense policy to deny Japan its coveted oil. The colonial Dutch were even being discouraged by ABDA from seriously defending Sumatra and were coerced into focusing on Java instead, as the so-called Malay Barrier of Java was intended to shield Australia from future Japanese attacks. In the end it didn't really matter, as ABDA had nowhere near enough resources to defend Java either.

Sumatra meanwhile received an intense focus from Japan because of the vital oil reserves, which prompted them to take control of the Palembang region as quickly as possible. The necessary haste required less orthodox means than a routine invasion by sea that had been the carefully planned technique for Malaya, Borneo, and the Philippines. For Palembang, they would use paratroopers as a first strike to capture the coveted prize.

It was the airborne paratroopers that Singapore had mistaken for a bombing raid when they alerted JJ Howell and others in Sumatra. On 13

February—even before Singapore was fully subdued—a cloud of three hundred parachutes filled the sky near Palembang, focused on the Royal Dutch Shell refinery at Pladjoe. The paratroops, whose objective was to prevent sabotage of the oil wells and refinery, were advance shock troops for a larger seaborne invasion force that had been underway for several days from Cam Ranh Bay, Indochina, and would arrive at Sumatra's northeast coast the following day.

Just as Admiral Ozawa's invasion fleet was arriving off eastern Sumatra the morning of 14 February, there came a bizarre moment of high drama. In a feat of great daring and courage, a small Chinese-built Yangtze River passenger boat conscripted by the Royal Navy as HMS *Li Wo*—in the process of being detached from Singapore to Batavia on Java—came upon Admiral Ozawa's invasion fleet. Without hesitation, the little ship's commander, Temporary Lieutenant Thomas Wilkinson RNR, with resolute support from the entire crew, had the ship's battle ensign hoisted and charged at the Japanese transports, its skillfully handled 4-inch gun (with only 13 shells available) setting one transport afire, and its machine guns damaging another. After being set upon by a Japanese cruiser, *Li Wo* began sinking, at which point Lt. Wilkinson decided to ram the damaged transport. After the hectic one-hour battle, *Li Wo* sank with the loss of 77 crew members out of 84, including Lt. Wilkinson who was later awarded a posthumous Victoria Cross, the only VC of the entire NEI campaign. Ten other officers and men were also given awards for bravery, some posthumously, making HMS *Li Wo*—scarcely 50 feet long—the most decorated small ship in the entire Royal Navy during WWII.

By contrast, an ABDA fleet of 5 cruisers and 10 destroyers under Dutch Admiral Karel Doorman leaving Java on 15 February, made an abortive attempt at intercepting the same Japanese fleet, but Doorman's fleet was driven off by planes from aircraft carrier *Ryujo* and land-based aircraft.

During the Japanese parachute drop at Palembang, Wing Commander JJ Howell, directing an antiaircraft battery at P2, was wounded by a Japanese bomb, unaware that Janice and her shipmates had been detained by Japanese soldiers just fifteen miles away from the P2 base, as they were struggling inland from the river where they had hidden the lifeboats from the abandoned Dutch freighter. JJ and other wounded were evacuated on a

Red Cross ship bound for India, which the Japanese fleet allowed to pass. Further along, however, their illuminated ship was nevertheless torpedoed by a Japanese submarine, but Howell and a few others were able to cling to some floating wreckage until a British seaplane rescued them. An Indian surgeon at the Bombay hospital (plus extensive saltwater immersion en route) had managed to save JJ's gangrenous leg, and he was eventually dispatched to London with other recovering patients from India.

Meanwhile Janice and her companions were taken by IJN army trucks to a hastily established internment center in the fenced-off Pladjoe (Plaju) suburb of Palembang, where a series of comfortable oil camp residences were being converted into the local Japanese headquarters. It was there, when her turn came to be interviewed, that Janice produced an identification card in French that showed her to be a middle-ranking official of the French diplomatic corps with diplomatic immunity, a fact not known to her less-fortunate traveling companions nor to her missing husband JJ.

In due course, Janice, three Texas oil engineers from Palembang, and the foreign staff members of several embassies in Batavia were repatriated to New Orleans in the United States by way of Buenos Aires, Argentina, a neutral country, in a lengthy series of adventures that occupied roughly six months of 1942. Upon arrival at long last in London two months after that, Janice found that JJ had beat her home by some six weeks, but was still recuperating at All Saints Hospital, Bromsgrove, Worcestershire.

Following JJ's eventual recovery, he resumed doing what he did best—attacking enemy installations and aircraft for the remainder of the war, this time in Europe. For his exemplary dedication to duty, he was awarded the Distinguished Flying Cross in 1945. Janice, meanwhile, after a big row with the leasing company for having destroyed their Lockheed Electra in Singapore, persuaded them to lease her a new single-engine Beech Bonanza, on the premise that the Singapore plane would have been destroyed or confiscated by the Japanese in any event. Her new contract was approved by Walter Beech himself.

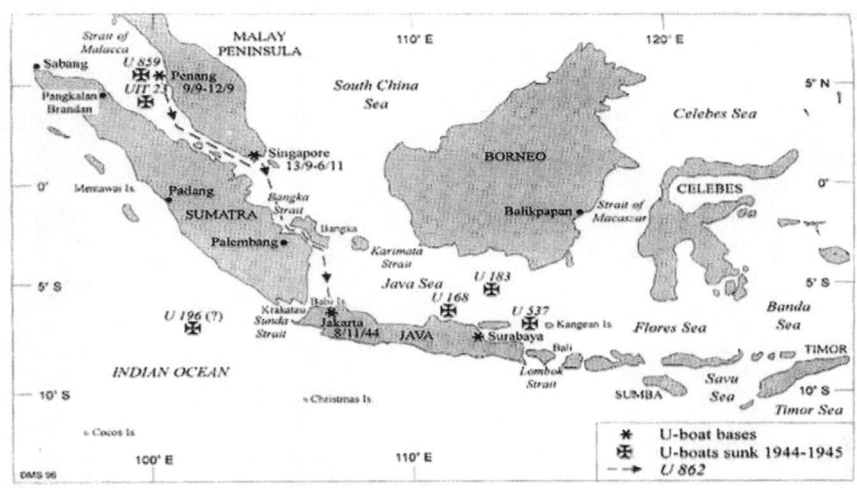

German bases in Malaya and the Netherlands East Indies, 1944–45

The simple map above, showing Nazi Germany's eventual U-Boat presence in Japanese-controlled territory, is also a useful reference to show where Singapore and Palembang are located with respect to each other in the preceding stories. Off the Sumatran coast near Palembang, one can also see Bangka island where some Singapore refugees went ashore.

SCENE TWO

French Indochina

Map of French Indochina,
courtesy http://www.gia-vuc.com/frenchindochina.htm

 In the pre-WWII era, French Indochina consisted of five distinct regions: **Laos, Tonkin, Annam, Cambodia,** and **Cochin-China** (the latter name to distinguish itself from an ancient Jewish colony called Cochin in southern India). The name Viet Nam (or Vietnam) did not, at that time, figure in the landscape.

The more northerly part of Indochina was **Laos**, with its capital at Vientiane. Formerly an ancient kingdom, many times fought over by Siam and China and extensively depopulated by slavery, Laos was a mountainous landlocked region and eventual French protectorate. It acted for the French as a barrier between the Kingdom of Siam to the west and the strategic rice-growing coastal flatlands of Indochina that girded the Gulf of Tonkin. Inside that gulf lay the large Chinese island of Hainan, recently occupied by Japan, which was also eyeing the French rice paddies.

The **Tonkin** region of Indochina was also a barrier—or buffer zone—like Laos, but in this case a buffer between China to the north and the rest of the French colony to the south. As one might expect for a buffer zone, Tonkin's language and culture had been heavily influenced by China during their long coexistence.

The Tonkinese capital of Ha Noi (Hanoi) was a busy city, often garrisoned by French Foreign Legionnaires. In the time-honored ethnic Han Chinese system of writing, at which Tonkinese and Japanese were both quite proficient, Ton-kin and To-kyo are written in the same ideographs (東京), meaning Eastern Capital, though they are situated thousands of miles apart. In this writing system, known in Japan as *Kanji*, the name of the older Japanese capital Kyoto has the ideographs reversed, thus Kyo-to (京東). The same is true of the syllables in English. There, wasn't that interesting?

The Tonkinese were good farmers and desirable emigrants for other French colonies around the Pacific such as New Caledonia and Tahiti, and even the New Hebrides Anglo-French Condominium. It is thought that these people originally came to Indochina from Java and Sumatra thousands of years before, when the last ice age lowered regional sea levels drastically.

To the south of Tonkin, a long, narrow, curved region followed the Indochina coastline. The French called it **Annam**, borrowing its old Chinese name meaning Pacified South (安南). Later in the century when the French went away and the Americans came, this coastal region would become known as Central Vietnam. A strategic deep-water harbor in southern Annam was and still is Cam Ranh Bay.

To the southwest of Annam was another ancient kingdom, **Cambodia**, which like Laos also functioned as a French protectorate and a buffer zone to Siam. The Cambodian capital of Phnom Penh is situated inland from the vast delta where the Mekong River drains into the South China Sea.

Cambodia was an original part of the diaspora from India long before the Christian era, when its early language was Sanskrit. Over millennia, it gradually morphed from an aggressive Hindu maritime outpost into a series of ever-weakened Buddhist communities that slowly contracted in the face of Siamese and Annamese incursions, until the battered rump of Cambodia was eager to accept France's offer of protection in 1863, becoming thereby a puppet monarchy.

Lastly (but by no means 'leastly') there was **Cochin-China**, a prosperous southern region of Indochina with its elegant capital Saigon, very much a favorite of French ladies, militia, administrators, tourists, and investors alike. The province's name is often written as Cochinchina, but we think it is more easily read in the hyphenated version.

Such was Indochina—or *Indochine* in French—at the outset of WWII. It is near the coastal plain of Annam, slightly south of Cam Ranh Bay, that our next story begins in late 1941.

*** WARSHIPS ON THE MOVE ***

"Brother Anlé! Please come, Brother Anlé!" the young Annamese schoolboy shouted as he burst into the simple lodging where two French monks lived in the almost-jungle, almost-forest, south of Cam Ranh Bay. Their crude monastery hut was yet unknown to the Japanese, which had been given permission by the Vichy French governor to use Indochina for staging their military assets toward British Burma. Those *Japoni*, as they were called locally, were starting to patrol the seacoast area north of Saigon.

It was still a dark December morning outside and there was very little moon. The boy had called to Brother André, his monk-tutor, because he knew Brother Georges was hard of hearing and sometimes difficult to awaken.

André heard the boy and hissed at him to be silent, meanwhile wrapping a light cloak around himself and sliding his feet into crude leather sandals. He lit a single candle, so they could faintly see each other inside the hut.

"Eh, what is it, little Thao? Why do you wake me so early today?"

"Come to see, Brother Anlé, come to see. Many *Japoni* big ship go now!" The excited boy was wearing his rumpled school uniform, a short-sleeve white shirt and simple blue cotton trousers with sandals. He waited impatiently at the open door, shuffling his feet.

Extinguishing the candle, the monk followed Thao outdoors. They began to hurry carefully through the dense vegetation despite the monk's floppy sandals and the lack of daylight. It was quite dark in the trees and the trail was hard to follow, but Thao's white shirt helped the monk guess where the boy was leading. Near the trail's end, the monk collided with a prickly bush when he failed to sense the boy turning abruptly to the left. Hearing a soft giggle from Thao did not improve his disposition. He knew the lad's name Thao meant 'polite' but making fun of a monk's discomfort was clearly not a namesake.

"Now, Brother Anlé, soon can see ships." Thao slowed to a crawl, then crept along the ground until they were underneath another dense bush not far from the edge of the cliff where he sometimes pilfered eggs from the tern nests. "There, see lights?"

The sun was close to dawning and a dozen wakes from the Japanese fleet were already quite visible as whitish traces on the dark sea. Dark hulls occasionally winked with signal lights, and a faint rumble from many engines reached them up on the cliff.

"Those ships leave from *Vinh Cam Ranh*, right Thao?" Brother André asked the boy, who whispered an affirmative.

"Look, I must get back and tell Brother Georges to prepare the wireless. Please stay here and count the ships. Soon you can see more easily. When the ships are all gone, run and tell us how many there were, all right?"

As the monk backed away to crawl under the bush, Thao nodded but kept his eyes on the fleet below. Each time he counted five ships he moved a little pebble into a hollow near his left hand. He was unsure whether some of them were already out of sight during the time he had run to awaken Brother André, but there were already nine pebbles in the hollow by the time the sun was fully up from the horizon, and more ships were still coming out.

The boy was just adding a tenth pebble when he heard gun shots in the forest behind him. He strained his neck to see how many more ships were still uncounted and realized that the fleet was nearly all underway.

Another shot made him rush to estimate the last few stragglers. Allowing for some ships to have left before he started counting, there were probably around fifty-five of them at sea, heading southward to pass Saigon and the *Mouths of the Mekong*, as the great river's enormous delta was known. Thao backed away from the cliff edge and started running once the path was clear of bushes. Now there was ample light and he made timely progress toward the monks' hut.

Suddenly he heard voices—*Japoni* voices! Thao came to a quick stop and slid behind a tree. He was not yet at the hut, though it wasn't far away. He crept carefully from tree to tree, then froze with fright as he saw two Japanese soldiers come out of the hut with the monks' clandestine wireless transmitter.

Thao had watched Brother André using it several times in the past few weeks and was flattered that both monks let him observe the procedure for contacting someone in Saigon. It made him feel like a team member.

Behind the tree near the hut he was still panting with fright. His mind kept screaming: *where are brothers?* A very nervous Thao watched the Japanese soldiers struggle with the transmitter as far as the opposite edge of the clearing, then he screamed aloud and practically fainted as a strong hand grasped his shoulder from behind. He had not heard a third soldier creep up to him.

From his hiding place the terrified boy was dragged toward the door of the hut by his captor, who was apparently the leader of the Japanese soldiers, perhaps a senior private or corporal. Through the open door he was shocked to see Brother Georges lying motionless on the floor with his head in a puddle of blood. As Thao was propelled inside he saw Brother André sitting half slouched against a wall with bloody streaks on his gown and face. Brother André was conscious enough to signal the boy with a slight headshake, to not recognize him. Thao somehow had the presence of mind to understand.

The senior soldier was shouting at Thao, while pointing at the wounded monk. With downcast eyes Thao replied softly in his language that he didn't understand Japanese, although it was clear that the soldier wanted him to identify the French clerics. Thao stood his ground, not belligerently but firmly and quietly.

Finally, in frustration, the angry soldier pulled a pistol from his belt and without hesitating even a heartbeat shot Thao in the back of the head. The courageous but terrified boy dropped like a stone, his fear-stained underwear discharging its rancid contents down his leg. The soldier kicked the boy over and glared at Brother André, who winced and prepared himself to be the next victim.

André did not understand the Japanese language either, and his heart was heavy from the loss of his long-time companion Georges lying dead nearby, and more so now from losing his pupil, the loyal schoolboy who had at least postponed the loss of his own life. But probably his life would soon end anyway, he imagined. He hardly thought it mattered now, with his wounds and depressed state of mind, but he was ashamed that they had been unable to warn their brethren colleagues in Saigon about the departed Japanese war fleet, so they could in turn have alerted the British in Malaya. The two monks had been so intent on getting the transmitter set up that they failed to hear the soldiers' footsteps outside the door. Sensing his death was near, André the monk began to pray.

*** THE COMBINED FLEET ***

On board the flagship of the principal Japanese fleet that had sailed a day before from the recently occupied Chinese island of Hainan, was an Imperial Japanese Army colonel named Tsuji Masanobu. Colonel Tsuji had been one of the main planners for the overall invasion of British Malaya. Being somewhat fanatical in his adoration of the emperor (and his disdain of Prime Minister Tojo whose protégé he theoretically was), he seldom left anything to chance. Although Rear Admiral Kondo, in charge of the fleet, well-outranked the colonel and was at least ten years his senior in age, the admiral knew better than to interfere with the army's plans for this crucial operation of theirs. Admiral Kondo would simply swallow his pride and deliver the army to the beachheads, just as the plan prescribed.

Colonel Tsuji was accompanied by three very junior IJA lieutenants to whom he would normally have paid scant attention, but—annoying though it was to have his thoughts interrupted by constant questions from the eager young men—his special indirect instructions from the emperor were foremost in his mind. One of the young officers, Lt. Tanamoto, was a nephew of the emperor's favorite sister, and the other two were his inseparable fellow-graduates from the senior IJA academy at Sagamihara. The three young men had all gone on active duty together just a year before, in December 1940, and had all achieved complimentary notations in their training records.

They were, moreover, the emperor's personally designated observers, not only for the forthcoming invasions but also for the implementation of Japan's fledgling *Greater East Asia Co-Prosperity Sphere.* His Majesty was extremely interested in the success of this new program, whereby the native peoples of East Asia would be admitted into Japan's sphere of influence in return for helping rid the region of European and American influences. Japan would then enlighten those liberated nations and train them to understand their roles in the overall economic development of the region.

Around 10 am, a lookout high up on the signaling mast of the flagship called down to the bridge that the expected smaller fleet from Cam Ranh Bay in French Indochina had been sighted and was closing slowly onto a parallel heading. Colonel Tsuji smiled to himself ever so slightly, pleased that this phase of the plan had gone off like clockwork. Now they would have 135 ships, including twenty-two transports loaded with infantry and artillery (whose plodding speed caused the convoy to proceed at a much slower pace than the admiral would have preferred).

The colonel asked the admiral's aide to verify the number and disposition of the combined fleet as quickly as possible, and to signal the colonel's compliments to General Yamashita Tomoyuki, overall commander of the 25th Army assigned to capture Malaya and Singapore.

General Yamashita had decided to sail with the auxiliary fleet from Cam Ranh Bay, to give himself an extra day for verifying that five hundred locally made bicycles were delivered to the port on time and loaded aboard the transports with his infantry. He wondered with amusement whether an army had in recent memory attacked a numerically superior force while mounted on bicycles. It had been Tsuji's idea, and the general was intrigued by the suggestion.

Upon receipt of Tsuji's signal, the general returned his own compliments accordingly although he was normally somewhat disdainful of staff officers.

It was 5 December 1941 when the two southbound fleets joined together. By mid-morning the combined fleet would pass Cochin-China and turn westward toward Siam. Meanwhile, an even larger Japanese fleet, unencumbered by any slow transport ships, was well on its way from Ulithi Atoll to Hawaii, where it was still December 4th.

The investment in Bunker-C fuel oil to move such large numbers of ships was taking a significant share of the empire's remaining reserves, after the American embargo. This fact preoccupied many of the army planners, the imperial observers and, in fact, the emperor himself.

*** *A MONK IN HIDING* ***

The French monk named André was left behind in the hut with the two dead bodies, seemingly under an assumption by the Japanese soldier in charge that he would soon be dead from his wounds. The soldier had used almost all his pistol ammunition in the initial attack on the hut, with the final round being expended on schoolboy Thao. The other soldiers had rifles, to be sure, but they were already fifty meters or so along a path back to the harbor as their leader had instructed and were struggling with the weight and awkward shape of the transmitter, plus those rifles. The leader decided not to call them back, and simply grinned evilly at the wounded monk as he departed the hut.

Grimacing, André murmured a short prayer of thanks for his life then stripped down to the waist to examine his wounds, for there were two of them. One pistol bullet had grazed his upper left arm while he was seated with Georges at the transmitter, and the wound was still oozing blood. André bound it with a strip of bath towel, after hopefully sterilizing it with a measure of good Marcell brandy poured directly onto the wound, a second measure of which he poured down his throat after toasting the two dead colleagues on the floor.

The other wound felt more serious but was probably not a threat to his life. A bullet was firmly lodged in his lower jaw, having entered somehow from behind. Perhaps it was a spent round that had bounced off the transmitter when the two clerics jumped up to flee from the Japanese soldier at the door.

I hope that also rendered the transmitter useless, André thought, flicking droplets of brandy onto the jaw—and over the jaw into the mouth. The wound was not bleeding, probably due to the tightly lodged bullet.

It can stay there for now, he decided, feeling vaguely happy and numb.

Knowing he had better leave the area soon in case the Japanese sent back a larger group to search for more useful booty, the wounded monk covered the two bodies with curtains painfully pulled down from the windows. He then prepared a haversack with some clothes and as much food and water as he could manage to carry. It was a sad business, preparing to leave the two unburied friends, but he felt there was no time or energy available to do otherwise. He carefully pulled the door closed to keep out any wild animals.

*** *COMBINED FLEET DISCOVERED* ***

After lunching with the senior naval officers on board Admiral Kondo's flagship, which was a modern heavy cruiser, Col. Tsuji summoned the three army lieutenants to his cabin where he had mounted the national flag to a bulkhead.

"Gentlemen," the colonel began, "you have all shown yourselves to be diligent and courageous officers in the glorious army of Nippon. We are soon to meet the enemy in his own territory, where you will be tested time and time again. Please form a straight line facing the flag. Now...*Tenko!*"

The three tall young officers came to attention and—one after the other—shouted their army serial numbers while staring straight ahead, avoiding eye contact while Colonel Tsuji buckled on his old cavalry saber and polished the round lenses of his spectacles. The colonel then stood with his back to the flag, facing Junior Lieutenant Tanamoto, the emperor's distant relative-in-law, and pinned a medal onto his tunic, reading aloud from a small slip of parchment:

"Junior Lieutenant Tanamoto, on behalf of His Glorious Majesty the Emperor I hereby present you with the Showa Grand Enthronement Commemorative Medal. You are to display the medal with pride on occasions when the Emperor is officially remembered, and otherwise you are to wear just the corresponding ribbon on your dress uniform. May receipt of this award keep you safe from harm on the battlefield. You may now pay homage to the symbol of our great nation!"

Tanamoto saluted the flag and then the colonel, who solemnly returned the salute before moving with precision to face the next young officer,

Junior Lieutenant Yamamura. The same award was presented to him, and finally their third companion—Uekuchi—was so honored as well.

Colonel Tsuji stepped back two paces and centered himself before the flag, facing the three honorees who were still rigidly at attention.

"Gentlemen, it is now time to place one of you in charge of the others, so that your efforts may be well-coordinated during the forthcoming conflict with the English and their colonial lackeys. The three of you are quite evenly matched in all aspects of your military careers to date, including your test scores and other accomplishments, your decorum and behavior both on and off duty, and your excellent marksmanship. It has been a difficult decision for me to select the one who shall now be promoted to senior lieutenant. When I announce his name, his two comrades need feel no dishonor nor inadequacy whatsoever. It is simply a matter that only one of you can be promoted now, and I have chosen that person to be ... Senior Lieutenant Tanamoto ... who may now step forward."

Just as Colonel Tsuji was pinning the insignia of higher rank onto Tanamoto's jacket collar a loud klaxon horn sounded on deck, its irregular repetitious code indicating the sighting of enemy aircraft.

"That will be all then, gentlemen. You are dismissed—and congratulations, Tanamoto; your promotion is well deserved."

"Yes sir, thank you sir." The three men dashed from the colonel's quarters towards their own, one deck below, to collect steel helmets and rifles.

"Moto, congratulations!" The friends paused to shake hands with their lucky companion.

"Thank you, Mura and Kuchi, but remember that you must not call me Moto any longer, except when we are alone like this. Please do not forget."

Up on deck, it turned out that an enemy patrol plane—a Lockheed Hudson with British markings—had been seen for a short while before it flew into a cloudbank. It was almost certain that the fleet had been spotted, so the admiral dispatched a coded message by wireless for a squadron of navy fighter aircraft from Indochina to give the fleet continuous daylight cover in case other enemy planes came to attack. At the same time, it was decided to disperse the fleet early next morning into its various invasion components—slightly ahead of schedule—to lessen the chance of loss in the event of an air attack.

Soon after dawn on December 7th, a Catalina flying boat—also with British markings—circled the fleet, which began firing antiaircraft guns.

The Catalina took evasive action but stayed in sight of the ships. It was a fatal decision for its crew, as the dawn patrol of Nakajima fighters arrived just then from Indochina and shot down the British plane.

Following the morning excitement, Admiral Kondo gave the order to disperse the ships into various individual formations. It was quite a complicated exercise to collect and dispatch seven columns of ships toward various parts of the Siamese coast, from Bangkok in the north to several southern points down the Kra Peninsula. The two largest, southernmost groups contained General Yamashita's 25th Army for arrival at Singora in the Siamese state of Pattani, just north of the Malay border. The five smaller groups of ships contained elements of the 11th Army under Lt. General Iida Shojiro, who would lead them across Siam to attack British Burma. General Iida had sailed from Hainan Island with the larger flotilla and was aboard one of the army transports.

Still more of General Yamashita's troops—in an eighth flotilla—would go ashore at Kota Bahru in Malaya itself, to neutralize an RAF airbase that might otherwise interfere with the general's main body of troops coming down south from the Siamese border. Well before dawn on the morning of December 8th, all the complicated landings would commence in the dark, just as six Japanese aircraft carriers would be launching their planes toward Pearl Harbor in Hawaii, far across the Pacific Ocean where it would be just past dawn on December 7th. Siam time was seventeen hours ahead of Hawaii (it would have been seven hours behind, but for the International Dateline).

*** *FRENCH VERSUS FRENCH IN SAIGON* ***

With help from a network of devoted Catholic brothers and monks imported from France, whose mission was to help the poor people of Indochina improve their lives in return for adopting the Roman Catholic faith, Brother André managed to drag his wounded self here and there from one 'cell' to another—receiving a variety of medical treatments, herbal medications, four-footed transportation, and very welcome nourishment along the way—until he finally reached Saigon the same fine morning that the Japanese combined fleet was commencing its dispersal near Siam into eight attack units. In Saigon, André sought out Brother Bernard, chief friar of the Franciscan order to which they all belonged by means of religious vows taken before leaving France. Brother Bernard had been alerted to the pending arrival of a wounded colleague and had arranged for a medical examination prior to their discussion. During the examination, the spent bullet was at long last removed from André's swollen and throbbing jaw.

Three long, painful days had passed for Brother André since the Japanese fleet had sailed from Cam Ranh Bay, since Brother Georges and schoolboy Thao had been murdered by the Japanese soldier, and since André himself had been wounded. He was hugely relieved to finally unburden his anxieties to Brother Bernard, whose acquaintance he had made some four years before, upon first arriving in Saigon from Marseilles. Bernard had assigned him to the coastal part of central Annam where he had labored ever since.

It was a matter of pride to André that virtually all the brother monks and friars shared not only a common devotion to the poor, but also a deeply shared belief that France should not have capitulated to Germany in the early days of the European war, and therefore that the Vichy government of France was illegal, or at least immoral. The same disgust was shared by the monks with respect to the current Vichy French government of Indochina, that had allowed the Japanese to take control of the colony.

The brotherhood was aware of a fledgling, alternative French government-in-exile under General Charles de Gaulle, presently based in England. The brothers secretly pledged to one another that they would rise and join de Gaulle, should the 'Free French' ever find their way to Indochina. Meanwhile they would carry on helping the poor but would remain mute about politics. They would also do their best to avoid outright cooperation with the Vichy government representative and his staff in Saigon, and especially with the *Japoni* that they felt were little more than brutish Germans with oriental faces.

The official Vichy French representative for Saigon, Monsieur François Bouvé, a balding gentleman who had been a private school headmaster in the south of France before the Germans invaded his beloved country, knew all about the Franciscan brotherhood's unrealistic political beliefs, of course, but apart from referring to them in private conversations with Madame Bouvé as a brotherhood of idiotic dreamers, 'Monsieur B' did not normally let that aspect of the religious order bother him in the least. He had far more important things to worry about, such as the Japanese delegation at that moment standing before his desk with a battered wireless transmitter that their soldiers had recently confiscated somewhere in Annam, near Cam Ranh Bay.

Monsieur Bouvé was struggling to take down accurate notes on what the Japanese major was telling him. Conversation with the *Japoni*, as his assistants liked to call them, was frequently difficult. Very few people of any nationality could manage both Japanese and French effectively, either written or spoken, therefore the usual method of conversing was (to the disgust of both parties) by means of the English language, which each party could manage with moderate degrees of success. The result was most often a linguistic muddle that produced, for any native English speaker invited to participate in such a discourse, no small number of amusing byproducts, best kept to one's self until sufficiently lubricated after hours by a pint of lager or a Gimlet in the sanctuary of the Saigon British Club.

What did the major just say? M. Bouvé asked his subconscious Francophone self in his own personal version of British English. *Was it* "*bruddah may-kee-reegar lady oh cahr?*" *Ah yes, he must have meant* "*The brother made an illegal radio call,*" *that must be it.*

Effusing confidence, the Vichy representative responded, with suitable seriousness in what, to Japanese ears across the table, could only be defined as Flangrish.

"'Allo, zaht ees note permiteh. Zees browzair ee weel ahv tyu hexplaine ahn-meh-dyat-uh-mahn whan ee eez cote."

Silly fool, how can one deal with these idiots, the Japanese major thought. *I must get myself transferred to some other place, like Singapore after we capture it. At least they will speak proper English there.*

*** THE PACIFIC WAR BEGINS ***

It was pitch black in the early morning of 9 December 1941 when transport ships among the first of seven Japanese flotillas began dropping landing craft into Siam's offshore waters and loading infantry to go ashore.

Not all flotillas from the original combined fleet would arrive in their target zones at the exact same time, despite best efforts to do so. Accordingly, the earliest wave of barges was fired upon by a Siamese coastal garrison nearly half an hour before the Japanese air attack on Pearl Harbor, Hawaii, which was seventeen time-zones behind by the calendar but seven hours ahead by the clock—the international dateline causing the apparent discrepancy.

Fortunately for the faraway just-launched carrier planes, the defenders in Siam were far too preoccupied with battling Japanese troops at the beaches to bother raising an alarm outside the country, thus the US Navy in Hawaii received no warning of its looming disaster, nor did the British Army in Malaya—until just before daylight when it was too late.

While the British high command had continued to dither over whether its troops and planes should or should not cross into Siam to deal with the Japanese before they could get through the mountain pass near Singora and fan out across the Malay Peninsula, Old Brooker had eventually decided to get a good night's sleep on the seventh and see how things looked in the morning, resulting in nothing at all being done that day to trap the Japanese in Siam. *Operation Matador* might as well not have existed.

As if in punishment for the oversight, sleep was disturbed for everyone in Singapore at 4am by a Japanese air raid launched from South Indochina. The raid caused considerable damage around Singapore City, which remained brightly illuminated because no one could find the night-shift supervisor who had the pass-key to turn off the city lights (he had apparently gone to watch a movie).

After the air raid, the Royal Navy did not dither at all. Hearing reports of a Japanese night-landing near Kota Bahru on the northeast coast of Malaya, Admiral Tom Phillips—only just back to Singapore by air from a hurried conference in Manila with US Admiral Hart—boarded HMS *Prince of Wales* and set out that night with battlecruiser *Repulse* and several escort destroyers as Force Z, to destroy the Japanese invaders. RAF Singapore was unable to provide air support before morning, but Admiral Phillips was eager to catch the Japanese before their landings were completed.

Unknowingly, the admiral was about to help consign the distinguished, centuries-long pedigree of capital warship design to the dustbin of history, but his immediate concern was the inability of his task force to locate the Japanese landing zone. What had been reported to Force Z from Singapore turned out to be a few Chinese junks moving down the coast, which in the dark had been mistaken by shore-based observers as enemy ships, whereas the real landing force for Kota Bahru apparently went unreported. The admiral turned Force Z back south toward Singapore while continuing to scout along the coast. Then he was told of another landing Japanese fleet heading from Indochina toward Singora, Siam, two days further north, so Force Z turned northward once again.

Along the way, the British ships were spotted by Japanese scout planes, which caused several squadrons of bombers and torpedo planes to be made ready near Saigon to intercept them. Force Z was also shadowed by a Japanese submarine that reported the British positions for several hours. Those reports persuaded the Japanese to turn their second Singora-bound invasion force back to Cam Ranh Bay until the British ships had been dealt with.

Suspecting that his fleet had by then been spotted by enemy planes, Admiral Phillips decided to abandon the Singora trek and turn the flotilla back south toward Singapore once again. Around midnight on the 9th he was sent a report of Japanese landings at Kuantan, which was between his current position and Singapore. The admiral moved his ships in toward the coast but was unknowingly detected at 3 a.m. by another Japanese submarine, which reported the new position of Force Z. Japanese planes on standby in Indochina were given their instructions and took off to hunt for the British fleet. It was by then almost daylight in the South China Sea between Cochin-China and Malaya where, in a matter of hours, the British warships would both be attacked and sunk by torpedo planes.

In Siam, upon receipt of the abrupt Japanese 'pass-through ultimatum' just before the actual invasions, local officials—most having been asleep—were unable to gather together and debate a timely response. It was nearly noon on the 8th before they officially gave Japan permission to transit the country, by which time all Japanese troops were ashore doing battle with a stout cadre of Siamese defenders.

Quite a few deaths occurred on both sides of the conflict that morning, but after the cease-fire was announced the Japanese 11th Army passed unmolested on its way to attack British Burma to the west of Siam. Meanwhile, the 25th Army's main contingent had already hurried south from Singora (through the mountain pass where they might have been stopped) toward the Malaya frontier.

After crossing the frontier, they would be joined by their Kota Bahru contingent that had dealt with an Australian bomber squadron at an RAF base. The two Japanese groups would strike all the way across Malaya to its western side, then south toward Jitra and Penang. The landing at Kota

Bahru was finally reported to British headquarters when RAAF planes flew down to Singapore for safety, but no word had yet reached Singapore from Siam about the other seven landings.

*** MONKS ON THE RUN ***

Back in Indochina, having promised a Japanese major to investigate the peculiar situation of a clandestine wireless transmitter being in the custody of two Franciscan monks, the Vichy French representative for Saigon, Monsieur François Bouvé, knew that he had better fulfill his promise in short order, before the Japanese undertook an investigation themselves. Accordingly, he paid a hurried visit to the chief friar of the Franciscan order.

"Brother Bernard, you well know that I have no choice in this matter but to report that your monks received their wireless equipment from a British agent who was here three weeks ago. I can give you twenty-four hours to get your wounded colleague—and perhaps your good self—away from here somehow, after which I must instruct the police to make a search of these premises and all other locations where your brotherhood has a presence. I hope they will not discover any other items such as a transmitter."

"Yes, yes, I understand your position," the friar replied, "and I am grateful for this warning and some time to react. You know that we brothers do not like the way Germany has divided France into an occupied zone and a zone of French collaborators at Vichy … and even Indochina … but your presence here today to help us gives me hope that one day we may restore our faith in one another and be completely rid of the Germans and Japanese. All right then, we will trust in St. Francis and be gone before twenty-four hours. I have already sent Brother André to Cambodia to recover from his wounds, and I shall go there myself tonight to join him. *Merci autre fois, monsieur Bouvé; Vive la France !*"

*** BRITISH TROOPS ON THE DEFENSIVE ***

Japanese troops that landed at Singora on December 8th were soon on the southward march into Malaya to join comrades who invaded Kota Bahru.

A somewhat disorganized British 11th Indian Division was trying frantically to prepare a blocking position near Jitra in the western Malay state of Kedah. Having failed to trap the Japanese in Siam, as originally planned but never executed, small units of British troops attempted a series of delaying actions to slow the Japanese advance, such as blowing bridges or manning anti-tank positions, hoping to give the main body of the division more time to dig themselves in across a fourteen-mile defensive line.

Leading the Japanese attack was the venerable 5th Infantry Division under Major General Matsui Takuro, who had been in command since 1940 in China. In the Malayan Campaign, his 5th Division was part of Lt. General Yamashita Tomoyuki's 25th Army. As the spearhead of the attack, the 5th Division included a platoon of light tanks and a company of engineers. Generals Yamashita and Matsui were both experienced campaigners from many years of fighting in and around China.

*** *SINGAPORE AWAKENS* ***

The emphasis of the Japanese attack plan for Malaya was on speed, to keep the British off balance and to enable an outnumbered 25th Army to overcome a larger British defensive force. To this end, the advance elements moved on tanks, trucks, and the many bicycles purchased in South Indochina or purloined from local people in Malaya. An unexpected psychological advantage of the bicycles, that surpassed even their modest improvement in deployment speed for the infantry, was the rattling noise that they made as tires disintegrated and the riders moved along on metal rims, convincing nervous Indian troops and their British officers that the enemy possessed hundreds of tanks rather that the two dozen actuals. Often in the following days as the tanko-cycles approached British lines, Indian troops would break and run before the threatened advance.

Between December 11th and 13th, the British were routed at Jitra. They were withdrawn in haphazard fashion to a prepared position further south, with their rear guard hotly pursued by Japanese infantry. Meanwhile, from December 8th, the important British colony of Penang Island off the west coast of Kedah state had been bombed daily by IJN planes with great loss of civilian life, after which—scandalously—the European community was evacuated while local people were left to fend for themselves, as Japan achieved air superiority over northern Malaya. With the sinking of HMS *Prince of Wales* and *Repulse* on December 10th, Japan had gained naval superiority as well. Sleepy Singapore was suddenly wide awake!

*** *AUSTRALIA BECKONS* ***

On January first—New Year's Day 1942—Wendy's ship was already a day and two nights east of Singapore, bound—eventually—for Darwin Australia. Peter had badgered her incessantly in his letters from Canton Island, to close their house on the reservoir and take John away from Singapore. Finally, after hearing the depressing war news from Malaya, Wendy had agreed with Peter that it would be smart to do just that.

She was pleased when the ticket office found her and John a small cabin on a slow Dutch passenger-freighter that would be calling on Batavia to offload cargo, sailing a few days later for Darwin. Peter had promised to meet her in Sydney after his contract was completed on Canton Island.

Some lights were already visible ashore as the ship nosed in toward Batavia, the capital city and main port of Java and the NEI. Wendy, standing with John at the rail, was sorry that there wasn't time available for meeting Maggie Rees briefly in Soebang or even here in Batavia. She had written Maggie about her plans for leaving Singapore, and even urged Maggie to join her and John on the same ship for Australia when it called in at Batavia. But Maggie, it seemed, had joined the Home Guard as an air raid warden and was determined to stay and help protect the town where her husband had died. Soebang was close to an important Dutch air base, and there were concerns about the Japanese bombing it from the Philippines.

"Look, dear," Wendy said to little John, who was holding her hand as well as the ship's rusty rail, "there are the big docks where we shall tie up for a day or so. Do you remember going to England on a big ocean liner when you were three?"

Yawning, the boy shook his head, for it was just six in the morning and Wendy had awakened him to see the busy port city in the hope that he would recall their home leave trip four years earlier.

"Can we go to breakfast, Mummy, please?" John pleaded.

"Of course, darling," Wendy replied, stroking his head, but as she turned to go below her eye caught the flutter of the Union Jack and white ensign on the stern of a grey hull across the harbor.

"Look John, there is a British warship!" Wendy exclaimed. "Doesn't she look ever so smart?"

One of the passenger ship's Dutch officers standing nearby at the rail, spoke to Wendy in heavily-accented English: "Yah madam, she is HMS

Exeter, a heavy cruiser. Glad we are that she is here to help protect our islands, because she is a very famous ship."

"Really?" Wendy said, "Did you hear that, John? This British ship is famous. Why is that, sir, may I ask?"

"Ach, *Exeter* she was one of those brave ships what did, um, fight the big German battleship *Graf Spee* in South America. It was two years past. Could you remember that story?" the man asked. "Now she is here in our world-side to help us Dutchmen fight Japan," he laughed. "Yah, they are ready on that ship, and we also are ready."

*** *A SPY IN THEIR MIDST* ***

It has been said by some historians that Japan achieved much of its tactical success in Malaya and Singapore because of assistance from a malcontented captain of the British Indian Army named Patrick Heenan, who acted as a Japanese spy to feed them information about the British airfields and other strategic defenses. However, Japan was also said to already have a large network of spies in Singapore, some of whom were photographers, plus consular and other Japanese visitors who reported to Tokyo on their observations. Whichever way it was that they obtained it, Japan clearly had a thorough knowledge of British defenses prior to the invasion of the Malay Peninsula and Singapore.

Just how much of their success could be attributed to Heenan is conjectural, but it appears that he was arrested on 10 December, court-martialed in January, and then incarcerated until the Japanese were literally at Singapore's back door. On 13 February—two days before Singapore's surrender—Heenan was allegedly executed by his guards on their own initiative, his body being dumped into the sea. The reader is invited to peruse *Odd Man Out* by Peter Elphick, listed in our bibliography, for more coverage of this intriguing story.

*** *WHAT'S IN A NAME?* ***

From their initial defeat at Jitra near the northwest coast of Malaya, the defending British Commonwealth ground forces seem to have been continuously off balance during the nearly two months that Japan pushed them—mile by mile—down through successive defensive positions, right to the very southern tip of the Malay Peninsula. After the British remnant had scurried across the causeway to Singapore Island on February 1st, with engineers blowing away a large chunk of it behind them, General Yamashita paused at the Malayan town of Johore Bahru for several days to rest his men and take stock of his resources.

The Japanese name for Singapore was *Syonan-to*, meaning 'Light of the South.' The general was certain that Syonan would soon be his.

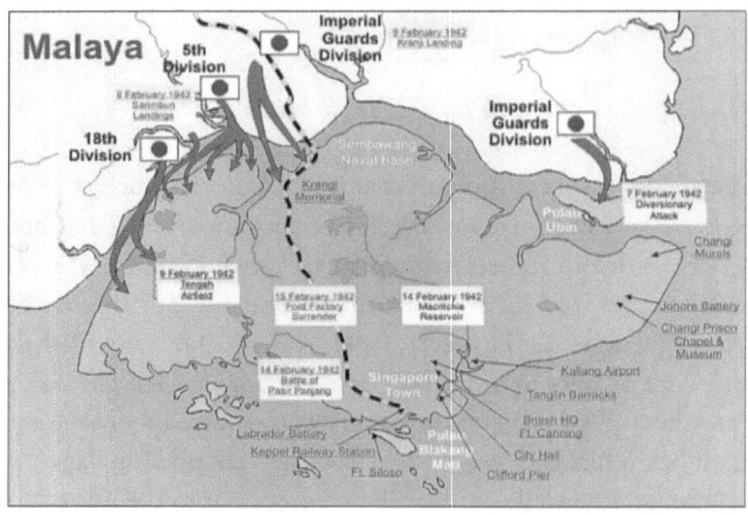

"Singapore Battlefield," courtesy Glenn Griffin (glenn1g.tripod.com)

Temporarily safe across the Strait of Johore, the relatively narrow and shallow waterway that separated Singapore Island from peninsular Malaya, the British had little time for rest as they frantically assembled Hurricane aircraft that had only just arrived in crates, and assessed the fuel, food and water supplies to see how long they could sustain their forces—recently boosted by last-minute Australian recruits. In addition, a large civilian population had been persuaded to stay in Singapore by misleading British propaganda which assured them daily over eight weeks that "all is well; no need to panic," while passenger ships sailed away nearly empty.

When panic finally *did* set in, with nearly constant Japanese artillery and aircraft poundings from Johore, and queues of Europeans at the passenger ticket offices trying to squeeze themselves aboard the final few ships still able to leave; with local Chinese, Malay and Tamil populations fleeing the town for more rural sectors of the island, and bewildered, newly-arrived Australian troops wandering the streets; with overworked medical and civil defense volunteers, and city engineers trying frantically to keep water and electric supplies going and to put out the many fires; Singapore was transformed from a prosperous trading post into a ghastly scene from Hades.

Facing the Japanese across the Johore Strait, overall commander of the British forces (now that 'Old Brooker' was safely off in retirement) Lt. General Arthur Percival dispersed his defending units along Singapore's north shore. Percival assigned a smaller sector, west of the partly demolished causeway, to Lt. General Gordon Bennett's 8th Australian Division, while the lengthier northeast coastline was assigned to various British units such as the Gurkhas, the regular Indian Army, the Scots, and so forth. Because this longer sector had a small island—Pulau Ubin—in the center of the waterway where the Japanese could theoretically mass their troops, General Percival placed his strongest defense in that vicinity.

On 8 February 1942, after feigning an attack on Pulau Ubin, two reinforced Japanese divisions struck the Australian lines, crossing the shallower waterway in small boats that they had collected here and there. As fighting intensified and it became clear that the Australians could not hold, General Bennett, figuring himself too important to be taken prisoner, escaped by plane to his homeland, for which he was afterwards heavily censured. He must have wondered at US General MacArthur doing the very same thing a month later in the Philippines to loud applause.

While there are many larger islands than Singapore in the world, it is not a particularly small island either, having an area in 1942 of around 223 square miles (278 square miles today after extensive coastal land reclamation). The preceding map shows what unfolded over the final week before the definitive battles of February 14 at Pasir Panjang and MacRitchie Reservoir (which demolished the former Perry and Rees/Van Noorden residences that were being used by British artillery spotters). These final conflicts brought an end to hostilities and a formal British surrender at the Ford Factory on February 15th.

*** JAPANESE ATROCITIES ***

General Yamashita's 25th Army had three components: the 5th and 18th Infantry Divisions and the Imperial Guards. It is hard to assess whether all his troops were guilty of barbaric acts but certainly many were. Although Japan was not a signatory to the 1929 Geneva Convention on the treatment of prisoners, it had earlier signed similar agreements that restricted atrocities and specified humane treatment of prisoners and the wounded. Somehow their troops and junior officers could circumvent those restrictions without fear of punishment by their superiors. Several examples came to light during their initial conquests, and many more were reported by handfuls of emaciated survivors after the war had ended.

A post-war military tribunal known as the Tokyo Trials would deal with crimes charged against senior Japanese officers for having caused the war in the first place, whereas the investigation and trial of more junior officers and troops for atrocities would be left to the civil courts of individual Allied nations. As the battle for Singapore came to an end, one such atrocity was the murder of patients and staff at the Alexandra Military Hospital where some three hundred nurses and bed-ridden patients—including survivors from Force Z—were killed by rampaging soldiers with bayonets. A similar hospital massacre had already occurred in Hong Kong at St. Stephen's College, and yet another was to occur a month later at the Soebang Hospital in Java.

Amid the frantic confusion of the final two days before Singapore capitulated on 15 February 1942, the remaining airworthy RAF planes were flown off to join Dutch forces on Java and Sumatra. Many people—both military and civilian—managed to escape Singapore in small boats as well. Most headed towards the Rhio Archipelago, a chain of nearby islands belonging to the Dutch colonies, that stretched southward to Sumatra.

Some of the escapees did manage to reach Sumatra and cross over mountains to its south coast, where occasional rescue ships collected them and took them to faraway Ceylon. Most escapees were intercepted, however, and either killed or taken prisoner. Two dozen Australian army nurses that had struggled ashore on Bangka Island after their little ship—the *Vyner Brooke*—was bombed and sunk were machine-gunned on the beach, just one of their number—nurse Vivian Bullwinkel—escaping, wounded. A book, *White Coolies*, about that harrowing event was later published by Betty Jeffrey. It was later speculated that the nurses had all been sexually assaulted by Japanese soldiers, then murdered to prevent them bearing witness to that earlier crime.

The many European soldiers, sailors, airmen, and civilians who had not been able to escape Singapore were collected at the Padang sports field near St. Andrew's Cathedral. Military prisoners, including the hundreds of bewildered young Australian troops just recently arrived, were then marched by Japanese guards some twenty miles to the east end of the island for internment in Changi Gaol (Jail), from which former criminal inmates had been set free.

Civilians and their dependents were prodded along to camps on Sime Road, five miles away in the center of the island. Alternately weeping or sneering at the sad spectacles, masses of former Chinese and Malay servants, employees, business associates, debtors, lovers, entertainers, and adversaries lined the two routes to stare disbelievingly as the humiliated Caucasian throngs shuffled by in silence. An occasional brave soul would rush from the roadside to offer water to some familiar face among the ragged phalanxes. It was clearly the end of an era.

*** THE KEMPEI TAI ***

Near the city center, Japanese Kempei Tai military secret police moved quickly to establish their headquarters at the Singapore YMCA Building. The Kempei Tai lost little time beginning their grizzly task by dragging in suspected pro-British locals for interrogation. During a period of weeks, over 30,000 Singapore Chinese were murdered in numerous ways, many being tied together in 'bundles' of three and tossed into the coastal waters from boats, where—being unable to swim in that encumbered state—they soon drowned. These and many other Kempei Tai atrocities in Syonan were a systematic purge of perceived hostile elements among the locals.

These brutal military police had their origins in the 1880s, based upon Japanese studies of European secret police tactics. The Kempei Tai originally had both civilian and military responsibilities, but their civilian duties were later usurped by the *Tokko* 'Special Higher Police' which insured that no western ideas could flourish among the citizenry.

The Kempei Tai had both army and navy divisions, the more brutal by far being that of the IJA. Kempei Tai units were attached to and in theory reported to the senior commander of each army division in the field but were really directed by their own internal command structure.

The Kempei Tai had their own training schools too—originally located in Tokyo and Seoul then later in Singapore and Manila—which explains the uniformly aggressive behavior of Kempei Tai units in each of the conquered islands.

The Kempei Tai even had one of its own in the highest elected position of power in Japan. Prime Minister Tojo Hideki had formerly been commandant of the Kwantung Army Kempei Tai unit in Manchukuo during the period 1935-37.

*** THE GREAT CAMPAIGN MANAGER ***

The overall Malaya Campaign was largely planned by IJA Colonel Tsuji Masanobu, who traveled in the second echelon to attack Malaya via Siam as part of Commanding General Yamashita's headquarters staff. Two of his three young lieutenants were kept safely in the rear out of deference to the Emperor, but Lieutenant Uekuchi—the least inquisitive of the trio in Colonel Tsuji's opinion—was directed to join the colonel for interrogation of some troops from Bajura, Nepal, that had been captured from the retreating British rear guard.

"Uekuchi, you will have an opportunity to study the makeup of the British Indian Army as we go through the Malayan campaign," said the colonel. "When we interrogate two men from Nepal in the morning, you will doubtless observe that they are fiercely loyal to their British officers— therefore we shall have to eliminate them after the interrogation is over, do you understand?"

"Yes, sir," Lieutenant Uekuchi replied, hesitantly, "but aren't we supposed to keep our prisoners alive until the war is over?"

Seeing Colonel Tsuji's exasperated expression, the nervous lieutenant added hurriedly: "I mean ... I thought...sorry, sir, I..."

The colonel smiled as if speaking to a child: "The British are already having trouble governing India, Lieutenant, which provides an opportunity for us. Have you heard of Subhas Chandra Bose, by chance? Well, I can see that you have not. Let me quickly explain."

After the colonel's lecture about the clandestine Indian National Army's founder, he assigned Lt. Uekuchi to a mobile detachment of Kempei Tai that followed behind the front-line troops, interrogating local people who had survived the Malayan Peninsula battles.

One of his two remaining protégés, Junior Lieutenant Yamamura, would be assigned to the Singapore Kempei Tai to gain instruction in the finer points of enemy territory occupation. In assisting the Kempei Tai with its reign of terror, young Yamamura quickly lost his innocence, but the murderous treatment of so many Chinese civilians sickened him.

The colonel had other plans for his principal understudy, Senior Lieutenant Tanamoto. The two of them were soon on their way from Kuala Lumpur to Manila, where the Imperial Japanese Army had pushed General MacArthur's American defenders of Luzon onto the Bataan Peninsula and a nearby fortified island in Manila Bay, called Corregidor.

Colonel Tsuji was seemingly not a Kempei Tai member himself, but he certainly shared their hostility toward Western prisoners. It seems more likely that Tsuji was a member of some ultranationalist secret society in Japan, of which there were several still in existence from the First World War and even earlier, but with his disappearance in 1945 for several years until the general amnesty for war crimes was announced, and his subsequent return to Japan and election to the Diet, the truth may never be known. Those who might have helped bring him to trial have remained silent.

*** *A MONK'S PAST PROFESSION* ***

With the early defeat of France in Europe and its partial occupation by Nazi Germany, Vichy French Indochina became a tempting target for neighboring enemies. One such predator was the Kingdom of Siam which had long disputed parts of Cambodia and Laos. Although Siamese shock troops quickly drove French colonial forces from Laos in 1940, the Siamese and French reached a military stalemate in Cambodia until Japan intervened in mid-1941 (before the Pacific War began), bringing the parties to Saigon for negotiations. Unfortunately for France, Laos, and Cambodia, the result was that Siam gained the territories it wanted, most of which were taken from Cambodia. By appeasing Siam in this way, Japan was skillfully preparing for an eventual right of transit through that country so that its armies could attack British Burma and Malaya without having to subdue Siam first.

Requesting Germany to put pressure on Vichy France—by dint of the Tripartite Act—Japan also received French permission to establish prewar military bases in Indochina, including Cambodia. Ostensibly this was to cut off supplies going to Nationalist China, but after Japan itself entered the world war the Cambodian bases were used in conjunction with Siamese territory for attacks upon neighboring British colonies. Japan allowed the French colonial regime to continue operating in Cambodia and the rest of Indochina until early 1945, when it took direct control of Indochina in a *coup d'état* in parallel with Germany's full occupation of Vichy France, after the Allied liberation of Paris in August 1944.

Japan also restored Emperor Bao Dai's position in Annam, and placed King Norodom Sihanouk on the Cambodian throne. When the war ended, King Sihanouk negotiated with France to obtain independence for Cambodia. That, and a bountiful rice harvest in the postwar years, made Sihanouk one of the most popular monarchs in Cambodian history, although his later political views oscillated between US-lead policies and those of Communist China and North Vietnam. In 1955 he abdicated in favor of his father, and upon his father's death in 1960 Sihanouk became Cambodia's prime minister rather than its sovereign again.

It was against the early part of this background that André, the French monk from Cochin-China, appeared on the Cambodian scene, having slipped away from Saigon with the approval of the Vichy French administrator in early 1942. The reader may recall the circumstances that propelled André from the Cochin-China territory, for fear the Japanese Kempei Tai might arrest him for illegal possession of a radio transmitter at his hut near Cam Ranh Bay, where he was wounded by Japanese soldiers, and his fellow monk and their young student understudy were killed.

Before taking his vows in France to become a Franciscan monk, André—whose full name was André Séguin—had been a police sergeant in one of the Paris precincts. Upon arrival in Phnom Penh, the new Cambodian capital, to heal his wounds and his psyche, André decided to seek employment in that field once again rather than keep up appearances as a wandering monk. He still possessed his French police dossier and could explain away the recent year's missing record by pretending to have spent the time with an uncle in New Caledonia, knowing that Vichy-ruled colonies were quite unlikely to contact those of the Free French to verify information. Being desperately short of police leadership in Phnom Penh, the police commissioner received former-sergeant Séguin enthusiastically and promptly swore him in as a police lieutenant, with a bachelor apartment as part of his tax-free allowances.

Unaware of his prior identity as a monk, Japanese authorities approved the assignment and André promptly went to work. He was given oversight of the city's gambling, prostitution, and opium dens, with orders to insure they continued operating quietly behind the scenes while paying their ongoing twenty percent royalties to the police commissioner, who in turn would distribute half of those funds to the mayor of Phnom Penh. If André could entice the owners of those clandestine establishments to disburse a bit more than the customary monthly average, then he was free to 'keep the change' for himself, so to speak.

When, in March 1945, the Japanese *coup d'état* took place against the French colonial rule throughout Indochina, André went into hiding with an attractive Cambodian woman friend named Duong Mey, meaning "Little Sister of the East," whom he subsequently married while in exile. Mey and her relatives helped André avoid Japanese patrols that occasionally appeared in her village, and in return he made use of his background as a policeman to help improve the village's security. André even began a police cadet training school, with positive results, and he also trained Mey—whom he referred to as "my moon-faced cadet"—in police tactics.

During this half year of tension from fear of discovery by the Japanese, André and Mey developed a ritual of love-making that helped calm their nerves. Frequently on Friday evenings after the stress of the week began to abate, the newlyweds would retire to a private little garden behind the thatched cottage that Mey's parents had lent them, there to imbibe cups of strong hot tea laced with cinnamon sticks, the latter acting as a mild aphrodisiac. They customarily dressed in simple robes under which they were naked.

One attribute about Mey that had attracted André when they first met was the fact that she shaved under her arms, just as high-society French ladies were doing (although many French secretaries and local Cambodian girls did not yet follow that new custom). After they married while in exile, André discovered that Mey also shaved her pubic hair, which surprised him. Her response was to say that she wanted to appear to him like a very young girl, to better excite him when they made love. She could indeed take on that role, with her small breasts and short stature, even though being in her thirties when they wed. "After all, *mon amour*, my name Mey means younger sister, just like *Mei-Mei* in Chinese," she teased.

Mey had acquired at some emporium a small but noisy forerunner of today's ubiquitous electric shavers. The clever little tool was operated by a pair of small disposable batteries that the French called *mignons*, which were being produced in Singapore. After pouring André a second cup of cinnamon tea in the garden, Mey would retire to their bathroom from where André could hear the funny little shaver at work. He would always imagine it moving over the nether parts of her trim little body, and its buzzing noise eventually became for him an erotic stimulant as the Friday afternoon sessions evolved. He suspected that Mey, being aroused by the little shaver's vibrations, was probably oiling and satisfying herself afterwards. She usually did not come forth for fifteen minutes or so after the shaver stopped buzzing, whereupon she seemed flustered and somewhat breathless. She was always ready for him, though, and would lead him by the hand to their bedroom, her robe already opened and her hand groping to untie his.

One day they heard news of the atomic bombs and Japan's surrender to the Allies. "Oh, my beloved, this is wonderful!" shouted André, as he burst into the hut with a sheet from the newspaper. "Now we can go to Cochin-China to find better work. Aren't you excited?" he said, suddenly noting Mey's forlorn expression.

"Yes, I am excited about getting rid of the *japoni*." she replied earnestly, "but why do we have to leave Kampuchea (using a local name for her beloved country)?"

"You will see why, once we reach beautiful and vibrant Saigon," André replied, kissing her forehead, remembering a Saigon of 1941 when the Japanese were only background noise. "Cambodia has a lot of fascinating history and monuments, that's true, but Saigon in Cochin-China is like Europe in Asia. You will love it there, I promise."

And, as often seems to happen in novels—historical or otherwise—a shadow passed over the room.

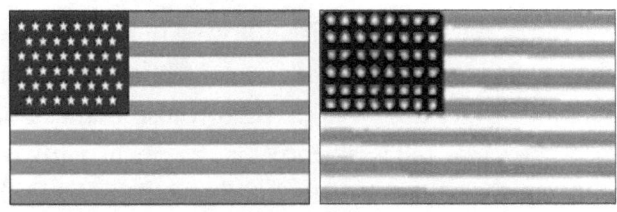

SCENE THREE

The US Territory of the Philippine Islands

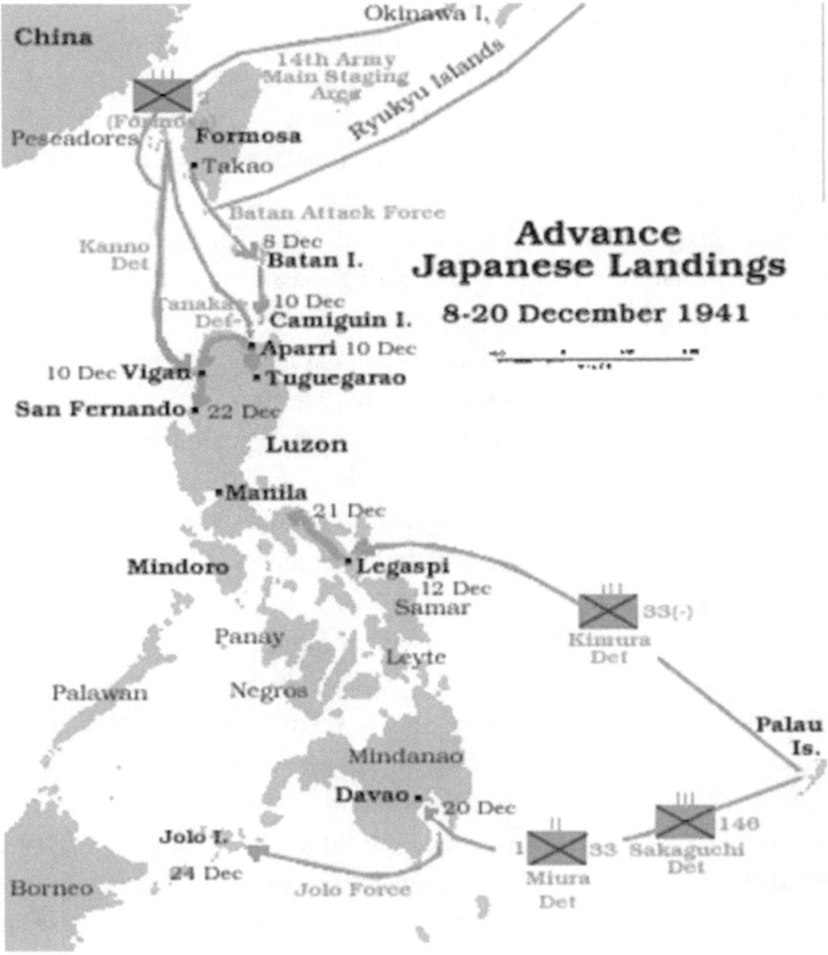

Advance Japanese Landings
8-20 December 1941

China

Okinawa I.

14th Army
Main Staging
Area

Ryukyu Islands

Pescadores

(Formosa)

Formosa

Takao

Batan Attack Force

Kanno
Det

8 Dec
Batan I.

Tanaka
Det

10 Dec
Camiguin I.

Aparri 10 Dec

10 Dec Vigan

Tuguegarao

San Fernando

22 Dec

Luzon

Manila

21 Dec

Mindoro

Legaspi
12 Dec
Samar

Panay

Leyte

Palawan

Negros

33(-)
Kimura
Det

Palau
Is.

Mindanao

Davao

20 Dec

146

Jolo I.

24 Dec

Jolo Force

Borneo

1 33 Sakaguchi
Det
Miura
Det

 Whereas the Philippine Islands were indeed a prewar colony, having been under American control since the end of the Spanish-American War in 1898, those islands had already started a process towards independence by agreement with the United States Congress (the Jones Law of 1916 and the Tydings-McDuffie Act of 1934). During World War II, the Philippines were invaded and occupied by Japan under similar harsh conditions to those of the European colonies, but Filipinos did not have to fight their colonial masters for independence in the postwar era, hence their story differs from those of the European colonies. Filipinos would be promptly granted independence by the US in 1946, although American influence would linger.

Before the Spanish arrived in the 16th Century, the islands of that region were an eclectic mixture of seafaring settlements with trading links derived from Indian, Arab, Chinese, and even Japanese relationships. Constant inter-island warfare was the hallmark of the region as each society strove to exert control over its neighbors.

How these squabbling communities eventually came to be united under Spanish control is an interesting story in itself—that the author hopes to explore in his third historical novel about the Asia-Pacific region—but in a nutshell, it had to do with Spain's earlier massive forays into the lands known to Europeans as 'the Americas.'

After Spain had conquered and expanded its control over Mexico by the mid-1500s, Spanish expeditions sailed westward from Acapulco to first explore and then exert control over remote Pacific territories, using the time-tested combination of soldiers and monks to discipline the natives physically and spiritually. The first Spanish conquests in the Pacific were the islands of Samar and Leyte, which they named *Las Islas Filipinas* after King Phillip II of Spain.

In this manner, Christianity was introduced as Spanish control of other islands expanded. Roughly halfway between Mexico and the Philippines, the Mariana Islands—notably Guam—were occupied and used as reprovisioning stopovers for Spanish ships sailing in both directions.

In early 1898, with the mysterious sinking of battleship USS *Maine* in Havana Cuba, the Spanish-American war broke out, in which the US was helped by existing anti-Spanish insurgencies in Cuba and the Philippines. When the war ended later that year, the US had acquired not only the

Spanish insular territories of Cuba and Puerto Rico in the Caribbean region, but also Guam and the Philippines in the Pacific. Spain later sold the remaining Marianas to Germany, since the US was only interested in Guam. With Germany's defeat in the First World War, Japan inherited those orphaned Marianas from the League of Nations, along with all other German colonies in the Pacific. It took them very little time to capture Guam as well, once the Second World War began.

*** NO ONE SAID IT WOULD BE EASY ***

During the early years of Philippine occupation by the United States, a fervent Filipino nationalist and guerrilla general named Emilio Aguinaldo was determined to continue a fight that he had been waging against the Spanish occupation for several years, that had resulted in his being exiled to Hong Kong by the Spanish, together with some of his fellow-insurgents. Aguinaldo, a short, thin, dignified-looking man who appeared more like a professor than a general, was determined to rid the Philippines of any and all foreign interlopers.

Soon after the American Asiatic Squadron under Commodore George Dewey (flying the US 45-star flag, above L) defeated the Spanish fleet in May 1898 at the Battle of Manila Bay, Aguinaldo—ever the opportunist— seized the moment and declared independence for the Philippines, with himself quickly elected as its first president. The US, of course, did not go along with Aguinaldo's declaration, but was at first unable to take up arms against the Filipino rebels. It was several more months before Dewey's small force of sailors and marines was reinforced by some 20,000 army volunteers from all over the United States, led by Brigadier Generals Francis Greene and Arthur MacArthur (father of General Douglas MacArthur, and eventual military governor of the Philippines for a year).

In February 1899, war broke out between the Philippine insurgents and the American army, which lasted until April 1901 when the Americans cleverly captured the Filipino leader at his remote hideout. Afterwards, an embarrassed Emilio Aguinaldo swore allegiance to the United States and lived on through the Japanese occupation of his beloved Philippines during World War II, until his passing in 1964.

*** *A SOLDIER'S LIFE* ***

Among the 20,000 USV (volunteer army) troops sent to the Philippines to assist Admiral Dewey was a young private soldier named James Coe Gibson of Company L, First Battalion, 20th Kansas Volunteer Infantry Regiment, Col. Fred Funston commanding.

Coe, the name by which he had lately chosen to identify himself (out of respect for his maternal Coe ancestors that had come from England to America in the 1500s) was 19 years old when Kansas 20/1 shipped out from San Francisco aboard transport *SS Newport.* He was very excited to celebrate his 20th birthday when the troops were given a few days shore leave in Honolulu on the way to Manila.

Coe wrote several well-composed letters to his parents during the year-long Philippine adventure, some of which they later had published in the *Chapman Standard* of Chapman, Kansas. Coe's first letter after leaving California on November 12, 1898, was posted from Hawaii, describing the fascinating birds and plants that he observed while climbing a nearby mountain with some fellow soldiers. He also mentioned his sadness at learning of the Hawaiian monarchy's demise. He described the (Polynesian) Hawaiian natives to his parents as quite handsome and intelligent looking. A bigger surprise was the many people of Portuguese ancestry that he encountered on the Honolulu streets, apparently descended from a migration that occurred when sugarcane was introduced to Hawaii by American business interests during the monarchy era.

After *SS Newport* sailed for the Philippines, Coe's next letter dealt briefly with that 11-day voyage and his arrival in Manila Harbor soon after another chartered troopship *SS Indiana* that carried the 2nd and 3rd Battalions of his regiment. Volunteers for the campaign were coming from all 45 US states, he learned once his battalion's barracks were hastily converted from tobacco warehouses and made ready for occupancy. Colonel Funston's 20th Kansas regiment comprised 1500 or so men, divided into three battalions of four companies each. Private Coe Gibson was part of Company L in the 1st Battalion that arrived aboard *SS Newport* together with Companies A, B, and K. Keeping a protective eye on the newly arrived transports in Manila Harbor, the American Asiatic fleet was moored nearby at Cavite Bay.

Coe learned that the army volunteers had been requested by Admiral Dewey to help put down an insurrection by a young populist Filipino general named Emilio Aguinaldo, who had raised a local militia in 1896 to harass the Spanish but had been caught and exiled to Hong Kong with his co-conspirators.

When the Spanish began leaving the Philippines in December 1898 after Admiral Dewey's fleet destroyed their ships in Manila Bay and the Treaty of Paris had been signed by US and Spanish representatives, General Aguinaldo quickly returned from Hong Kong after first declaring the Philippine Islands' independence. Upon his return he was elected as its first president.

Having acquired a large stash of abandoned Spanish weaponry and gunpowder, Aguinaldo reignited the passions of his former militia and greatly increased its size, feeling thereby capable of containing the American navy and eventually dispersing it. Admiral Dewey, with his relatively small contingent of sailors and Marines, was unable to do much more than defend his ships at anchor in Cavite Bay, biding his time until USV troops could arrive to boost his resources.

After a few quiet months in Manila, during which Coe wrote about the nice weather, the local people he met, the many languages heard on the streets, and the downcast Spanish soldiers and civilians who were leaving Manila during the handover of power, Emilio Aguinaldo no doubt became concerned with the buildup of American troops, and decided to act before becoming outnumbered.

On February 4, 1899, the Philippine–American war began, about which Coe told his parents in his fourth overseas letter. He added: "I have heard the dreaded Mauser sing, and the brass-tipped Remington buzz, but here in the trenches before Maloban we can sleep quite comfortably while lead flies over our heads." It was almost a poem.

By February 13, 20th Kansas and USV auxiliaries drove the rebels from their fortifications at Caloocan. Around two thousand American troops and artillery divided and put to route some eighteen thousand natives. Colonel Fred Funston led his men from the very firing line, excitedly waving his hat to urge them on. It was doubtless then and there that he gained the nickname 'Fighting Fred.'

By the end of March, the insurgent capital at Malalos had fallen to the USV, so Aguinaldo moved his headquarters to Palanan, a location that was unknown to the Americans. He continued to direct the insurgency through a trusted group of friends, known as the *Kapitunan*, and eventually changed his methodology to hit-and-run guerilla warfare instead traditional military tactics.

After encounters with the insurgents at Calumpit and St Thomas in April and May, the 20th Kansas and other USV troops were gradually being replaced on the line by regular army units that had been steadily arriving from the US. Meanwhile Fighting Fred Funston had been elevated to Brigadier General—the same rank as Arthur MacArthur, the new Philippine Governor—and was detached from the 20th Kansas Volunteers to join the regular US Army in its quest to capture Aguinaldo and end the guerrilla warfare.

[Please try https://filipinoamericanwar.com/captureofaguinaldo1901.htm to see the fascinating result of the Funston-Aguinaldo battle of wits: Ed.]

On September 6, 1899, the 20th Kansas, which was down in strength by almost 50%, boarded transports for its return to the US, where on October 28 it was mustered out of service. Coe Gibson had achieved the rank of corporal during his Philippine service. He returned to civilian life as an oil and gas operative, marrying Neva Baker of Missouri. They had five children by the time Coe passed away in 1923 at the young age of 45. Neva, known to her grandchildren as Doppy, outlived him by 45 more years.

*** *A HOTEL FOR ALL SEASONS* ***

Part of the settlement for the US acquisition of the Philippines and Guam, was a payment to Spain of 20 million dollars. Soon after the Spanish-American war and the Philippine insurgencies were ended, President William McKinley ordered a face-lift for the city of Manila, the former Spanish capital on the island of Luzon. It was McKinley's intention to turn Manila into a showcase city for the Far East, just as he had suggested for Havana Cuba and San Juan Puerto Rico in the Caribbean, which were other spoils of the Spanish-American War. Having appointed Howard Taft as the first civilian Governor-General of the Philippines, McKinley directed Taft to develop a master plan for Manila's modernization.

After an extensive search, Governor Taft appointed Daniel Burnham as the city planner for Manila, Burnham having already developed comprehensive plans for several US cities including Chicago, Washington DC, Cleveland, and San Francisco. The usual scope of Burnham's work included aspects of civic beauty as well as improved transportation networks so that his cities would be both livable and enjoyable.

Upon acceptance of his preliminary plan for Manila, which envisioned a long tree-lined boulevard along the bay shore (known as Shore Road, Cavite Boulevard, Dewey Boulevard, and Roxas Boulevard over the years), Burnham in turn recommended William Parsons to be the on-site consulting architect to the government for the plan's implementation, a recommendation that Taft gladly accepted. Parsons had studied at Yale and *l'École des Beaux-Arts* in Paris and was a fellow admirer of the European classical style of architecture that Burnham preferred. Parsons was engaged in Manila from 1906 to 1914 with a retainer salary but was permitted to continue in private practice as well with his Parsons School of Design in New York City. He was initially put in charge of all public park design and development for the colony.

An 'anchor' at one end of the new seaside boulevard was planned to be a prestigious hotel, the design and oversight of which was also assigned to Parsons. His concept for the hotel was an H-shaped floorplan in the style of a California mission, but far grander. There would be five stories of well-ventilated high-ceilinged rooms with spectacular views of Manila Bay in front, and to the rear the Intramuros walled fortress-city that had long served the colony's Spanish governors. Whereas Intramuros had originally overlooked some ugly mud flats at the edge of the bay, the American enhancements—including the hotel and boulevard—were built on reclaimed land that covered up the muddy shore between the bay and Intramuros.

Construction of the Manila Hotel, as it was named, began in 1909 and was completed three years later. The roof covered a viewing deck with attractive plantings, where guests could sit and enjoy a fascinating panorama or watch the American navy at play in the harbor. By 1935, however, when the seaplanes of Pan American Airways also used the bay for landing, the entire top deck of the hotel was under construction as a penthouse for the enjoyment of General Douglas MacArthur and his small family.

1935 was also the first year of elections in the colony, whereby a newly formed Commonwealth of the Philippines would replace the former US colonial governor with an elected president and vice-president, for a transitional period of a decade or so until full independence would be granted. The 1935 election placed Manuel Luis Quezon in the office of President, with Sergio Osmeña as Vice President.

President Quezon had previously been good friends with retired US Army Lt. General Douglas MacArthur, who had served until retirement with the US Army of Occupation in the Philippines. The new president lost no time in contacting MacArthur with an offer to return from retirement and develop a national Filipino army for the Commonwealth government. Being offered a handsome salary and the local rank of Field Marshal, MacArthur readily agreed to the assignment upon further confirmation of substantial quarters with seven rooms to use as his home and office. Thereby, the Manila Hotel Penthouse was created, and the viewing deck disappeared forever.

While the penthouse was being built, the hotel underwent its first major renovation, this time under the direction of Paris-trained Filipino architect Andrés Luna, who added an airconditioned annex and some large function rooms that were completed in time for the Commonwealth inauguration ceremonies.

Both before and after MacArthur's penthouse tenancy, the Manila Hotel became world famous on its own merit and was visited by numerous renowned authors and other international celebrities. It underwent several more renovations between 1935 and 1945 and can now offer more than 500 rooms because of an 18-story annex tower that was added in the modern era.

*** *PEARL HARBOR ECHOES IN MANILA* ***

At US Naval Station Cavite on December 8th, and at the Manila Hotel where General MacArthur maintained both his Philippine headquarters and his residence, teletype messages were continuously arriving from Hawaii about the devastating Japanese air attacks. Most US battleships moored at Ford Island in Pearl Harbor had been severely damaged, and in some cases sunk, rendering the US Pacific Fleet virtually useless apart from three aircraft carriers and their escorts that had fortunately been away on assignments. Destruction of the US battleships was a preamble to the dramatic script that British admiral Tom Phillips was soon to write in Malaya with the loss of Force Z, both US and British catastrophes being orchestrated by Japanese air power.

The alarming Pearl Harbor news was also a warning to General MacArthur to be alert for Japanese threats in the Philippines, so the general immediately dispatched his Army Air Corps to scour the seas for enemy activity. Finding nothing after extensive searches, the planes returned to base for refueling but were strafed next day by a surprise Japanese attack from Formosa. MacArthur's air force was virtually destroyed on the ground despite the ample warnings, a disaster that would render the Philippines indefensible, as time would tell.

Later that day the naval base at Cavite—which had also been used by Pan Am for its seaplanes before war broke out—was likewise pummeled, having just been deprived of air protection. Some capital ships of the US Asiatic Fleet escaped to the port of Balikpapan in Borneo and onward to Soerabaja in Java under Admiral Thomas Hart and his flagship USS *Houston* (CA-30), where a hastily planned ABDA (American-British-Dutch-Australian) defensive line was being formed on the Dutch island of Java.

Cavite's half-dozen PT Boats were also moved to sea in time to escape the raid and were afterwards based close by ruined Cavite at Sisiman Cove, from where they sank several Japanese warships and freighters over the following few weeks. But the gallant little boats also incurred losses themselves. In March 1942, three surviving PT Boats moved General MacArthur with his staff and family to the big island of Mindanao for an ongoing flight to Australia.

*** *A CUNNING PLAN* ***

Japanese strategy for the capture of the Philippines—a massively complicated objective with several very large islands and numerous smaller ones—was cleverly planned and masterfully executed. As with their other attacks in the southern Pacific region, the invaders were on the move by December 8, with the bulk of their Philippine attack forces having been gathered at the Japanese colony of Formosa (Taiwan). The principal force was the 14th Army under Lt General Homma Masaharu, advanced elements of which attacked the north coast of Luzon on December 10, as shown on the preceding map.

To deter MacArthur from concentrating all his troops against the 14th Army, three secondary attacks were launched from the former German colony of the Palau Islands that Japan had received as a mandate from the League of Nations after the First World War (and soon afterwards illegally fortified and militarized). Those smaller forces reached Samar and the large island of Mindanao only a few days after Homma's 14th Army landed on Luzon, making the point that the Philippine campaign was to be a complex undertaking, requiring an equally complex response.

*** *A GALLANT BUT FUTILE RESISTANCE* ***

With Japanese air and naval superiority and the main body of the 14th Army coming ashore at Lingayen Gulf on December 22, PA (Philippine-American) ground troops were unable to defend the invasion beaches. General MacArthur then executed a standard pre-war plan that involved concentrating his Luzon-based resources onto the Bataan Peninsula that jutted into Manila Bay, and onto the nearby island of Corregidor—but it wasn't enough.

Lacking reinforcements, which the Allies were in no position to provide, the PA defenders suffered constant attrition, having battled

Japanese invaders from 7 January until 9 April 1942. The relatively few who with General MacArthur managed to escape the Bataan surrender, confined themselves to the small island of Corregidor where they held out for another month, the last weeks being under the command of General Wainwright after MacArthur had left for Australia.

Corregidor defenders included the North China Marines, the salty 4th Marine Regiment evacuated at the last minute from garrison duty in the American concession at Shanghai, China. Those hardy veterans manned the heavy guns and patrolled the perimeter of Corregidor, to help protect the medical staff and their wounded in the bomb-proof hospital below ground. The story of a former 4th Marine Sergeant Major is told in Scene 8 of this book.

Among the starved and emaciated survivors who eventually surrendered at Corregidor with General Wainwright were several dozen Army nurses and their senior officer, Captain Maude Davison. Sent to the internment camp at Santo Tomas University with civilians who had been captured in Manila, these gallant nurses continued to treat the sick and wounded until liberation finally came in 1945. They are commemorated in the book *We Band of Angels* by Elizabeth Norman.

*** *THE BATAAN DEATH MARCH* ***

Prior to the initial American surrender on Bataan, the ever-devious Colonel Tsuji left Malaya with his remaining understudy lieutenant to join the 14th Army staff. Tsuji's basic plan was simple: "kill all American prisoners," but after seeing that an astonishing 70,000 PA troops had surrendered at Bataan—an unthinkable situation according to Japanese Bushido code— Tsuji realized the impracticality of dealing with so many corpses at one time. When the prisoners were ordered to walk the 60 miles to Camp O'Donnell, where those who were fit enough to reach the camp would be retained for further use, prisoner escorts were instructed to show no mercy in cases where captives were unable to complete the long trek. Many wounded or sick prisoners dropped out of line on the way to the camp, and Colonel Tsuji's mandate caused them to be bayoneted to death by Japanese guards.

The hellish ordeal, with little food or water available, caused some twenty percent of the struggling captives to perish. The grisly event became known as the Bataan Death March when it was finally learned about by Americans at home, more than a year later.

In typical Tsuji fashion, Senior Lieutenant Tanamoto was assigned to the Manila Kempei Tai, where he resolutely followed Tsuji's orders to help eradicate pro-American Filipinos, and to publicize Japan's *Greater East Asia Co-Prosperity Scheme* to the remainder of the local population.

Tsuji himself had moved onward to Formosa to expand a fledgling School of Jungle Warfare for the Japanese Army, and to help draft the final plan for capturing oil supplies on Borneo and Sumatra, which was implemented after Singapore surrendered on February 15, 1942.

Prior to the surrender of his Bataan troops, General MacArthur had declared Manila to be an Open City in the hope that the Japanese invaders would not destroy its historical buildings (and his private property in the Manila Hotel). He then withdrew to the island of Corregidor with his staff and a bunker-type militia.

MacArthur also hoped the US or Allies could send reinforcements before the little island ran out of food and medical supplies, although he knew the chances of that were very slim. In his mind, he blamed his present circumstances on the decision by Admiral Thomas Hart to withdraw the remainder of the US fleet to Java, rather than protecting the Philippines from being over-run by Japs. To anyone who would listen, which included his many US supporters (the general was still in radio contact with Washington), he blamed the Navy over and over for his present sorry circumstances.

Admiral Hart—who outranked Lt.-General MacArthur by 4 stars to 3 when the Pacific war began, but was often treated by the general as an underling—had tried over and over to explain to MacArthur that a navy was quite ineffective in those modern times without the protection of an air flotilla, hoping the general would get the point that his Army Air Corps which had been destroyed on the ground was the key strategic loss that had brought about the sad sequence of events in which the US found itself.

In Washington, the few clear thinkers realized that neither MacArthur nor Hart could individually or collectively have stopped the Japanese invasion. Had most of MacArthur's planes not been destroyed on the ground, they soon would have been lost to an overwhelming number of more modern Japanese aircraft, whereas the paltry US Navy in the Philippines was little more than a token fleet as well.

Great Britain found itself in a similar predicament with Singapore and Malaya, having barely enough military and naval resources to contend with civil disobedience, but nothing to match the secretive build-up that had taken place in Japan since it began its war with China a decade earlier.

Soon it would be time for the Dutch on Java to defend their so-called Malay Barrier that might conceivably stop the Japanese onslaught and prevent it from attacking Australia, but—those same few clear-thinkers in Washington realized—it was quite unlikely that the hastily-assembled ABDA resources would achieve much more than a brief slowdown to Japanese momentum.

*** *TIGERS ALOFT* ***

Following Japan's prewar occupation of strategic bases in southern Indochina after Vichy France came into being, President Roosevelt and some members of Congress had realized—when calling upon the Dutch East Indies in 1941 to join the US in cutting off oil supplies to Japan—that there would come a Japanese reaction of some sort, but the President hoped that any military moves could be contained until Japan was brought to the negotiating table and stability was returned to the Far East.

To aid in this imagined containment, he authorized the formation of a covert military air group to assist China and its President Chiang Kai-Shek with their ongoing battles against Japan. The Auxiliary Volunteer Group, or AVG, was organized by USAAC Major General Claire Chennault with 100 pilots and 200 ground crew from the US Army, Navy, and Marine Corps—each of whom was required to resign from his branch of service and join a holding company that eventually became a special unit of the Chinese Air Force.

Chinese soldier guarding P-40 figher planes of the Flying Tigers

Flying P-40 fighter aircraft painted with distinctive shark-tooth cowlings, the AVG became known as the Flying Tigers, achieving highly successful results during its year of operations. Its performance was one of very few bright lights amid the general gloom that beset the US in the first half of 1942, until the battles of the Coral Sea, Midway, and Guadalcanal began to turn the tide against Japan.

Scene Four

British and Dutch Territories on Borneo

 In the center of the previous map, one can see the large island of Borneo southwest of the Philippines. Mountainous jungle for the most part, Borneo is the world's third-largest island after Greenland and New Guinea (Australia being considered a continent rather than an island).

Roughly one quarter of the island to the north and northwest of Borneo was effectively British before WWII—including **British North Borneo** (that was later known as Sabah), the semi-autonomous Sultanate of **Brunei**, and the Sultan's former kingdom of **Sarawak**—while the remaining three-quarters were Dutch and was known as **Kalimantan.**

Both British and Dutch territories had extensive oil production, which Japan coveted and was determined to capture. Japan was counting on thirty percent of its oil requirements coming from Borneo, with most of the remainder being supplied from Sumatra once the Allied forces and Dutch colonial government on Java were neutralized.

A pre-war understanding between Great Britain and the Netherlands resolved that Borneo would not be defended in case of war with Japan, but that oil facilities would all be destroyed to prevent their use by the Japanese. This understanding was not widely followed, however, since the British did send some troops to help defend Sarawak once it was realized that captured Borneo airfields would put Singapore in range of Japanese aircraft. The Dutch also used their limited resources to harass the Japanese invaders quite aggressively, for which they paid a high price if captured.

*** THE WHITE RAJAHS OF SARAWAK ***

A territory that would become the British Colony of Sarawak after WWII was located in the NW sector of Borneo island, and today is part of East Malaysia. A century before, it was part of the Sultanate of Brunei, and had a unique history thereafter. In 1841, an India-born English adventurer named James Brooke was awarded the governorship of Sarawak by the Sultan of Brunei, whom Brooke had assisted in suppressing an uprising within the Sultan's population of mostly Dayak headhunters. In time, Brooke became the Rajah of Sarawak, thus its absolute ruler in perpetuity. In one of those amazing stories from the East, this eccentric Englishman and his descendants ruled Sarawak for a century from Government House in Kuching, their fief having become a British Protectorate in 1882.

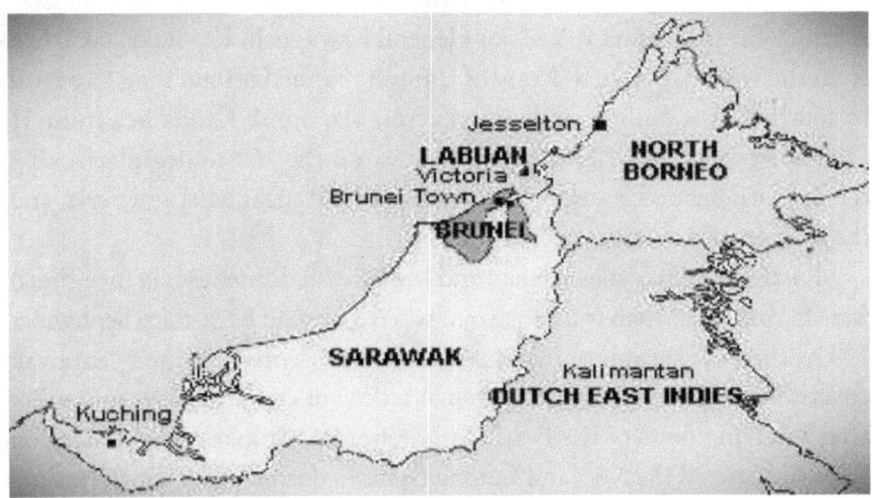

Map of northern Borneo, courtesy Sarawak Specialists Society (www.s-s-s.org.uk)

Only in 1946, after the Japanese had occupied and plundered Sarawak and British North Borneo, did Charles Vyner de Windt Brooke, the third and last rajah, sell the Sarawak fief to Great Britain for a suitable fee, making the new Crown Colony of Sarawak Britain's last-ever colonial acquisition. The colony lasted until 1963, when Sarawak became a charter member of the new nation called Malaysia.

The small independent but oil-rich rump-Sultanate of Brunei—to which Sarawak had once belonged—still exists today, surrounded by East Malaysia. The preceding map shows what these northern parts of Borneo looked like in 1941.

*** DESTRUCTION OF THE OIL FIELDS ***

As mentioned, Japan's military government was intensely interested in Borneo because of oil reserves in both the British and Dutch sections of the large island. Japan resolved to capture Borneo, as well as Sumatra where the Palembang oil fields were even more productive.

Yet another example of precise Japanese planning, the invasion force for northern Borneo was mustered at Cam Ranh Bay, Indochina, right on the heels of the earlier Japanese fleet that had departed for its invasion of Siam, Malaya, and Burma.

The Kawaguchi Force aboard the Borneo-bound fleet was the 35th Infantry Brigade under IJA Major General Kawaguchi Kiyotake, detached from the veteran Japanese Army of Canton that had fought long and hard in south China. Sailing undetected across the South China Sea from 11 December 1941, this fleet arrived at dawn on the 16th to begin attacking the lightly defended Sarawak and Brunei oilfields near Miri and Seria, and the refinery at Lutong.

Rajah Charles Vyner Brooke and his wife the Ranee Sylvia (née Brett) were in Australia when war broke out, where they had been since September 1941, thereby escaping imprisonment but depriving their Sarawak government of important leadership at a time of crisis. On December 8th, after receiving news of the Pearl Harbor attacks, Brooke's government on Sarawak ordered the Miri and Lutong facilities decommissioned according to a rehearsed plan that was successfully carried out by the same evening, and the Brunei wells at Seria were then sealed with cement.

Some months before, unbeknownst to Japanese spies on Sarawak, these facilities had already been throttled back in oil production by seventy percent, then on the 8th all operable wells were capped, and skilled workers were sent off to Singapore with critical parts from the wells and refinery. After Singapore fell to the Japanese in mid-February 1942, those skilled workers were rounded up and sent back to Miri to restart oil production under duress. Over the next four years of Japanese occupation, still running at just thirty percent of true capacity, the Miri wells nevertheless produced nearly a million barrels of oil despite ongoing allied bombing raids on the wells and refinery.

[As an interesting historical note, Miri had been known for centuries for its petroleum from shallow, hand-dug wells, as recorded in Chinese chronicles. Eventually the Brookes convinced Royal Dutch Shell to drill the first modern well in 1910. Known as The Grand Old Lady, its wooden structure was operational into the 1970s and now reposes outside a local museum. This Well #1 was joined by hundreds of other onshore and offshore wells thereafter, while the population of Miri township grew apace from 2,000 people in 1941 to over 200,000 today—Ed.]

In addition to the oil facilities of Sarawak and Brunei, a major production field at Sandakan in British North Borneo was also disabled prior to the arrival of IJA troops on 17 January 1942. Sir Robert Smith—governor of that region which the British had leased in 1878 from the Sultan of Sabah—signed the surrender at his official residence on the small offshore island of Labuan, which was administratively linked to the Straits Settlements Crown Colony of Singapore, Malacca, and Penang. 'Offshore Management' was a hallmark of the British Empire in the Pacific Region.

Sandakan later became a notorious Japanese POW campsite as did many of the Dutch coastal settlements on Borneo.

*** LAST-MINUTE BRITISH DEFENSES ***

[The following story about the exemplary SARFOR Defense Force in British Borneo is condensed from unpublished documents of The Soldier's Burden *at https://kaiserscross.com/304501/521701.html – Ed.]*

By prewar agreement with the Dutch, Britain at first provided only minimal defensive measures in Sarawak, but after realizing that the Bukit Stabar airfield near the seat of government at Kuching—far south of the Sarawak oil fields—could put Japanese planes in easy range of Singapore, just 350 miles distant, the 2nd Battalion of the veteran 15th Punjab Regiment from British India was dispatched from Singapore to Kuching, together with gunnery, medical, and engineering resources. Japanese invaders knew about this airport and proceeded to engage its defenders on December 24th.

2/15th Punjab Battalion was commanded by Major Charles Malet Lane, who was promoted to Lieutenant Colonel soon after his arrival at Sarawak when given the additional command of 1500 local Sarawak Rangers and the local police force. Collectively known as SARFOR (Sarawak Forces), Lt. Colonel Lane's 2500 combined Indian and Sarawak troops had an interesting racial makeup. The 2/15th Punjab Battalion, with both English and Indian officers, consisted mostly of Muslim Punjabis but there were also several hundred Sikhs, Khattacks, and Jats from the same Punjab region of India. The para-military Sarawak Rangers included former head-hunter Dayaks and local Muslim Malay Volunteers, both with British officers.

The local police force, a platoon of Royal Engineers, and one company from the battalion were left at Miri to assist with decommissioning the oil facilities, while the rest of SARFOR was billeted near Kuching to defend the airfield. After Major General Kawaguchi's troops landed at Miri and discovered the unusable oil wells and refinery, they left one battalion of infantry behind to subdue Brunei, British North Borneo, and the small island of Labuan, while the rest of the invasion force sailed south for Kuching, which was bombed on December 19th and invaded on the 23rd. Following the bombing, Singapore gave orders for the Kuching airfield to be destroyed, and sappers exploded charges in 50 predrilled boreholes that had been placed across the runways, rendering the airfield unusable.

The next morning, 24 December, twenty enemy landing craft approached the river mouths that led to Kuching, becoming engaged in a fierce fight with the Sarawak Rangers and the rear guard of 2/15th that resulted in the sinking of seven of the barges. Kuching had been declared an open city, to spare the civilian population, so SARFOR withdrew toward the airfield as the Japanese gradually outnumbered them.

On Christmas morning, Colonel Lane ordered SARFOR to further withdraw southward into the jungle toward the Dutch border. A group of British women and children was sent on ahead with the hospital contingent during a lull in the fighting. As these movements were proceeding, a large Japanese force attacked the 2/15th rear-guard in strength. After a stiff fight, particularly by the Khattacks who machine-gunned a considerable number of advancing Japanese, four British officers, six Indian officers and 230 sepoys were killed or taken prisoner, wounded prisoners being bayoneted by the Japanese.

Five days later and after a 60-mile march, the rear-guard remnant joined 2/15th at Sanggau in Dutch Borneo. Colonel Lane, who next morning found that his black hair had turned white overnight, kept his weary men moving on foot. The local Sarawak units were disbanded at Sanggau, as their military commitment did not extend beyond the state borders, but several Volunteer and Ranger officers and senior ranks chose to fight on with the Battalion as did a Malay Ranger, Suhail Ali, who impressed everyone with his tireless energy and commitment. All the Sarawak additions were extremely useful because of their intimate knowledge of Borneo.

The wounded, the sick, and the women and children were sent on to the nearby Dutch airbase Singkawan II, escorted by those Sarawak Volunteers who chose to stay and fight. The strength of SARFOR was by then seventeen British officers—including seven from the Rangers—fourteen Indian officers, and 790 men. These numbers included the Royal Engineers, Indian Medical Service, and RAF personnel who had been attached to the Battalion in Kuching, plus the few remaining local state personnel—including Ranger Suhail Ali.

The slimmed-down SARFOR—roughly one third its original size—proceeded along jungle tracks to Sanggau, arriving there on 29 December. At the Singkawan II airbase, good accommodation was found in barracks built for RAF personnel. Food and clothing could be obtained and on December 31, three Blenheim aircraft from Singapore dropped one thousand pounds of rations for the Punjabis onto Singkawan II.

Colonel Lane signaled his thanks to Singapore, requesting that the Punjabis now be withdrawn from Borneo, but was informed that the Battalion would thereafter be under Dutch command. Accordingly, the civilians and surplus administrative troops in SARFOR were ordered to proceed to Pontianak for evacuation to Java, while the fighting troops were told to defend the Dutch airfield.

Eventually the Japanese tried to break through to Singkawan II airfield. Their progress was blocked by Subedar (Warrant Officer) Faramurz Khan and two platoons of Muslim Punjabi sepoys (soldiers) from B Company. Khan exhorted his men to fight to the end. After an all-day action the Punjabis were finally overrun in the early evening, having expended their ammunition. Faramurz Khan and many of his men were already dead but the Japanese were angry and vengeful because of the 400 or more casualties that they themselves had suffered. Only three Punjabis from these two platoons were ever seen again, and one of them, Lance-Naik (Lance-Corporal) Sher Khan, later reported that the Japanese had wired the Punjabi prisoners together, doused them in gasoline and burned them to death.

The ammunition state of the Battalion was by then just 60 rounds per man and one fully charged magazine for each Bren gun. There were no reserves of ammunition, and the clothing and boots of the sepoys were worn out. Colonel Lane decided to withdraw the remaining men of SARFOR to the south Borneo coast with a view to arranging an evacuation to Java.

The colonel had been seriously ill with malaria since mid-January and he was not fit to march further. The Dutch agreed to evacuate him by air to Java along with some senior Dutch officials, but the seaplane took off before Colonel Lane could reach its river mooring, leaving him to make his own way to the south coast with his battalion.

Although the Punjabis did not yet know it, they had fought the last of their major actions against the Japanese. What lay ahead of them was an exceedingly tough march through hot, wet, and often inhospitable jungle. Lt. Colonel Ross-Thompson, assuming command from sick Colonel Lane, organized SARFOR into two columns—a West Column with under-strength A and B companies, and an East Column with likewise debilitated C and D companies, that were to march separately to different coastal villages. There was also a Blitz Party whose task was to move rapidly to the closer coastal village of Sampit and contact the British HQ in Java, either by radio or small boat. These men achieved their mission by struggling through 100 miles of jungle in five days and then finding a useable radio, although the seaplane that had taken off without Colonel Lane had already alerted Java to the battalion's intentions.

Nearly a month later, after epic treks and river crossings, both East and West Columns reached their destinations. Apart from a lack of rations—foraging in villages having produced very little spare food—mosquitoes, leeches, soldier ants, snakes, and wild bees attacked the men as they made their way south. Many weapons were lost on river crossings when homemade rafts capsized. By then, most of the sepoys were physically shattered and debilitated from the lack of food, and those who fell out on the march faced an uncertain future as many villagers were unfriendly towards foreigners. In the larger towns, anarchy reigned, and armed civilians were attacking the remaining Europeans and Chinese and looting their offices and stores.

Both SARFOR columns travelled down rivers when possible on rafts or launches supplied by cooperative Dutch officials. When near the coast at Sampit, a Japanese force landed ahead of East Column, and two Khattack patrols fought a delaying action to allow the remainder of the column to withdraw. Even so, many men were left behind, some too exhausted to move quickly. The Japanese soon rounded them up. The remainder of East Column then marched westward to join West Column near Pangkalanboen.

Then a staff officer arrived from Java to advise that the Punjabis were not to be evacuated after all but were to defend Kotawaringen airfield and then operate in the interior as guerrillas, along with a Dutch unit. The troops were to live off the land. But this plan came too late to be viable. The battalion was no longer physically capable of facing the exertions and privations of jungle-living. The staff officer unfortunately broadcast the intentions of East and West Columns throughout the area, perhaps in a misguided attempt to contact any stragglers, but his efforts resulted in the Japanese becoming aware of SARFOR and its intended movements.

A boat did arrive from Java for SARFOR bringing welcome rations. It also brought weapons and ammunition, but the cargo had been incorrectly loaded, as Bren guns were without magazines, grenades were without detonators and much of the ammunition was for Dutch 6.5-milimetre carbines. Colonel Lane met up with the Battalion and assumed command of SARFOR again. Concerned about the physical condition of the men, Colonel Lane and Lt.-Colonel Ross-Thompson decided that further resistance would be futile, and SARFOR surrendered to a Japanese naval brigade on 3 April 1942, thus ending their heroic ten-week ordeal in the jungle a month after the Japanese had invaded and occupied Java.

In captivity SARFOR was split up and placed in several camps in South-East Asia. All the British officers of the 2/15th Punjab Regiment survived captivity. Some were held in the Batu Lintang camp at Kuching, and mention is made of them in Don Wall's book *Kill the Prisoners*.

It was the Indian officers and soldiers who suffered the most from Japanese atrocities in the camps. Most sepoys and NCOs, led by their Indian officers, refused to join the Japanese-sponsored Indian National Army under the collaborator Subhas Chandra Bose. This infuriated the Japanese, and at the Kuala Belait camp in Brunei, Subedar Makhmad Anwar was flogged and hung by his heels until he was dead. Four jemadars in Kuala Belait camp were made to dig their own graves before they were beheaded. It appears that fifty sepoys who had refused to collaborate were tied up and bayoneted or otherwise murdered.

Malay Ranger Suhail Ali stayed with the Battalion throughout its time in Borneo and went into captivity with it. The Japanese offered him repatriation to Sarawak, but he chose to stay with the Punjabis. He was a tower of strength in captivity, and after release from a camp in Rabaul at the end of the war he went with the Punjabi survivors back to Ambala in India where the Battalion was reorganized, returning to Sarawak later. Captain Philip Crosland later wrote of him: "A braver and more honorable man you could not find anywhere."

*** DUTCH BORNEO ATROCITIES ***

The principal Dutch oil facilities were at Tarakan, Samarinda and Balikpapan on the east coast. The Imperial Japanese Navy was given the logistical responsibility of capturing the Dutch portion of Borneo, known as Kalimantan, and was assigned army units to make the actual invasions. The fleet set about this task in January 1942, with a landing at Tarakan Island on 11 January by Major General Sakaguchi Shizuo's 124th Infantry Regiment, plus armored vehicles and artillery.

Two major fields at Tarakan were producing over four million barrels of crude oil annually. Outnumbered Dutch troops destroyed the 700 wells to prevent Japanese use, in return for which the Japanese executed all surrendered Dutch POWs the following day.

On January 24th, the Sakaguchi elements were landed at Balikpapan, where they occupied the town and oil facilities without serious resistance, although their ships were attacked by a flotilla of American destroyers dispatched from Java by Admiral Hart. The following month the Japanese executed Dutch POWs and civilians for having destroyed the oil facilities prior to the occupation.

[This type of inhumane reaction seems to have manifested itself throughout the territories that Japan conquered, making it probable that a common thread was involved—such as the wily Colonel Tsuji Masanobu. He was certainly a 'dark force' within the Imperial Japanese Army and seems to have intimidated even some senior officers. But at least one exception was Major-General Kawaguchi Kiyotake who oversaw the Japanese force that attacked Sarawak in December 1941. Although some of the general's infantry officers seemed to condone summary executions of captured prisoners, he himself was

publicly on record afterwards—while stationed in Cebu, Philippines—as being vehemently opposed to Tsuji's inhuman tactics. Tsuji, who could not in turn rebut his accuser openly, did use his personnel connections to get General Kawaguchi transferred to various dangerous battlegrounds—such as Guadalcanal, where the general's troops were on the losing end of the Battle at Edson's Ridge—in the hope that his adversary would not return.

General Kawaguchi did return, but ironically after the war he was tried, convicted and sentenced to some years in prison for allegedly participating in one of Tsuji's revenge murders of a leading pro-American Filipino politician. Perhaps the court tried the wrong man, but after the war Colonel Tsuji managed to disappear in Thailand for a while, surfacing eventually in Japan and getting elected to the Diet, at which point he had the audacity to publish his own book, Singapore, the Japanese Version. *He was never brought to justice - Ed.]*

The modernized Balikpapan oil center could in those days produce aviation fuel, diesel oil, kerosene, and lubricating oil, and its delayed startup was a serious setback for the Japanese. Although they eventually made all the Borneo oil facilities operational again, a further setback for Japan was the loss of a ship that was carrying hundreds of their civilian technical, medical and administrative people to run the captured territories and oil centers. Army transport *Taiyo Maru* was sunk by American submarine USS *Grenadier* on 8 May 1942.

The Dutch East Indies of Java and Sumatra

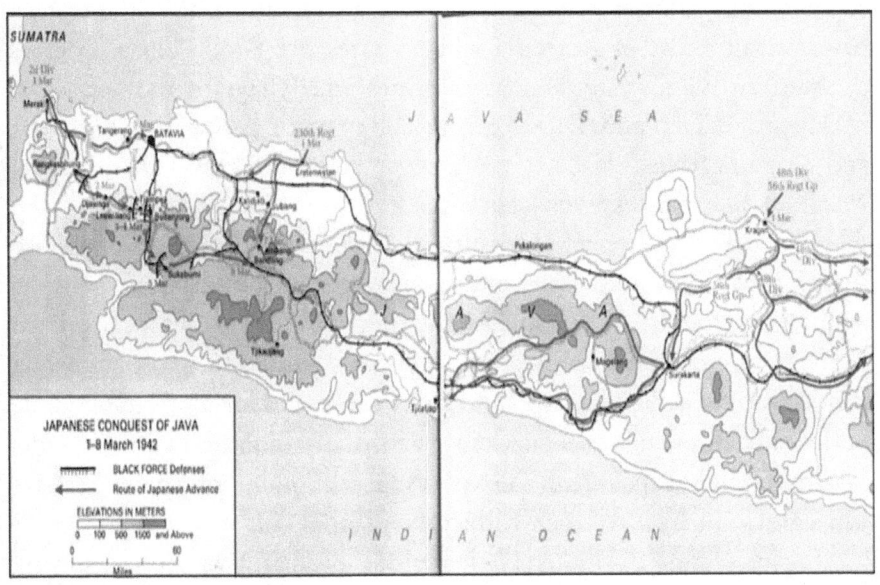

Java Jive
The Ink Spots (1940)

I love coffee, I love tea
I love the java jive and it loves me
Coffee and tea and the jiving and me
A cup, a cup, a cup, a cup, a cup! …m'boy

Songwriters: MILTON DRAKE, BEN OAKLAND
© Sony/ATV Music Publishing LLC, Warner/Chappell Music, Inc.
Data from: LyricFind

 The Republic of Indonesia today comprises the very extensive Dutch colonial holdings that existed in SE Asia for some 300 years prior to WWII. Even before Dutch rule, the region's seafaring legacy brought it considerable prosperity through trade with other lands, in the process of which its people came under the sway of several major religions—Hinduism, Buddhism, Islam, and Christianity.

The territory is a collection of islands large and small—nearly 14,000 of them—spread over an archipelago of comparable East-West magnitude to the United States of America. With rugged terrain that is still difficult to traverse, the region's coastlines and waterways have always been of primary importance to its development.

Straddling two tectonic shelves—the Sunda and the Sahul—has resulted in an unusual ecological diversity. Flora and fauna of the eastern parts mimic those of Australia which shares the Sunda Shelf, whereas the western islands have similar creatures and foliage to the jungles of Malaysia and Thailand. Due to the instability of the two shelves; both Java and Sumatra have a dozen or more active volcanoes each. The resulting volcanic soil mixtures favor Java's crops over Sumatra's.

The region's physical, agricultural, and social development is also shaped by summer and winter monsoons, with wet and dry seasons as the winds blow from the NW and SE for each half of the year. From the dawn of the Common Era (CE) over two thousand years ago, those monsoon winds brought sailing ships to and from the Indies for a profitable trade in rice and spices with other nations, particularly India and China. Trade, in turn, brought exposure to the world's great religions, of which there are still significant traces of each within the islands.

Explorers from the Dutch Netherlands arrived around 1600, following earlier Portuguese navigators who had developed the first oceanic trade routes to the Far East from Western Europe that would rival more ancient overland routes to China, known as the Silk Road.

Lured by the profitable spice trade, the privately held Dutch East India Company, or VOC (*Vereenigde Oost-Indische Compagnie*) was established in 1602 as the world's first corporation to issue bonds and shares. In addition, it had quasi-governmental powers including the ability to wage war, to imprison and execute convicts, to negotiate treaties, and to issue its own coinage. The VOC lasted for two centuries, until it was wound up during Napoleon's occupation of the Netherlands.

In 1795, Napoleon's troops and cavalry invaded the Dutch Netherlands and the Austrian Netherlands, intent on adding the Low Countries of Europe to an expanding French empire. By 1803 Napoleon had merged those two conquered territories into one, naming it the Batavian Republic (Batavia being an ancient name for a region of Holland). After his defeat, they split apart again, this time into three, and became the Netherlands, Belgium, and Luxemburg.

Napoleon seemed unstoppable in his early days of conquest, but one powerful nation did not have to fear him for it was protected from continental Europe by a wide waterway and patrolled worldwide by a fleet of warships that the French could not subdue. That nation was the United Kingdom of Great Britain and Ireland, with which the Dutch government-in-exile hastened to establish unofficial relations after Napoleon's French armies took over their homeland.

A few years later—far away in the Pacific Ocean—a French-controlled Dutch fleet based at Java began to harass British shipping along the lucrative trade route between India and China. Having replaced the now-defunct VOC, the Dutch colonies of Java and Sumatra became essentially a French client state under the supervision of a French governor, with support from the French navy in the Indian Ocean at Île de France (today's Mauritius) and Île Réunion.

British fleet commanders in India resolved to destroy the French ships, which they did during 1806-7 with many a swashbuckling adventure at sea (the general plot for the *Master and Commander* books by Patrick O'Brian). In 1811, British sailors and marines invaded Java and took away control of the Dutch colony from France, although the Dutch homeland was still under Napoleon's thumb in Europe.

It is likely that the exiled Dutch government had encouraged Great Britain to occupy Java and expel the French with promise of a reward for doing so. What the reward might be is unrecorded, but it was certain that compensation of some sort would be demanded by Britain in due course. Even though the exiled Dutch government was on somewhat cordial diplomatic terms with the British when it came to harassment of their mutual French enemy, they were otherwise fierce competitors in the world marketplace for spices and other Asian plantation products. It was probable, therefore, that the reward Britain might claim, would somehow advance Britain's competitive position in the Far East, and so it came to pass.

Once the French fleet was destroyed and the remaining Dutch administrators on Java were won over, Lord Minto—British governor-general of India—personally visited Java to assess the opportunities. He had become impressed with the talents of a young up-and-coming functionary named Stamford Raffles, who was based at Penang Island off Malaya, on the very eastern fringes of the British Raj. Much to the astonishment (and jealousy) of the Penang cadre, Lord Minto brought Raffles along on his inspection visit and in due course appointed him Lieutenant Governor of Java.

The British Foreign Service was shocked at this abrupt elevation of an obscure junior official to such a prominent position, but Raffles more than fulfilled Lord Minto's expectations. Being of inquiring mind and possessing a deep fascination with the countries, languages and cultures of the East, Raffles instituted numerous reforms to improve the lives of the Javanese peasantry, and was responsible for the discovery and restoration of a huge ancient Buddhist temple at Borobudur (today a World Heritage site). Furthermore, upon finding the VOC treasury practically bankrupt, Raffles proposed that the British government press the exiled Dutch into a concession that would procure funds for Java's administration. This proposal became the basis for Britain's claim for services rendered in chasing the French away from Java four years earlier.

It was a clever scheme, which involved providing British investors with an option to buy shares in a vast collection of West Java plantations that became known as the P&T Lands (*P&T Landen* in Dutch, meaning *Pamanoekan en Tjassemlanden*). The original P&T concession exceeded 200,000 hectares and was duly registered in 1812. We shall hear more about P&T Lands in a later section.

Raffles remained at his Java post until 1816, when it reverted to Dutch administration (but with P&T Lands still under British ownership). Three years later, upon receiving instructions to establish a British sovereign presence somewhere within the Dutch sphere of influence—the British and Dutch being serious competitors once again—newly-knighted Sir Stamford Raffles founded the British colony of Singapore on a virtually uninhabited island at the southern tip of the Malayan Peninsula.

This fine achievement brought Raffles everlasting fame, having given Britain a strategic outpost along the trade routes of the Orient. In 1826, Raffles died in London of ill health, just 45 years of age.

Stamford Raffles is world-famous to this day as the founder of Singapore, and even vaguely remembered for the restoration of ancient Borobudur. Much less is known of P&T Lands, however, his other important achievement.

After Napoleon's defeat, and the end of British custodianship of former VOC territory, the Netherlands East Indies (NEI) was formed as a Dutch colony to continue development and expansion of their Far East holdings. Effectively, the NEI lasted until the Japanese invasions of 1942.

*** THE REES FAMILY IN JAVA ***

Everything in Java had seemed in good order when Alan Rees and his wife Margaret—known to friends as Maggie—arrived in Batavia upon their return from a final Singapore-funded home leave. The slow ocean voyages from Singapore to Southampton and Rotterdam to Batavia in the spring of 1938 had been uneventful, and Alan was eager to get into his new job with P&T Lands as quickly as possible. Alan was a few years older, a few inches shorter, and an inch or so stouter in the waist than his Singapore successor, Peter Perry, but still reasonably fit. Like Peter, who was a fellow Welshman by origin, Alan enjoyed Rugby football very much, and had acquired a fondness for horseback riding in Singapore that he hoped would be available to expatriate managers such as himself at P&T Lands.

Alan's wife Maggie instinctively tended to compare herself to young Wendy Perry, whose husband had acquired Alan's former post with the Singapore Municipal Engineers. Maggie was convinced that she was considered more attractive than Wendy, at least to the English, but she acknowledged that Wendy had a nicer figure. *And that often appeals to some sorts of men more than a pretty face*, she mused at times. *Well, my face may not be my fortune, but Alan and I do make a reasonably handsome couple*, she was certain, having been told so by more than one older couple in Singapore and aboard ship. She couldn't help wondering, though, whether she would be considered attractive by the Dutch people that they would meet in Soebang, the company town. *So many of them are blond and rosy-cheeked*, she remembered from her few Dutch friends in Singapore. *I sometimes wish I were a blond too, instead of a plain brunette. Well, why am*

I so nervous? she asked herself as the ship was being tied up to a bulkhead of the passenger wharf.

A sedan and lorry from P&T awaited their morning arrival at the Batavia docks, so Alan and Maggie decided to load the steamer trunks into the lorry and drive in caravan to Soebang that same day, a journey of some six hours back then, rather than sending their things on ahead with the lorry. They would wait and explore Batavia some other time.

Java's capital was five hundred miles below the equator, but not so far east of Singapore that it caused many problems for one's body clock. Nonetheless, because they had sailed directly from Europe around the Cape of Good Hope and across the Indian Ocean, Maggie dozed most of the way to Soebang while Alan and the driver kept up a constant chatter as they whizzed through little villages set into windblown fields of sugarcane, followed closely by the lorry that lurched along with their possessions. Alan admired the distant hazy mountains that made Java look so different from Singapore's cultivated and almost-flat landscape.

Now and then they stopped so Alan and Maggie could take photographs of each other against some unusually exotic background, at which point they would invariably be surrounded by smiling villagers, offering to sell them exquisite wood carvings, strange-looking knives, multicolored batik cloth, and scenic watercolor paintings that were amazingly realistic.

The languages they heard around them were distinctly different from the chatter of Chinese and Malay dialects which characterized Singapore's marketplaces. Instead they heard an unintelligible local tongue—which their driver said was the Soendanese language, mixed with Dutch words that he could understand but apparently Alan and Maggie could not.

"We have some work ahead of us, darling," Maggie observed, "and did you see that gorgeous watercolor painting of a volcano, by the way?"

"I did indeed," Alan replied, "and its price—forty-eight Rix Dollars, which would be around twenty Dutch Guilders, or forty Sing Dollars. Are you sure you'd like to have it?"

"You're so clever, darling. Perhaps another day, then," Maggie replied, thinking ahead to her probable food bill for the month.

*** *A HUGE PLANTATION COMPLEX* ***

P&T Lands, when the Rees family moved there in March 1938, was enjoying renewed prosperity after a period of decline and near bankruptcy. The original prosperity had to do with Sir Stamford Raffles; the subsequent decline came about through greed.

Soon after Raffles got permission to float the P&T shares in 1813 they were snatched up on the London Exchange, but the initial English investors were simply speculators who resold their holdings later for a profit. Then, surprisingly, a single investor repurchased nearly all the London shares in 1840.

The new investor was an enterprising Dutchman named Peter William Hofland who, after acquiring control of the company, spent his lifelong energies and talent developing the various plantation estates of P&T Lands into a viable agricultural conglomerate that was—to the relief, no doubt, of the NEI government—fully under Dutch control once again. A large commemorative statue of Peter Hofland in the old Christian cemetery at Soebang attests to this man's tremendous achievement during his lifetime.

Upon his death, however, Hofland's two sons gradually squandered the company proceeds and allowed the P&T estates to decline into virtual ruin through lack of ongoing investment and maintenance. In due course, the banks called in their loans and appointed an overseer to dispose of the debt by selling off the assets. For lack of any Dutch buyers, the P&T shares were refloated in England where a group of new investors took over the estates in the early 1900s. The new English owners formed a holding company, Anglo-Dutch Plantations of Java Ltd, and were pragmatic enough to bring the estates back into productivity before paying out any dividends to the investors.

In 1919, the NEI government expropriated 355,000 of 528,000 acres of P&T land for the sum of seventeen million guilders, but the remainder was still highly profitable considering that the English owners had a virtually captive home market of customers, which the competing government-owned estates did not. In addition, it was the custom for plantations in Java to allow local village tenant farmers to work a share of the different estates for their own account, upon payment to the plantation owners of twenty percent of their profits, a practice which was known as *tjoekee* (sounds like *chuckee*).

For the remaining unexpropriated estates, *tjoekee* was a significant source of P&T income that supplemented the revenue from the company's own exports abroad. During the heydays of the 1920s P&T Lands managed to acquire additional estates elsewhere in Java and Sumatra to make up for some of the terrain lost to the government.

Thus, more than a hundred years after P&T's original founding, life in Soebang—the company headquarters town—was once again good. The town certainly appealed to the Reeses, once they had settled in and met some people from both the British and Dutch communities.

Alan was delighted to find that P&T had a Soebang rugby team, and in short order he was elected captain because of his experience playing in England and Singapore. He lost no time inviting his old Singapore XV to visit Batavia for a match in the coming year against a combined Soebang and Batavia side. What surprised Alan most was that both the Soebang and Batavia teams had Dutch players as well as English, and that the Dutchmen gave a good account of themselves without the benefit of having played the game during their school days in Holland.

Rugby match at the Soebang Club, 1939, Soebang in white - Photo H. Price

Of further appeal to Alan and Maggie was the semi-tropical climate within the P&T estates that varied from warm to cool according to various elevations around the company's boundaries, from sea-level in the north up to the high southern mountains. Soebang's elevation on the wide plain at the base of the mountains was just 300 feet above sea level, so it was often hot—or warm at best—whereas Bandoeng, just outside the company's southern boundaries across the central mountains, was around 2,500 feet high and considerably cooler, although Bandoeng was a large and busy city and not a place for weekend relaxation.

The best location of all for Soebang residents to spend their weekends—in those pre-war, pre-air-conditioning days—was Lembang, at over 4,000 feet elevation and only 40 miles away from Soebang, in coffee country. Situated near the crater of a semi-active volcano, Lembang's climate was excellent all year long and could be reached by road from Soebang through a narrow mountain pass called Tjiater. The Grand Hotel in Lembang was always ready to welcome weekend or long-term visitors.

Alan's new job appealed to him greatly as well. During his first year in Java he travelled to all corners of the P&T territory, visiting each of the company estates in turn to assess their future needs for electricity and water supply, for roads and equipment, and for telephone service. The directors had given him a fairly-free hand at modernizing the company infrastructure for the future, with an eye to better communications and more efficient handling of the many valuable products that P&T Lands provided to nearly all corners of the earth.

Alan and Maggie were thrilled to be part of this forward-thinking organization that was the world's third or fourth-largest supplier of plantation-based products. With such a prestigious international position came highly important responsibilities, however, because many of the P&T products—such as rubber—were by then on the critical lists for Allied military services.

Toward the end of 1938, Alan was put in charge of design and construction of a new headquarters building in Soebang, for which the company directors had just allocated funds on condition that the building would be completed well before 31 August 1939 for Queen Wilhelmina's birthday celebrations.

For this large project, with its many key details and a mere ten months available for completion, Civil Engineer Alan Rees—who had also dabbled in architecture—was provided with three assistant engineers and eight supervising foremen, plus some four hundred workers.

In the middle of 1939 after the building's design phase had been completed, Alan picked the more promising of his assistants—Ronald Van Noorden, a Dutchman very fluent in English—and sent him off to Singapore with his wife and son to work under Peter Perry and learn everything possible about the Singapore water treatment and sewage systems. Peter wrote back that the former Rees residence at MacRitchie Reservoir was still vacant, and the Van Noordens would be housed there as Peter and Wendy's new neighbors.

Much of the Soebang headquarters building construction took place at night, seven days a week. The project was completed a full month ahead of schedule—even with the pleasant distraction of a 'friendly' rugby match between Batavia and Soebang at the Soebang Club in January, then an international cup match in Batavia in February between Singapore and a combined team from Batavia and Soebang. Although Singapore won the cup, it was great fun for Alan to be with his old team-mates again for a couple of days, with a rematch promised for 1940 in Singapore.

P&T Lands headquarters in Soebang, Java, 1942 – photo R. van Veen

In due course the P&T headquarters building was officially opened to much fanfare, with many high-ranking official government and civil guests in attendance. Alan was pleased to hand over the keys to Daphne Jackson, the managing director's wife, who then opened the doors for the hundreds of guests and onlookers. Daphne's husband, the Managing Director Charles Jackson, led the many speeches of the afternoon by stating that the new building represented the company's confidence in three important aspects: confidence in future prosperity from the company's products, confidence in an ongoing cordial relationship with the NEI government, and confidence in the company's talented staff members.

*** A FOOLISH TRAGEDY ***

By 1941 when Alan was well into his third year with P&T Lands, the company had around 250 British and Dutch employees, and of course thousands of village natives working on the estates as laborers, who were primarily Soendanese from West Java rather than Javanese. For the most part, the individual plantation estates were run by Dutch managers, while P&T's corporate, financial and technical staff in Soebang was mostly English. There were exceptions in both cases, but this was the general situation.

Although quite congenial during workdays, the various cultural groups—including the many Chinese shopkeepers of Soebang—tended to dwell apart during evenings and weekends, primarily because of language preferences. Of course, the Europeans managed to learn enough Soendanese to direct the work of their native employees, and most well-educated Dutch people also spoke English. Nonetheless, very few English people could manage a conversation in the difficult Dutch language, which they referred to sarcastically as "a throat disease." The English throughout their history were never famous as linguists, and that was certainly true in Java (*Americans abroad generally share that stigma as well; it must be a Mayflower gene – Ed.*).

Despite their cultural and linguistic differences, the English and Dutch of P&T Lands depended on each other for their livelihoods and therefore got along together reasonably well. They were also highly competitive in sports and games whenever an off-duty opportunity arose, a competitiveness which often extended to drinking contests by younger staff members since social functions—such as company parties—usually included both groups.

There was never a better annual opportunity for Anglo-Dutch competition in Soebang than during the festive week before the Dutch Sovereign's birthday observance on August 31st each year, which continued to be observed in the Dutch colonies despite the terrible war with Germany in Europe. Queen Wilhelmina of the Netherlands was officially feted at many places throughout the East Indies, especially in major cities like Batavia, Soerabaja, and Bandoeng in Java, and Palembang in Sumatra. In the smaller city of Soebang, it was mostly P&T Lands that provided a budget for the Queen's birthday celebrations, even though the head of NEI government from Batavia usually attended as did members of ancient Javanese royalty.

One of the favorite events for the Queen's birthday during the 1930s and 40s that inflamed the hearts and souls of the entire population of Soebang, was horse racing! With betting! In those days it was not the staid and dignified variety of horse racing over which society editors of leading newspapers salivate, but a much more primitive—and exciting—version. Evenly matched English and Dutch teams of four riders each would race wild mountain ponies, bareback, through the city streets of Soebang while people along the way cheered and shouted, urging the riders to ever-more daring speeds toward the finish line, a predetermined spot outside of the town.

So highly intoxicating was the mutual-betting pony racing for the populace of Soebang—at the start of a four-day holiday for the Queen's birthday the following Sunday—that the betting pot had reached an all-time high by Thursday afternoon 28 August 1941, just before the annual race began.

On that same Thursday, Alan and Maggie were returning to Soebang from a few relaxing days up at Lembang where they had recently bought a small plot of land to build a weekend cottage, intending to put an end to hotel expenses. Their deed certificate was not yet registered by the NEI bureaucracy, however, and construction could not start without the certificate. They looked forward with great anticipation to their eventual private bungalow in the cool mountains—an option that would have been unthinkable in flat and equatorial Singapore.

[Singapore expats tended to gravitate to the Cameron Highlands in Malaya to gain respite from the tropical heat, but those mountains to the north of Kuala Lumpur were a long tiring drive each way – Ed.]

Upon arriving back home in Soebang that afternoon as the heat was beginning to dissipate, Alan was surprised to be accosted in his driveway by several young men from the engineering department, pleading for him to join them in a wild pony race later that day.

"Please, Alan, we need you! The Dutch have four riders, but we only have three because Jones is ill, so we will probably be blocked by the Dutch riders from winning! And the winning team's share of the betting pot is over four hundred guilders this year, never so high. Please, Alan!"

Alan decided to consult with Maggie, although she was very likely opposed to the idea of him going out again after they had just returned home.

"What do you think, dear?" Alan asked Maggie, who was unloading the car.

"I think you should tell them to go away, and come inside to tidy up and relax, that's what I think. You have no experience riding those ponies without a saddle. Please send those boys away," Maggie insisted.

In his heart of hearts, Peter knew she was right. He had never ridden a horse bareback but did have considerable experience riding in Singapore with a saddle and had often careened along at a gallop beside the manicured banks of MacRitchie Reservoir; he had already done a bit of riding in Java too, but with a saddle always. Nevertheless, he knew the young engineers looked up to him as an all-around athlete, who captained the Soebang rugby side against Batavia or occasional British navy teams that came up to Soebang for a jolly weekend. Alan found their adoration quite flattering, in fact.

"Please Alan; Mr. Rees," the lads went on. "It would be terrible to let the Dutch walk away with that big pot of money, now wouldn't it?"

"Oh, all right then, I'll ride with you three. I could certainly use a hundred guilders. What time do we start?" Hearing this, Maggie sniffed and went inside without a backward glance.

"Er, in twenty minutes, over at the headquarters building," one of the lads replied. "Sorry the start-time is so close. We were terribly afraid that you wouldn't arrive here in time!"

"Good grief, that means I haven't time to freshen up and change into some better riding kit," Alan sputtered. "Well, no matter, let's hop to it. Have you a car, or shall we take mine?"

Twenty minutes later, the mad race began with a pistol shot in the air from one of the umpires. This unusual noise so startled the ponies that they dashed frantically down the headquarters driveway, at the end of which the eight riders—four English and four Dutch—fought for position while turning their ponies sharply onto a dirt track that bordered the tidy lawn. Noting that his floppy weekend trousers were quite useless for gripping the animal with his knees, Alan held onto his pony's mane for dear life, as he fought to keep himself upright.

Beyond the dirt track was a hard-surfaced road that led toward the town center. The unshod ponies slipped and clattered along this unfamiliar surface, as their positions quickly transposed from a disorganized clump into a drawn-out line, with riders striving to block each other as they raced along, so that someone else from their team could hopefully escape the blockade and rush on to claim the prize. Alan was feeling more confident then, on the straightaway, but suddenly everything changed for the worse.

There was another road intersection ahead, with big, temporary signs pointing to a hard-left turn onto a narrow lane bordered by tall trees. A rider in the lead failed to make the turn, and carried on straight ahead with his pony, crashing into a hedge and scattering the excited crowd. Two other riders succeeded in turning into the lane, kicking their mounts to yet faster speed, while along came Alan in fourth place, followed closely by four other excited ponies.

His spirited mount had somehow already sensed that a left turn was required, and abruptly lurched in that direction even before reaching the row of trees, apparently seeking a shortcut. Alan was meanwhile attempting to brace himself and hang on, not yet ready to pull the reins over until the first tree was closer.

The result was a catastrophe. As the pony suddenly dashed off to the left, Alan flew on ahead, airborne, bisecting the original trajectory and slamming up hard against a large tree that marked the corner and entrance to the lane. The pony, freed of Alan's weight, carried onwards at a gallop outside the line of trees, every so often slowing to kick its heels in the air with sheer delight.

Excited, chattering people standing along the road, rushed back to Alan, lying crumpled at the base of the tree, to help him stand up. Alan knew he was badly injured, sensing—as he tried to catch his breath—that he had one or more broken ribs. *God, Maggie will be livid*, Alan thought. Then he yelped aloud as several well-meaning people began to lift him up.

"No, no, don't move me, please don't touch me," Alan mumbled in semi-conscious English. As luck would have it, most people at that early part of the course were locals, who failed to understand Alan's mutterings, and continued to lift him with well-intentioned coordination. Suddenly Alan fainted as a broken rib pierced his lung. Someone finally had the sense to realize that all was not well and called the others to lay Alan back down at the roadside. It was some twenty minutes before an ambulance arrived, that one of the officials had thoughtfully summoned while Alan lay gasping by the roadside. Meanwhile, a considerable crowd was gathering, that impeded the ambulance's progress and made its arrival even later, before an unconscious Alan could finally be transported to the Soebang hospital.

The Queen's pre-birthday activity schedule continued while Alan lay in the small P&T hospital at Soebang for three more days. The head nurse, Sister Catharina Jansen, assisted doctor Jentink as best she could, but the doctor was not a surgeon, and all they could really do was try to keep Alan comfortable and sedated. Bandoeng had a Dutch surgeon, but he was away in Sumatra at a conference and could not reach Soebang in time to save Alan, although he tried.

It was very hard on Maggie when she paid visits to the hospital. During the first two days, Alan would drift in and out of consciousness, while Sister Jansen did all she could to control his worsening fever. She and Maggie were about the same age, they learned from each other, born in 1906—Margaret Rees in Wales and Catharina Jansen in Sumatra.

Whenever Alan was lucid he was certain that his days were numbered, so he advised Maggie to go back to Singapore where they had more friends and a better chance of getting help for the future. It would be impossible to return to England with the war on, so Alan suggested Maggie consider Canada or Australia as a place to live after Singapore.

Alan also asked Charles Jackson to get in touch with Peter Perry in Singapore and have Ron Van Noorden sent back to Java immediately, to continue with the water purification projects for which Alan had ordered a small fortune in materials. It was then that they learned that Perry had been commandeered by the US Army to help design a water system for a small Pacific island somewhere near Hawaii.

Alan died near midnight Saturday, on the very eve of the Queen's 1941 birthday, while the company's invited guests were watching a commemorative film presentation. As a courtesy to Alan's new widow, the next day's events and speeches in Soebang were all canceled.

Back in 1939, Queen Wilhelmina's birthday celebrations had already been canceled in the Netherlands for the duration of the war, but not in the colonies. The Queen and her retinue had been granted asylum in England, from where the she made frequent radio broadcasts to her people in exile or captivity, just as Sir Winston Churchill and King George VI were doing for British people at home and abroad, while the Nazi machine gradually crushed all resistance on the European continent.

Most of the company's European managers and staff in Java had already been inducted into the NEI Home Guard as auxiliary officers or soldiers. Although the 1941 celebrations had been canceled in Soebang following Alan's fatal accident, Queen Wilhelmina's birthday was still celebrated in the rest of the Dutch colonies that year, with Home Guard units parading in uniform throughout Java and elsewhere on 31 August 1941.

Soon after Alan's death, Charles and Daphne Jackson vowed to do all possible to get Maggie off to Singapore on the next ship, and the British consul's wife in Bandoeng invited her to stay at their home while the paperwork was being processed. Daphne even offered to sell the Rees household furnishings for Maggie, that they had brought over from Singapore, saying that she would send the proceeds to her in Singapore rather than making her wait in Java.

But Alan's funeral made Maggie realize that she was suddenly alone in the world, and she was overcome with a feeling of obligation to try helping with the looming war effort. Practically everyone she knew was involved with war preparations in one way or other, and Maggie began to feel that she should not return to Singapore after all but stay instead with her more recent friends in Java. Furthermore, although Alan was dead and buried, she felt guilty about deserting her husband's memory, and his grave in the Soebang Christian Cemetery. One afternoon, a week after Alan's burial, she approached Daphne and asked whether she could be of any use to the P&T organization if she stayed in Soebang. To Maggie's great relief, Daphne was delighted at the offer, and took her on immediately as an assistant to help with all the many further details that needed attention because of the likelihood of war with Japan.

As if by some magic plan, Maggie received a letter the following day from Wendy Perry, who had heard about Alan's death and offered to help in whatever way she could "if Maggie intended to leave Java rather than stay where she might have a good future with the English company there." Wendy's letter seemed providential indeed.

*** THE INDOS ***

During her time in Java before Alan's tragic accident, Maggie Rees was exposed to an aspect of Dutch society that was far different from her earlier life in Singapore. It was the inter-marriage of colonial Dutch and native people. To the modern reader of this book, such inter-marriage between white and brown races may no longer seem in any way peculiar, or at the very least would probably be an acceptable practice nowadays, but to the English of the pre-war era (and even afterwards), inter-racial families were not readily accepted in polite society.

Englishmen brought their women along with them wherever in the world they settled, whereas the pragmatic Dutch (like the Spanish and Portuguese in the New World) had no problem with finding women of other races at their destinations, to educate, marry, and bear their children. Initially it was the bachelor KNIL—military personnel—who began to cohabit locally from their earliest days in the Dutch colonies, and many of them remained in Java and Sumatra after their terms of service were over.

At first, Maggie was taken aback by the many mixed-race people that she invariably encountered in Batavia, Bandoeng, and Soebang (although not among the few Dutch members of the mostly English P&T Lands headquarters staff, whose hiring was governed by English attitudes), but she and Alan eventually made friends with a few such couples. In this way, the Reeses came to realize first-hand that a good education and fluency for languages were what mattered most in life, rather than what the British called 'good breeding' and a path to sustained snobbery.

After several centuries of coexistence with the natives of Java and Sumatra, the Dutch gene pool was well dispersed, and the resulting genetic mixtures would often produce people of striking beauty and intelligence. Among their new friends in Soebang, one such combination stood out among the rest as far as the Reeses were concerned. Paul and Iris Meijer and their daughter Stephanie were as handsome a family as the cast of a Hollywood film. Petite and black-haired Iris especially, who said she was part Javanese, had inherited fair skin and striking light blue eyes thanks to some early Dutch ancestor. From Iris and brown-haired, brown-eyed Dutchman Paul Meijer, young Stephanie somehow emerged with green eyes, blondish-brown hair, and a slightly darker complexion than either parent. She was probably destined to become a great beauty also, though quite unlike her extraordinary mother.

Such mixed-race people were known among the pre-war Dutch as *de Indische*, which had the connotation of 'the mestizos' or 'the creoles.' The Dutch term wasn't particularly derogatory like the Anglo-American 'half-breed' but was just used by the European Dutch or other Caucasians to differentiate a specific official population category from the local Javanese or Soendanese natives. Research has shown that 80 per cent of the 'Europeans' living in the Dutch East Indies at the outset of WWII were born there, and that the majority had at least one Asian parent or ancestor.

Indeed, most government jobs were filled by Indies-born Europeans. Many of the *Indische* were highly educated (usually in Holland) and held positions of responsibility throughout the Dutch colonies. A key point, however, was that children of mixed unions were considered European only if legally adopted by their European fathers.

Later, during and after the Japanese occupation of Java and Sumatra when the term 'Indonesian' was being bandied about, the mixed-race Dutch speakers began to call themselves Indos. We shall read about the Indos' unusual wartime and post-war history in the second act of this book.

*** *A FUTILE DEFENSE* **

Meanwhile in the Java Sea after the fall of Singapore, where the remnants of the US Asiatic Fleet had arrived from the Philippines to join with British, Dutch and Australian naval elements, Admiral Hart was recalled home due to a chorus of disgruntled complainers. Some complainers were ABDA peers, who felt the admiral's leadership style was too conservative, and others were pro-MacArthur political figures in Washington, since the general was by this time blaming his looming defeat in the Philippines on the US Navy's lack of protection, with little mention of his demolished air force that was supposed to have guarded both the army and navy.

Upon Admiral Hart's departure, the ABDA fleet, known as ABDAFLOAT, was turned over to Dutch Vice Admiral Conrad Helfrich, who undertook the unenviable task of trying to coordinate a maritime defense of Java with American, British, Dutch and Australian warships that had never held exercises together, that lacked even a common signal code system, and that had quite differing strategic objectives (deficiencies that might well have been resolved during the prior twenty years of Peace). The Dutch admiral and his fleet commander Rear Admiral Karel Doorman were intent on defending the NEI with their last drop of blood, whereas the other three allies felt a better plan was to send the surviving ships off to Australia, so they could live to fight another day.

The result of this dilemma was predictable, but each ship gave its best effort to the common cause so long as that possibility existed. After losing a destroyer while trying to intercept a Japanese landing at the island of Bali, Admiral Doorman took the entire fleet to sea to block larger Japanese landing forces from coming ashore on Java itself. In the resulting **Battle of the Java Sea** on 27 February 1942, between ABDAFLOAT and the Japanese Eastern Invasion Force that had sailed from Lingayen Gulf in the Philippines, the Allied fleet was badly mauled, losing three of five cruisers and five of nine destroyers. Admiral Doorman was lost when his cruiser-flagship *De Ruyter* was sunk by torpedoes.

The Japanese Eastern Invasion Fleet with the IJA 48th Division under Lieutenant-General Tsuchihashi Yuitsu, and Major-General Sakaguchi Shizuo's 124th Infantry Regiment collected from Balikpapan, Borneo, landed at Kragan Java 100 miles east of Soerabaja on March 1 as scheduled.

After the disastrous naval battle, the light cruiser HMAS *Perth* and heavy cruiser USS *Houston*—Admiral Hart's former flagship—were given permission to run for Australia during the night of 28 February. They were told to proceed through the Sunda Strait between Java and Sumatra that was thought to be clear of enemy ships. As luck would have it, however, the two cruisers ran straight into the Japanese Western Invasion Fleet from Cam Ranh Bay that was making a large night landing at Bantam Bay in the Sunda Strait, and were immediately set upon by Japanese escort cruisers and destroyers defending the army landings.

Both Allied ships fought heroically, even after two days of round-the-clock action in the previous Battle of the Java Sea. They inflicted some damage to the landing barges and escorts but had no hope of escape in view of the many torpedoes that were fired at them (that in the confusion of darkness sank some Japanese ships as well).

Perth was lost first, soon after which *Houston*, with her rear turret inoperative from a previous action, went down with her forward 8-inch and all 5-inch guns blazing. *Houston's* Captain Rook was killed during the final melee (and was awarded a posthumous Congressional Medal of Honor in later years, after the fate of those ships was finally learned by the Allies). Several hundred survivors from both ships were captured and added to the growing collection of Allied army prisoners, for eventual transfer to work on the Japanese-operated Siam-Burma railroad, where many more of them would die.

*** *THE JAPANESE MOVE ASHORE* ***

On 27 February 1942, Infantry Colonel Shoji Toshishige and Col. Tsuji's remaining understudy Lt. Tanamoto, landed with the 230th Regiment of the 38th IJA Infantry Division, at Eretan Wetan—a North Java river port used in happier days by P&T Lands to export plantation commodities. The Japanese objective was to capture Kalidjati Airfield near Soebang, an unusually large piece of flat ground on hilly Java that had been donated by P&T Lands to the NEI Government back in the early days of aviation. By denying this airfield to the ABDA defenders, Japan could quickly achieve air superiority over northwest Java, where ABDACOM—under British General Archibald Wavell—had established its headquarters at the cool and scenic hill station of Lembang.

KNIL soldiers and Home Guard civilians initially put up a stout defense of Kalidjati Airfield but were well outnumbered and soon captured by the invaders. Japanese vengeance was swift and predictable, as it had been in Hong Kong, Singapore, Borneo, and the Philippines. Once the airfield was theirs, Japanese troops rushed into the Soebang hospital where Nurse Jansen and other medical personnel were wearing pistols to protect the building from native looters, but the weapons marked them as combatants in the eyes of the Japanese. After bayonetting the wounded in their beds, Japanese soldiers marched the hospital staff, the surrendered ABDA soldiers and the NEI home guardsmen to a nearby rubber plantation, where they—over 300 in all—were murdered and dumped into a mass grave.

[The 230th regimental commander Colonel Shoji was tried after the war for this crime, although the hand of Colonel Tsuji was seemingly behind the atrocity. Both colonels had ended up on Guadalcanal towards the end of 1942, trying in vain to stem the loss of that territory to American Marines and the US Army's Americal Division reinforcements, but both colonels survived the war–Ed.]

The next day, 8 March 1942, just a week after landing at Eretan Wetan, the Shoji Detachment—as it was also known—pushed on through Dutch and British defenders at the Tjiater Pass between Soebang and Lembang, forcing ABDACOM to dissolve and the military and civil Dutch administrations of Java to capitulate. Colonel Shoji was rewarded for his Tjiater Pass boldness by receiving the surrender of Dutch Major-General Jacob Pesman at the Isola Hotel in Lembang.

Other Japanese forces quickly occupied the NEI colonial capital of Batavia and all major cities of Java and Sumatra. The war was over for the NEI, and captivity would begin for surviving Allied troops and civilians including Charles and Daphne Jackson, Maggie Rees, and other management and staff of P&T Lands, and their children.

It was there in the Netherland East Indies colonies, with their vital sources of oil, that Colonel Tsuji installed the last and most intelligent of his protégés, Senior Lieutenant Tanamoto. Foreseeing a quick end to the war in the Pacific region and the humiliation of the Americans and their allies, Tsuji instructed Tanamoto repeatedly to continue planting the concept of independence among the native leadership in the big cities, and then in the kampong villages, so that these islands would be ready to join Japan's post-war economic zone as willing partners.

That this plan could and would work was already visible when Tsuji toured the captured Dutch territories with various IJA units. Local

Indonesians, as they were now being called, would invariably turn out by the thousands to cheer the Japanese motorcades, waving little Japanese flags that they had made by hand. It was an inspiring sight that lifted the colonel's spirits immensely.

This will be much easier than I ever imagined, Tsuji thought to himself smugly, envisioning great honors being showered on his person by the emperor. *Perhaps I shall make Tanamoto the Lieutenant Governor of Java. Yes, that's it! The English will cringe at the thought of an oriental filling the shoes of their beloved Stamford Raffles!*

INTERMISSION

This book is laid out (somewhat tongue in cheek) like the program for a two-act stage play, as shown in the Table of Contents.

Acts One and Two cover around fifteen to twenty years each—the prewar and postwar periods in the Pacific region—which are separated by this nearly four-year Intermission during which WWII takes place from December 1941 to August 1945.

Act One has five choreographed scenes, in which actors of international standing are in competition for a valuable prize—the de-militarization of Japan—but not one of them can claim the prize before the contest ends. This failure is the result of inadequate investment throughout the British, French, Dutch and American colonies of Southeast Asia, which were essentially being used as 'cash cows' by their colonial masters. In Act One, nevertheless, the beginning of WWII in the Pacific gives readers a feel for how people lived during the 1930s and '40s, where their priorities and loyalties lay, and how they felt about their fellow competitors. That all the competitors would be subdued by Japan early in the war, is testimony to the strain and intensity of the unfolding event.

This Intermission includes two sets of activities that are usually not included in books about the grisly battles of World War Two in the Pacific, but which are nonetheless quite important to know about: the repatriation of diplomatic personnel and the abysmal treatment of prisoners by the Japanese and their agents.

In Act Two, which follows this Intermission, a new cast of characters begins to appear on stage in the former colonies. Eager to be rid of the colonists once and for all, the new actors include President "Bung" Sukarno of Indonesia, Prime Minister Lee Kwan Yew of Singapore, Prime Minister Tunku Abdul Rahman of Malaysia, Presidents Ho Chi Minh and Ngo Dinh Diem of North and South Vietnam, and President Manuel Roxas of the Philippines.

As for the Pacific War details themselves, many excellent books have been written on the subject, those listed in our bibliography among them. Because *Colonies in Ruins* is primarily about the transformation of prewar colonies into independent nation-states, there is only a little detail about the war itself in this Intermission, but—for those who would like to know more—an overview of the major actions of World War II in the Pacific Theater is available after the End Notes.

*** *DIPLOMATS REPATRIATED* ***

Before we discuss the harsh Japanese-run camps throughout the colonial territories, let's consider one small group of captured foreigners that did not end up being interned in those camps. They were the diplomatic corps of ambassadors and consuls, with their families and staff. These vulnerable people are seldom written about in a historical context because the relatively small size of their group is not statistically significant, even though they often play a key role in unfolding events and dramas.

His Excellency Joseph Grew was the prewar US Ambassador to Japan who, immediately after Pearl Harbor had been bombed, was politely informed in Tokyo that a state of war existed between Japan and the US, and therefore he and his entourage would be confined to the US Embassy property in Tokyo until further notice, pending an eventual exchange of personnel with his Japanese counterpart in Washington, H.E. Admiral Nomura Kichisaburo and staff.

Popular legend, even today, has it that Japan—with the back-and-forth pre-war negotiations—was deviously attempting to catch the United States off guard with the blow that was to come, thereby stabbing us in the back with the Pearl Harbor bombing and other simultaneous attacks in the Far East. The reality, however, was that Ambassadors Grew and Nomura were both trying their best to bring Japan and the US to a high-level negotiation table for a face-to-face meeting (in Alaska, Hawaii, or some other halfway point) between President Franklin D. Roosevelt and Prince Konoye Fumimaro the Japanese Prime Minister, with the promise that Japan would offer concessions at the meeting that would bring the parties back from the brink of war. Unfortunately, FDR's then-Far East advisor in Washington was quite hostile to a diplomatic solution that did not include China, Japan's enemy, and this in turn catalyzed the president's negative response to Prince Konoye's proposal for a face-to-face meeting. As a result, an opportunity was lost that might have averted the calamity of war between Japan and the US, or at least could have provided more time for the US and its allies to get better prepared for a conflict. In either case, many lives might have been spared had such a meeting taken place.

But it was not to be. FDR was unwilling to meet with Prime Minister Konoye without first knowing the details of the Japanese proposals, whereas Prince Konoye was unwilling to announce the concessions in advance of a face-to-face meeting for fear of a leak to code-breakers among the militant factions in Japan, who would probably have him assassinated had there been proof that Japan was offering to negotiate with the United States. Consequently, a fantastic opportunity was missed to perhaps avoid the holocaust to come, and the US population was forever after convinced that Japan had acted in a perfidious manner by deliberately lulling the US into blissful ignorance of the forthcoming attack on Hawaii (and the Allied colonies).

Following a not-uncomfortable confinement of nearly six months in the Tokyo embassy grounds, Ambassador Grew and his people were finally loaded aboard the Japanese liner SS *Asama Maru*, while in Washington the Japanese embassy staff were loaded onto SS *Gripsholm*, a chartered Swedish liner. Both ships would collect other diplomatic and business personnel en route to the port of Lourenço Marques, Mozambique, where the actual exchange of diplomats would take place. US and British diplomats from Hong Kong, Saigon, and Singapore, with their horror stories of the Japanese Army's invasions of their territories, would thereby join the *Asama Maru* on its voyage to Mozambique.

Upon arrival in Washington (on the *Gripsholm*), Ambassador Grew's lengthy report to US Secretary of State, Cordell Hull, was received with shock and anger at Grew's criticism of FDR's failure to negotiate with

Japan. Grew was ordered to destroy the report and all copies on penalty of public censure, which he reluctantly did. The record of Grew's position only came to light after the war in a publication by his former personal secretary Robert A. Fearey, but this revelation has been unable to change the historical perception of deliberate perfidy on the part of Japan.

As an unfortunate postscript, the moderate anti-war Prime Minister Konoye was soon replaced by militant General Tojo, and Konoye committed suicide after the war when the US included him on the list of Class-A suspects to be tried for war crimes, despite his having tried strenuously to avoid war in the first place.

*** THE JAPANESE CAMPS ***

It must have come as a terrible shock to Japan to realize how many Western people—both military and civilian—were willing to surrender their persons to a conquering nation, instead of fighting to the bitter end as Japanese civilians and military were trained to do from infancy. Planners like Colonel Tsuji completely underestimated the number of Western prisoners that Japan would have to feed, house, and guard. As Japan was not a signatory to the Geneva Convention on the treatment of war prisoners, Tsuji's initial solution was to kill them all, the way that Japan's army usually dealt with captured Chinese. But perhaps someone in Tokyo belatedly issued instructions for the army to deal more benignly with Western-origin prisoners, that would eventually number several hundred thousand civilian and military personnel by the time all the colonies were occupied.

This belated instruction to look after the prisoners presented Japanese field commanders with a serious dilemma: how and where to find enough guards and food to sustain the many prison camps that were springing up in the wake of Japanese conquests, and which were already depriving the army of combat troops. Before the POW situation became somewhat better organized (by replacing combat soldiers with less qualified Korean guards), instructions from Tokyo were being ignored in many cases such as the hospital assaults in Hong Kong, Singapore, and Soebang, where wounded warriors and their caregivers were routinely massacred.

Also ignored was the proper treatment of captured combatants that the Japanese could identify as having caused harm to their troops—perhaps by aggressively blocking their advances or defending strategic airfields, or by destroying useful colonial property such as oil production and refining stations. It apparently meant little to the invaders that opposing troops were operating under valid orders from their own commanders, both in the defense of the colonies and in the scorched-earth treatment of certain assets. Perpetrators of such acts were in many instances punished by losing their lives. It was almost as if they had personally disobeyed <u>Japanese</u> orders!

*** SOME OF THE MANY HORRORS ***

Malaya-Singapore: The Japanese conquest of Malaya and Singapore took approximately ten weeks, from 8 December 1941 until 15 February 1942. Both civilians (men, women, and children) and combatants (mostly men) were taken prisoner in large numbers. Civilians were eventually interned at camps on Sime Road in the center of the island, with men and older boys being segregated from women and younger children. Although suffering great privations throughout the war, the percentage of civilian survivors in Singapore far exceeded that of military POWs. Military (including naval) prisoners were confined to—or processed through—Changi Gaol at the eastern end of Singapore island, which rapidly became over-crowded to three times its design capacity. There the POWs were put to work clearing swamps and beginning the construction of an airfield that today is Singapore's showcase international airport, Changi Field.

Siam: Hundreds of the Changi POWs were eventually shipped to Siam to work on the infamous Siam-Burma railroad, where a high percentage would die from exhaustion and disease. Singapore POWs in Siam were joined by groups of Allied prisoners captured in Java, including survivors from the sunken cruisers USS *Houston* and HMAS *Perth*.

While conditions at the Changi Prison camp were quite inhumane, with meager rations, poor sanitation and harsh punishment being the rule rather than the exception, at the railroad camps in Siam things were even worse for the captives. More strenuous work was required and a harsher climate and living conditions took a huge toll on the walking skeletons that were forced to work under hellish circumstances. An acclaimed 1960s movie *Bridge on the River Kwai* only begins to depict the barbaric conditions of the Siam-Burma railroad prisoners.

Tragically, after the railroad was completed and the emaciated surviving prisoners were dispatched to Japan to continue working at manual tasks such as coal mining, several of their dilapidated transport ships, not being appropriately marked to show that they contained prisoners, were torpedoed and sunk en route by US submarines.

Philippines: The five-month battle of the Philippines began on 8 December 1941 and ended on 8 May 1942 with the surrender of the starved US garrison on Corregidor Island in Manila Bay. Prior to the last few weeks on Corregidor for the remnant of MacArthur's cadre and the Fourth Marine Regiment, and for the Army nurses, the bulk of MacArthur's PA troops had already been surrendered after the battle of Bataan peninsula and had been on half rations for some time as Japanese prisoners.

The story of the Bataan Death March has already been written in the earlier chapter about the Philippines, where sick or wounded prisoners unable to make the 60-mile walk to Camp O'Donnell were summarily executed at the side of the road. The slightly healthier majority did reach the camp, although in a weakened state. From their arrival at Camp O'Donnell we will pick up their ongoing story, below, and in the next section about the Borneo camps we will read of the Sandakan Death Marches that took place a year or two later, where all British and Australian prisoners who started out from Sandakan were already debilitated, and none survived the brutal treatment except for a small handful who had managed to escape en route and were nursed back to health by local natives.

At Camp O'Donnell, which some fifty thousand exhausted PA troops finally managed to reach after straggling on foot for 60 miles and then riding like sardines inside old unventilated boxcars for an hour, plenty of Filipinos and Americans had died during both legs of the trip. After the war, General Homma was executed for war crimes because of this cruel march that his subordinates had organized at Colonel Tsuji's instigation. Once again, justice punished the wrong man!

A few months after arrival at Camp O'Donnell, the prisoners' Filipino majority was paroled under pledges that they would not become guerillas, with their tribal chiefs' lives at stake if the parole was violated. That left 500 or so American prisoners who were soon transferred to another camp at Cabanatuan. Camp O'Donnell was thereafter closed. During the next three years until the war ended, Cabanatuan's Allied—mostly American—POW population was frequently changed as prisoners died or were transferred to other locations such as Japan for forced labor. Eventually, after some parts of the Philippines were retaken by MacArthur's troops, a daring raid by Army Rangers and local guerillas was made into the Japanese-held region under concerns that the Cabanatuan POWs would soon be executed. The raid was a remarkable success in which all Japanese camp guards were killed, and the emaciated prisoners were transported away in oxcarts. Many other camps were liberated as American troops quickly fought their way into Luzon and the remaining islands.

Borneo: POW camps were operated in both British and Dutch sections of the large island. One of the earliest was at Batu Lintang near Sarawak's capital, Kuching, the former site of the Second Battalion 15th Punjab army barracks. An unusual feature of this sprawling camp was its containment of male and female civilian internees (mostly clergy) as well as British, Australian, Indian, and Dutch military POWs. Batu Lintang was also the office site of Lt. Colonel Suga Tatsuji, who could speak English and was the commandant of all POW and internment camps on Borneo. Most British and Australian prisoners had been transferred there from Singapore, whereas the Dutch KNIL prisoners had fought on Borneo itself.

Conditions at this camp, like all others within Borneo and Java, were abysmal, with minimal food, cramped quarters, non-existent medical care, frequent beatings, and debilitating work routines. More than half of the Batu Lintang POWs died of malnutrition and disease and the civilian internees fared almost as badly. When the camp was liberated, instructions were found in Col. Suga's desk ordering all prisoners—men, women, and children—to be exterminated by shooting, poisoning, or having their barracks set on fire.

Although Suga did not carry out these orders, he was indirectly responsible for many other serious crimes and would no doubt have been found guilty and executed had he not killed himself rather than stand trial with the guards and Kempei Tai personnel, many of whom were found guilty, then hanged or shot. Agnes Newton Keith was an American internee in Camp Batu Lintang with her husband and small son. Her best-selling 1947 book *Three Came Home* describes her ordeals. It was made into a movie as well, starring Claudette Colbert as Agnes.

Another horror story that certainly would have been Suga's undoing was known as the **Sandakan Death Marches**. Although less publicized after the war than the larger Bataan Death March in the Philippines, the Sandakan Death Marches had a far worse outcome.

Sandakan, an oil town on the northeast coast of British North Borneo (Sabah), became the site of a POW camp soon after the Japanese conquest. In 1942 and 1943, Australian and British POWs who had been captured at the Battle of Singapore were shipped to Sandakan to construct a military airfield and POW camp. As on the Siam-Burma Railway, the prisoners were forced to work at gunpoint and received very little food or medical attention. In August 1943, with the intention of better controlling the enlisted men by removing their commanders, most officer prisoners were moved from Sandakan to the Batu Lintang camp at Kuching. Conditions for the remaining prisoners deteriorated sharply following the officers' removal. Rations were further reduced, and sick prisoners were also forced to work on the airfield.

After construction was completed the surviving prisoners were initially retained at the camp, but in January 1945 the advancing Allies managed to successfully bomb and destroy the airfield. With Allied landings anticipated shortly, the camp commandant Captain Susumu decided to move the remaining prisoners westward into the mountains to the town of Ranau, 160 miles away. He later claimed that this was an order of Lt. General Baba Masao, commanding officer of the 37th Japanese Army.

The first phase of marches across wide marshland, dense jungle, and then up the eastern slope of Mount Kinabalu occurred between January and March 1945. Several groups of malnourished POWs, many of whom were suffering serious illnesses, started the journey. Any who were not fit enough or collapsed from exhaustion were either killed or left to die en route. Upon reaching Ranau the survivors—many with dysentery—were ordered to construct a temporary camp.

A second series of marches began on 29 May 1945 with over 500 prisoners. The new Sandakan camp commander, Captain Takuo, ordered the prisoners towards Ranau in groups of about fifty with accompanying Japanese guards. The marches lasted for twenty-six days, with prisoners even less fit than those in the first marches. They were provided with fewer rations and often forced to forage for food. Less than 200 prisoners managed to reach Ranau. Upon their arrival on 24 June 1945, they discovered that only six prisoners from the first series of marches during January were still alive.

Some 250 prisoners were left at Sandakan after the second march departed. Most were so ill that the Japanese initially intended to let them starve to death, forcing many to scavenge in the surrounding forest for food. However, it was eventually decided to send the remainder on a final march to Ranau. Most of these men were so weak that few survived beyond 30 miles. As each collapsed from exhaustion he was shot by a guard.

Due to a lack of food and brutal treatment at the hands of the Japanese, there were only 38 prisoners left alive at Ranau by the end of July. All were too unwell and weak to do any work, and it was ordered that any remaining survivors should be shot. They were killed by the guards during August, possibly up to 12 days after the end of the war on 14 August.

Six Australian servicemen managed to escape during the second march or after arrival at Ranau, and they became the only survivors of the original POWs at Sandakan, all the rest having died at the hands of the Japanese. Assisted by local people, these escapees were eventually rescued by Allied units. Of the six that were rescued, only four survived the lingering effects of their ordeal to give evidence at various war crime trials in Tokyo and Rabaul. Their testimonies resulted in several of the Japanese camp officials being hanged or shot.

Java: Japanese troops landed in Java on 28 February 1942, soon after Singapore's capitulation. By March 2nd the Shoji Regiment had captured Soebang and the Kalidjati Airfield. By the 8th they had breached the Tjiater Pass to help bring about the surrender of Dutch forces at Lembang and the civilian government at Bandoeng, the ABDA command having been dissolved a week earlier. It was the loss of Bandoeng in the high plateau of Central Java where the KNIL central command was located, that convinced the Dutch civil government to capitulate.

As on Sumatra, which had been captured earlier by Japanese paratroopers, Java was soon populated with separate camps for civilian internees and POWs. The camps were not further segregated by language but only by gender. Women and younger children were separated from men and older boys. At all the camps on Java, English- and Dutch-speakers were housed together, although they tended to segregate themselves internally.

Interestingly, the Japanese at first categorized the mixed-race Indos as natives, leaving them free from camp confinement until the later years when the war was going badly for Japan. Equally interesting, as Indonesia began its post-war struggle for independence and Dutch former-internees had been repatriated to the Netherlands, the Indos were rounded up by native Indonesians and confined to internment camps for a lengthy time, being effectively held as bargaining chips.

A post-war book *Java Nightmare* by British author Daphne Jackson, wife of P&T Lands managing director Charles Jackson, records many details of the spartan conditions that women endured in confinement while policed by Japanese and Korean guards. She famously wrote of her Japanese captors: "I was often to live in fear of these little men, but seldom hated them, since they seemed largely medieval in their outlook, and were not deliberately retrogressing from a state of culture, as were the Germans."

[The author and his wife were privileged to meet Daphne in 1989 at her home in Cornwall, where she was working on another book about her Java adventures. She told us that Charles had been tortured severely by the Kempei Tai during the war, which affected his ongoing health. Although he and Daphne made several postwar trips to Java from England to help train Indonesians to run the plantations, he passed away a few years after the war ended.]

ACT II

Turbulent Transitions (1945-65)

SCENE SIX

British Legacy - Malaysia and Singapore

Although collectively exhausted by the world war, European nations that had prewar colonies in the Asia-Pacific region tried to reclaim them as quickly as possible after the war's end—the Americans having already recaptured the Philippines half a year beforehand. Other, non-European, transformations were taking place in Taiwan and Korea as well. Read about those others in Scene Ten, the concluding chapter of this book.

*** *A WAITING GAME* ***

Euphoria at the end of the war was soon dissipated in Singapore after it became clear that the British would not be back in charge of the colony for at least a month, due to the logistics of organizing a relief force along with all the other pressing business of healing a broken world. In retrospect, it might have been better for Britain to have sent a token force to show the flag, as things turned out, but that did not happen. Finally, on 5 September 1945—three weeks after the official Japanese surrender—the British 5th Indian Division arrived by sea and began assessing the recovery situation, while gradually disarming the Japanese army and putting them to work on hasty reconstruction tasks. This was the beginning of a British Military Administration that was to last until 1 April 1946 when civilian government was reinstated.

On 12 September 1945, the official surrender ceremony took place at the Singapore Municipal Building opposite the Padang that had been hastily cleared of debris and bomb shelters by Japanese prisoners. The Japanese delegation was led by General Itagaki Seishiro, representing Field Marshal Count Terauchi who had been hospitalized in Japan by a stroke. The surrender was received by Lord Louis Mountbatten, Supreme Allied Commander for Southeast Asia (referred to on a friendly basis as *The Supremo*).

Also present at the ceremony—and awarded a place of honor inside the building—were some men and women of the jungle forces wearing five-pointed caps adorned with three stars, alternatively known as the Resistance Forces, the Guerrillas, or the Communists. They had harassed the Japanese for years from hideouts in the jungles of Malaya. The Supremo later awarded them medals for bravery, after which they were disbanded. Not long afterwards, however, the Malayan Communist Party under Chin Peng, reorganized those fighters and began a 12-year battle to oust the British from Malaya, which had the effect of delaying the granting of independence to Malaya and Singapore until 1957 when the Malayan Emergency was finally quelled.

*** THE MALAYAN EMERGENCY ***

In the Malay language, the Malayan Emergency was called *Darurat Malaya*. By any other measure than political it was a hard-fought twelve-year war of attrition between forces of the British Commonwealth and the Malayan National Liberation Army under Communist Leader Chin Peng, an adopted name. MNLA was the military arm of the Malayan Communist Party, and their term for the conflict was 'The Anti-British National Liberation War.' Although Britain  granted limited independence to Malaya in August 1957, to help gain more hearts and minds, the 'Emergency' lasted from June 1948 until the MNLA surrendered in July 1960, after which Mr. Chin was exiled from Malaysia, his homeland.

The brutal conflict, fought mostly in the Malay jungles, was defined as an emergency at the behest of the rubber and tin industries, which could not have their losses covered by insurance had it been officially declared a war.

Most MNLA guerillas were ethnic Chinese, though there were some Malays, Indonesians, and Indians among its members. MNLA camps and hideouts were usually situated in the more remote tropical jungle areas with limited access, but its supply organization had a network of contacts among the general population. Besides sourcing materials, especially food, the network was also important as a source of intelligence.

Initially, the government response to MNLA attacks and work stoppages was chaotic and disorganized. Its early strategy was primarily to guard important economic targets such as mines and plantation estates, since the British troop strength was only a dozen or so battalions for the entire Malay Peninsula. Eventually more Commonwealth troops were added from Australia, New Zealand, Fiji, and Rhodesia (today's Zimbabwe), along with more artillery and aircraft for bombing the MNLA jungle hideouts.

The government strategy then evolved into forced relocation of some 500,000 rural Malayans, including 400,000 ethnic Chinese, from their squatter communities on the fringes of the jungles into guarded camps called 'new villages.' The newly constructed sites were surrounded by barbed wire, police posts, and floodlit areas, meant to keep the inhabitants in and the guerrillas out.

Some British army units began a 'hearts and minds' campaign by giving medical and food aid to Malays and indigenous tribes. At the same time, they put pressure on the MNLA by patrolling the jungle with smaller and more frequent mobile units, based on intelligence gained in the villages. The MNLA guerrillas were consequently driven deeper into the jungle and denied essential resources. In the end, the conflict involved a maximum of 40,000 British and other Commonwealth troops, against a peak of about 7–8,000 communist guerrillas. Sadly, there were many more casualties among the civilian populations than in either of the official combatant networks.

Then in 1967, the exiled Chin Peng—perhaps emboldened by the recent expulsion of Singapore from Malaysia, or by a flare-up of Communist activity in Vietnam—resumed the Malayan insurgency, directing it from Beijing for 22 more years until 1989. After that the war-weary insurgent leader returned to Thailand until his death in 2013, because the Malaysian government continued to refuse his many requests to return home.

*** INDEPENDENCE ON THE HORIZON ***

After granting limited self-rule to peninsular Malaya in 1957 and Singapore in 1959, Britain eventually agreed to full and collective independence for all its former holdings of the Malay Peninsula and Borneo (Sarawak and Sabah) in 1963, to become the Federation of Malaysia. It was expected that they would go forth as a single, proud nation under a new flag (above left, at the beginning of this scene). For a brief time, such expectations were met, but lurking beneath the surface of a theoretical national harmony were racial and religious forces that ultimately caused the federation to rupture, with Singapore being expelled from Malaysia in 1965.

The Republic of Singapore's subsequent flag is shown above, to the right. Ever careful to acknowledge its original Malay heritage in spite of expulsion from Malaysia, Singapore's flag displays Islamic symbolism, while the country's national motto and anthem, *Majulah Singapura*, means *Onward Singapore* in the Malay language.

*** A REMARKABLE LEADER FOR SINGAPORE ***

Born in Singapore in 1923 of Hakka Chinese parentage, Lee Kwan Yew eventually became the longest serving prime minister in world history—31 years. 'LKY,' as he became known to his constituents, was a Cambridge University-educated lawyer who rose through the ranks of his country's political system to become Singapore's first prime minister in 1959, after negotiating limited independence from Britain in all matters except defense and foreign relations. Passionate about a merger for Singapore with Malaya, Sarawak, and Sabah, PM Lee vigorously promoted the concept of Malaysian federalism, and he was rewarded with that merger and full independence from Britain in 1963 in partnership with Tunku Abdul Rahman, the PM of Malaya (next photo).

This is when the world should have stopped still for Lee Kwan Yew, but much to his sorrow the merger did not last. After Chinese-Malay race riots occurred in both Singapore and Malaya, Lee was devastated to see Singapore expelled from Malaysia in  1965. At the heart of the matter was the fact that Malaysia would end up with a majority ethnic Chinese voting population with Singapore included, but would remain majority Malay without Singapore. Ah, pragmatism! PM Lee had made the mistake of having his Chinese-majority PAP (People's Action Party) participate in some Malayan national elections, which brought the racial issue to the surface.

By the 1980s, however, after LKY had successfully promoted Singapore to the world as a disciplined, high-quality industrial hub and financial center (and had banned chewing gum from the island because he once sat on a blob of it that stuck to his trousers), the small nation's standard of living and average income per capita was second in East Asia only to Japan's, a position held before the war by the (American-run) Philippines.

Lacking remote and undeveloped terrain at home, Singapore's military was secretly developed by the Israelis and trained in the rugged mountains of Taiwan, and the island's relatively small size was increased some twenty percent by reclaiming land from the surrounding sea.

LKY carried on as PM of Singapore until 1990, and even afterwards held positions of importance such as Minister-Mentor when his son Lee Hsien Loong took over the national leadership from Goh Chok Tong.

*** *SINGAPORE AIRLINES IS BORN* ***

The expulsion of Singapore from Malaysia also affected several new joint-venture businesses. One of those was an only-just-renamed Malaysian Airlines—previously Malayan Airlines—which in 1965 took on the convoluted name Malaysia-Singapore Airlines. By 1972, MSA was split into Singapore Airlines and Malaysian Airlines, two separate entities. With its slightly sexy Singapore Girl image of petite, mostly Chinese flight attendants wearing lovely (Malay-symbolic) batik sarongs, and its ongoing huge investment in the latest aircraft available from the US and Europe, Singapore Airlines grew rapidly into one of the world's finest and most reliable carriers, which it still is today. Many of its customer-satisfaction features have been widely copied by competitors.

*** THE SINGAPORE SLING ***

According to a Raffles Hotel brochure of the 1970s, the Singapore Sling, widely promoted as the national drink of the country, was first created in 1915 at the hotel by Hainanese bartender Ngiam Tong Boon (in case you wondered). Primarily a gin-based cocktail, the Singapore Sling of the 1970s—masquerading as a 1915 concoction—contained pineapple juice as its main ingredient along with grenadine, lime juice, and Dom Benedictine. This oft-quoted blurb seems to have been a harmless promotion for the hotel's Long Bar, but its recipe does not tally with earlier accounts of the generic 'Gin Sling,' which was a regional term for tall gin-based drinks that usually included just soda water and lime juice.

Joseph Conrad, in fact, wrote about his Raffles Gin Sling, but did not call it a Singapore Sling, so it seems that pineapple was a 1970s addition to coincide with the Tiki-type drinks in vogue around the world at that time. One is almost certain to receive a premixed pineapple version when ordering a Singapore Sling at the Raffles today. If a Gin Sling were to be ordered instead we cannot guarantee the result but would be quite curious to learn.

*** THE POST-WAR VIEW FROM MALAYSIA ***

Just what activities took place in British Malaya between 1945 at the end of WWII, and 1965 when the nation that became Malaysia decided to expel an over-confident Singapore, is a topic not often studied in our modern era. When Malaya and Singapore were under Japanese occupation from 1942 until 1945, Japan had rewarded Siam for its co-operation during this period by giving it the unfederated Malayan states of Perlis, Kedah, Kelantan, and Terengganu (that had been ceded to British Malaya by Siam in the first place), the rest of Malaya being governed by Japan from Syonan (Singapore) as a single colony. After Japan's surrender at the end of the war, Malaya and Singapore were initially placed under British Military Administration with a focus on Japanese troop repatriation and war trials of the former Japanese leadership.

Within a year, the loose administration of British Malaya became consolidated with the formation of the Malayan Union on 1 April 1946. The Union included Penang and Malacca, which had formerly been parts of the Straits Settlements, but Singapore was not included and was considered a crown colony by itself.

The new Union, however, was greeted with strong opposition from local Malays because of a reduction in the Malay rulers' powers. Due to this political pressure, the Malayan Union was replaced with the Federation of Malaya on 31 January 1948, giving the sultans more powers on Islamic matters. This initial federation achieved nominal independence from Britain on 31 August 1957, after which all the Malayan states formed a larger federation called Malaysia on 16 September 1963, to include Singapore, Sarawak, and Sabah (North Borneo).

The four unfederated Malayan states that Japan had ceded to Thailand during WWII, were returned to Malaya in due course. Because of that cooperation, Thailand—which had formed a type of military alliance with Japan during the war—was absolved from any postwar trials and allowed to join the United Nations.

*** BENEATH THE SURFACE ***

The previous summary makes it sound as though the transition from British rule to independence in Malaya was an orderly, inevitable process, but for twelve years it was anything but that. World Communism—sponsored by the USSR and China—was already on the march throughout East Asia before World War II and burst forth again once the war had ended—especially once Chiang Kai-Shek's Nationalist Chinese army was defeated by the Communist forces of Chairman Mao Tse Tung (Mao Zedong) in 1949.

In no time at all, it seemed, the colonial nations of the region were besieged by guerrilla movements wherever they turned. French forces in Laos, Cambodia and Vietnam had their hands full with Pathet Lao, Khmer Rouge, and Viet Minh insurgents; the Dutch faced off with the Communist Party of Indonesia (PKI); the Americans tackled the Communist Party of the Philippines (CPP); and the British went to war with the Malayan Communist Party (MCP)—even though they officially called it 'The Malayan Emergency' for insurance purposes.

The breadth and depth of postwar Communist upheavals—diligently prepared-for despite Japanese oversight during the war years—caused a sort of panic among military leaders of the United States. The Domino Theory, first mentioned by President Eisenhower in 1954, became a quasi-official doctrine in US military and diplomatic circles. It was a theory prominent from the 1950s into the 1980s, in fact, speculating that if one country in a region came under the influence of Communism, then the surrounding countries would follow in a domino-like effect. That theory led to a determined US resolve to strike down Communism whenever and wherever it appeared in East Asia.

*** RELATIONS WITH SINGAPORE ***

After the separation of Singapore from Malaysia in 1965, certain ongoing issues between the two new nations became quite volatile for a while. Chief among those was the supply and purification of water under agreements previously reached in 1961 and 1962. Singapore had always been short of fresh water for its densely populated island, even in colonial times, a situation that grew critical in the postwar period and brought about bizarre experiments such as the recycling of raw sewage into potable water.

In 1961 an agreement had been reached whereby Singapore would purchase high volumes of untreated catchment water from the Malayan state of Johore, in return for selling back to Johore a specified amount of potable water at a considerably higher price. This agreement had since expired. In 1962 an additional agreement—still in effect—gave Singapore the right to an even higher volume of untreated river water, in return for supplying two treatment plants and purification know-how to Johore.

Additional issues between the two countries have included a 40-year squabble over the ownership of a tiny islet the size of a football field in the Straits of Malacca, and the ownership of a railroad right-of-way in Singapore for the Malaysian railway that runs across the Singapore-Johore causeway. Happily, these and many other thorny issues—including mutual use of national airspaces—have been resolved in recent years, and Singapore-Malaysia relations today are dealt with in friendly fashion at an elevated level of maturity.

Both nations were founding members in 1967 of ASEAN, the highly successful and internationally respected Association of Southeast Asian Nations, together with Thailand, Indonesia, and the Philippines. Five other countries have since joined—Cambodia, Laos, Vietnam, Brunei, and Myanmar. The ASEAN headquarters are in Jakarta, Indonesia.

*** RELATIONS WITH INDONESIA ***

Because the new nations Malaysia and Indonesia were expected to share a former British-Dutch colonial era terrestrial border in Kalimantan (Borneo), there were serious tensions between them during the early postwar period, especially as Indonesia under its President Sukarno seemed determined to gobble up all former colonial territory in his vicinity, whether or not it had been historically part of the NEI in the colonial era. This had already become the fate of Irian Jaya, the former Dutch New Guinea that never was part of the NEI, and even looked for a while to become the fate of the former Portuguese colony of East Timor as well. There must surely have been concerns in Malaysia that Indonesia might perhaps have its eye on the smaller, formerly British portion of Borneo that was to become East Malaysia, so it could take control of the entire Borneo island as its own.

*** THE BORNEO CONFRONTATION ***

The *Konfrontasi*, a violent three-year conflict beginning in 1963, resulted from the pending formation of the Federation of Malaysia, to which Indonesia strenuously objected because Great Britain was intent on merging its Borneo colonies of Sarawak and Sabah (to become East Malaysia) with those of the Malay peninsula (to be called West Malaysia). Relying heavily at first on local Kalimantan volunteers trained by the Indonesian army, Indonesia began a series of infiltrations into Sarawak and Sabah, seeking to exploit the racial and cultural differences between those territories and the more homogenous Malay peninsula and Singapore, and thereby to unravel the pending federation of Malaysia.

A resulting series of battles were essentially ground engagements by small infantry units along the mountain-peaked border region that possessed few roads at the time. Both sides relied mainly upon air transport to move combat teams, and British Commonwealth forces possessed the advantage of more and better helicopters. Rivers were also used extensively, not only for boats but also as 'navigable roadways' for pontooned aircraft.

British naval units guarded the coastal regions from amphibious landings, while both sides gradually built up their troop levels. The British Commonwealth side that eventually numbered around 14,000 troops drew upon various detachments on routine duty in Singapore during the period, including Gurkhas and Royal Marines, while Indonesia replaced its poorly trained Sarawak volunteers with regular front-line army troops and eventually had over 30,000 soldiers involved in the conflict. Before the confrontation ended, British troops took the highly secret initiative of conducting search and destroy missions on the Indonesian side of the border, thereby changing from a defensive to an offensive strategy.

After diplomatic pressure from the US and UK, an end to the conflict came about in late 1965 with an attempted coup against Sukarno, in which several high-ranking Indonesian military leaders were killed and former General Suharto was given permission by Sukarno to reorganize the government. Suharto did this in short order and began a purge of the Indonesian Communist Party (PKI) that had been loosely allied with Sukarno. He eventually called for an alliance of leading politicians that did not include Sukarno, and by 1966 the conflict with Malaysia was ended and Suharto was the new president of Indonesia—an abrupt swing from the left to the right.

Malaysia and Indonesia then became charter members of ASEAN.

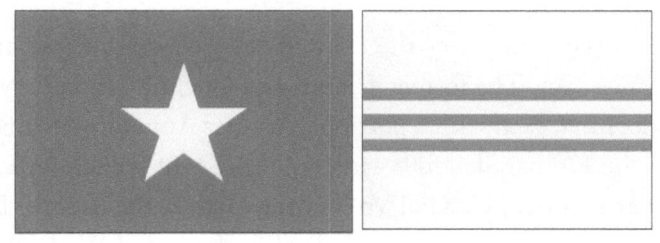

SCENE SEVEN

French Legacy – Vietnam, Cambodia, Laos

The adjacent flags shown at the start of this scene are those of North and South Vietnam. The former Tonkin and Cochin-China Provinces of French Indochina, each with a portion of former Annam, were divided by the UN at the 17th parallel, following the capture of French forces by the Viet Minh army under General Vo Nguyen Giap at the decisive Battle of Dien Bien Phu in 1954, nearly a decade after the end of World War Two.

The Geneva Accords that followed the military reality and insured the permanent departure of the French from Indochina, also restored the former French protectorates of Laos and Cambodia to their historical status as independent states, accompanied by United Nations memberships.

The Viet Minh (*Viet Nam Doc Lap Dong Minh Hoi*, meaning 'The League for the Independence of Vietnam') was formed by Ho Chi Minh

in 1941 while he was exiled in China. Although primarily led by Communists, it operated at first as a National Front open to persons of various political persuasions, then a year after Ho's 1945 declaration of Viet Nam independence, many other nationalists were purged and some even executed, probably to avert a drawn-out civil war as in China between Communist and Nationalist Chinese.

Nationalist sentiment in French Indochina had its origins in the late 1800s and was manifested when simmering anti-French protests burst forth on 1 May 1930 under Communist leadership. French retaliation was swift and deadly, with some 70,000 people being jailed and over 700 executed.

Ho Chi Minh and Vo Nguyen Giap were both exposed to anti-French rhetoric during their formative school years, and they plotted during the WWII Japanese occupation as to how they would fight to remove the French after the war.

The Battle of Dien Bien Phu was their triumphant achievement.

Fighting would continue after the 1954 French departure too, but this time the combatants would be the Viet Minh of North Vietnam and their insurgent Viet Cong allies in the south, against US-allied South Vietnam. That conflict would escalate in further horror for another two decades until General Giap would once again prevail in 1975, thereby uniting the Vietnam nation for the late 'Uncle Ho.'

*** RETURN OF THE FRENCH ***

When the French returned after World War II to reclaim their colony of Indochina, they found the northern part occupied by Communist-led insurgents that had raised a substantial local army with the help of Chinese Communists. These Viet Minh, as they were called, had also absorbed and benefited from some 1500 Japanese mercenary soldiers who had evaded repatriation at the end of the Pacific War. Although the French managed to reoccupy the Tonkin capital Ha Noi (Hanoi) in the spring of 1947 after months of house-to-house fighting, they had been unable to regain control of the Tonkin countryside.

The Viet Minh insurgents were led by Ho Chi Minh and his General Vo Nguyen Giap, who had been a former university professor of French history. Technically speaking, the former professor should have been known as General Vo, but being considerably younger than Ho Chi Minh, the people knew him throughout his brilliant career by his given name Giap.

General Giap (try saying *Zhénéral Zhee-ap* in a French accent) was a self-taught militarist who had studied many books about warfare, in particularly the campaigns of Napoleon Bonaparte which fascinated him. He joined the Indochina Communist Party (ICP) in 1937 and published several newspapers with anti-French rhetoric, a heavy workload that caused him to drop out of university before receiving his doctoral law degree.

Ho Chi Minh (born Nguyen Sinh Cung) was some twenty years older than his talented and eager young scholar-general (who had to be restrained on occasion for impulsiveness). Ho was a militarist too, but even more a politician who eventually convinced Giap that military efforts should always be subservient to the needs of the people themselves. Ho, who had been condemned to death in absentia, was frequently in self-imposed exile in China whenever French *Sûreté* Police sought his arrest.

He spent much of the Pacific War years in Mao's part of China, training, planning, and building relationships.

Regarded initially as a bunch of bandits by both Japanese and French administrations in their early days during WWII, the growing insurgency of Ho and Giap was not at first taken seriously. This would change in July 1944 with the collapse of Pétain's Vichy government in France, and the subsequent German occupation of all France not yet in Allied hands. Germany's ally, Japan, was quick to respond to those European circumstances by means of a complete *coup d'état* to remove all traces of French power in Indochina. Indochina, by force of arms, became an outright Japanese possession instead of an awkward ally. Many former French leaders were imprisoned or even executed.

Although Japan and its Kempeitai secret police quickly replaced French control of the cities, the rural areas of Indochina were effectively ignored. Into this vacuum the new clandestine army of General Giap rapidly expanded, village by village, as various tribes pledged allegiance to the Viet Minh throughout much of Tonkin Province.

Soon another unexpected benefit came to the Viet Minh, which found itself—through the fortunes of war—as a semi-official ally of American efforts to defeat Japan. Ho Chi Minh had the good fortune of meeting USAAF General Claire Chennault in Kunming, China, after which an OSS team was assigned to the Viet Minh and secret intelligence was exchanged in both directions. With US backing of its anti-Japanese tactics in Tonkin, the Viet Minh gained credibility with local people and acquired useful US military assets such as vehicles, weapons, and ammunition.

*** *A BROKEN TRUCE* ***

When in August 1945 the Comintern (Communist International) ordered Ho Chi Minh to declare Viet Nam a republic, Ho in turn persuaded the former French-then-Japanese puppet Emperor of Annam, Bao Dai, to abdicate in his favor, which gave Ho much more legitimacy in the eyes of the people. When French forces returned to reclaim their former colony, however, they decided to return Bao Dai to his throne to counteract the growing popularity of Ho Chi Minh.

It was initially the British who were tasked with postwar repatriation of Japanese troops in the southern part of Vietnam (as in Malaya-Singapore, Java, and Borneo), while the northern part of Vietnam was assigned to Chiang Kai Shek's Nationalist Chinese. A scraggly division of Chinese arrived at Hanoi from Kunming on 22 August, and proceeded to loot the northern territory, which the Viet Minh were unable to stop. Then British troops from Burma began arriving in Saigon on 11 September, with the unofficial aim of preparing the south for an eventual French return, which the Viet Minh were also unable to stop.

The immediate post-war struggles that followed Ho's declaration of independence even resulted in a short-lived formal written agreement on 6 March 1946 between France and the Democratic Republic of Viet Nam. This agreement ceded to France the territory of Cochin-China only, whereas the remainder—former Annam and Tonkin—became a Communist state under Ho's control.

At first this seemed a satisfactory compromise, as Cochin-China and its capital Saigon is where most of the prewar agricultural wealth had been generated for France, whereas the Viet Minh gained much land to the north. The new agreement did not last long, however, with Ho and Giap determined to take control of all Viet Nam, and with France clandestinely expanding northward from their Cochin-China territory into Annam.

The tension finally broke, with French troops arriving in force by sea and by air, fully determined to take back their entire Indochina colony. In no time at all, fighting broke out again between the two parties with the French taking control of Annamese cities and even Hanoi, and with Ho's Viet Minh being driven back into the countryside.

*** ANDRÉ AND MEY IN SAIGON ***

When the world war ended in August 1945, André Séguin had the freedom to return to Saigon, the capital of Cochin-China located on the Mekong River, which was for his wife Mey the first time she had ever been away from Cambodia. In their new city, with its name alternatively romanized in various ways as Sai Gon (Chinese), Sài Gòn (Vietnamese), Sai-Gon (British), Saïgon (French), or Saigon (American), both André and Mey played a visible role in mitigating the post-war anarchy that had begun to envelop the lovely metropolis during the month-long absence of an official government. For this assistance, André received accolades from the provincial governor of Cochin-China, newly arrived from France, and was promoted on the spot to Captain of Police. He and Mey were allocated a small but charming two-story colonial residence that had until recently been the quarters of a Japanese colonel. On André's new salary they could afford to adopt two young orphaned servants to assist with chores, a girl of eleven and her younger brother, nine. Their names were Tien and Huy.

Mey, who discovered she was pregnant soon after arrival in Saigon, busied herself with reorganizing the local hospital and two clinics, in preparation for her own—and other—childbirths. Whenever she and André could find the time to sit together and reflect upon their good fortune in avoiding the devastation of the war years, they gave thanks to their respective deities, his being Roman Catholic and hers the Hindu god Shiva. In other European colonies of the Asia-Pacific region, things had been much worse for the colonial populations than in Indochina, of this they were quite aware.

*** *A POLICEMAN'S LOT IS NOT A HAPPY ONE* ***

Not a single day of André's new role as a *Capitaine de Police Judiciare* was what one might call happy, however. His previous excitement at having secured a well-paying position with the security force for the fabled city of Saigon quickly evaporated as he was shown around the seamier sections that tourists and most residents scarcely knew existed. Although the *Commissariat de Police* itself was located on a pleasant avenue near the Hotel Majestic on the Mekong River, the territory that Captain Séguin would be responsible for was anything but pleasant. It looked to include a high rate of petty crime as well as many clandestine opium dens, a tax on the latter having been one of France's main sources of colonial income.

His guide that first day was grizzled police lieutenant Louis de Lourier, who was quick to tell André that he had been on the force for twenty-three years, of which fifteen had been in his current rank of lieutenant, and the last six months of which had been spent in a Japanese internment camp. That internment and his failure to secure any ongoing promotions had left him embittered and uncooperative.

André had already learned from the Saigon Commandant who hired him that the Colonial Police Force for Indochina (formerly known as *La Sûreté*) was headed by a superintendent named Perrier, recently retired from the French Army at Vichy where, as a brigadier general, he had overseen a corps of military police, or Gendarmes (*gens d'arme*). Indochina had a detachment of Gendarmes as well, which was responsible for security in the country towns and the borders. It was the collective task of the two police units—one civil and the other military—to provide security for the entire colony.

"Look, de Lourier, I am not interested in the past. You do your job well for me, and I'll see that you are rewarded properly. Is it a deal?" Reluctantly the lieutenant shook André's extended hand and muttered "*d'accord.*"

For the next four years, the French strengthened their control of Indochina by means of brutal law enforcement in the cities and equally stringent control of the countryside, using military might to supplement the Gendarmerie's roving patrols and spy networks, but gradually Ho Chi Minh's Viet Minh guerillas took back control of the country towns and villages to the far north despite massive French sweeps against them. Although the French had a tenuous hold on Hanoi, they were clearly losing overall control of Tonkin Province. Police officers André and Louis in Saigon were very busy as well, but thankful that their posting was in the south of the colony.

*** *THE MIGHTY MEKONG* ***

Thanks to a network of icy streams fed by melted snow that eventually merged to form its source in the mountains of Tibet, the lengthy river known to Westerners as the Mekong—but answering to many other local names along the way—meandered for some two thousand five hundred miles through Myanmar, China, Thailand, Laos, Vietnam, and Cambodia, to discharge its by-then warm and muddy waters into the South China Sea. The mighty river's local name near its muddy delta was Nine Dragons, the same meaning as Kowloon in the reoccupied British colony of Hong Kong.

Along the river's shallow banks in the flatland countries toiled some seventeen million fishermen and their families, most of them using nets to catch schools of small fry that were often repopulated by the fishermen themselves. Others used diving Cormorants to bring larger fish to the surface in their beaks, and still others with bigger boats and hours of patience lay in wait for giant catfish that very occasionally got outsmarted and captured. In all, there were some two hundred species of fish in the Mekong, from the tiny to the gigantic, that populated this mighty river.

Survival for certain fishing communities along the way—such as those in Cambodia and Cochin-China that glared with hostility at each other across their international border near the Mekong Delta—depended not only upon the river itself, but also on tropical monsoon rains that flushed the river and aided in its regeneration. With the development of modern fishing methods and the growth of riverine communities, the river became overfished and polluted but, like the Amazon in Brazil, the Mekong remained a vital River of Life both directly and indirectly for millions of people who fed on its fish and the rice and fruit nurtured during the river's flood cycles.

In the years immediately following World War II, the Mighty Mekong also carried boat traffic that had little to do with fishing. It was the job of Captain André Séguin and his assistant Lieutenant Louis de Lourier to investigate such river craft to ensure that their cargo spaces did not contain military-type weaponry or illegal quantities of opium. Upon discovery of either type of contraband, the offending boat's crew would be arrested by the police and the boat set on fire and scuttled, not necessarily in that order.

The colonial government's concern for illegal weaponry was motivated by a growing Viet Minh insurgency against French forces in the northern part of Indochina, and a suspicion that some weapons were reaching them overland from the Mekong region in the south, supplied by shipments from Communist China.

As for the illegal opium, its prohibition was not at all aimed at improving public health, but rather to prevent it from undercutting the price of government-sourced opium to which a twenty percent tax had been added when it was stored in government warehouses, ready for sale and distribution to the many opium dens in the city and beyond.

On a particularly ideal night for intercepting smugglers in November 1953, when the moon was full and police boats were stationed at several choke points along the river, André Séguin had just congratulated his assistant Louis de Lourier upon the latter's promotion to Captain of Police—with the caveat that the promotion would likely lead to a relocation in the near future to command some other police unit, probably in Annam—when suddenly the night sky erupted with the sound and light of multiple rocket and machinegun fire directed at each of the police craft that were lying in wait for smugglers.

These were clearly no ordinary smugglers, but more like a group of fanatics with the firepower and discipline of a military strike force, who seemed to know exactly where the police boats would be waiting. Their hit-and-run attack so close to Saigon, the center of French power for Indochina, marked a new phase in the battle with the Communist insurgency. Some surviving prisoners captured after the police called in French naval and air support, declared that they were not Viet Minh, but rather Viet Cong allies, a term not heard before in the south of the colony.

After the heavy skirmish was all over, it was found that some forty percent of the police personnel had been killed or wounded, and among the dead were Captains Séguin and de Lourier, both of whom had been aboard the control boat that was blasted apart and sunk early in the action, it being one of the more obvious Viet Cong targets.

A three-year war between South and North Korea had ended that year, 1953, so the Comintern was preparing for new mischief in South Vietnam once the French were routed in the north. To be ready for action in the south, some Viet Cong insurgents were being trained in China.

*** THE VALLEY OF DIEN BIEN PHU ***

After regaining control of Hanoi, a squabble between army Lt. General Henri Navarre and his subordinate Major General René Cogny, France's youngest general officer, led to *Operation Castor* in November 1953. The squabble was over how to finally defeat the Viet Minh insurgents who controlled much of Tonkin Province, particularly the western part bordering on Laos, thereby preventing French troops in Laos—already engaged with Pathet Lao Communists—from linking up with their French counterparts in Hanoi for mutual support.

A large valley called Dien Bien Phu (meaning 'Seat of the Border County Prefecture') lay close to Viet Minh territory near the Laos border, some 200 miles from Hanoi. Inside the valley was the village of Muong Thanh, inhabited by T'ai tribal people, who were part of a larger T'ai Federation in northern Tonkin that was loyal to the French, and which controlled a major opium growing area that was an important funding source for French special forces. Intelligence had revealed that the Viet Minh were intent on capturing the T'ai territory and acquiring the opium funds.

Dien Bien Phu—it was recalled by French veterans—contained a dirt airstrip that had been used in WWII for ferrying Free French and Americans away from Vichy/Japanese control, and General Navarre reckoned this airstrip could allow the French to bring in artillery and vehicles to turn the valley into a huge fortress. With a friendly population of T'ai tribesmen, the French forces should be able to install themselves with little interruption and then burst forth to exterminate the Viet Minh Communists.

General Cogny was uneasy about the idea. The primary Viet Minh unit that opposed French control of this region in the 1950s was Independent Regiment 148, which specialized in mountain warfare. In fighting these mountaineers, the French had already established two 'airheads' within Viet Minh territory, which were fortified villages with airstrips where the French could fly in supplies and paratroopers. This strategy was proving quite feasible because the Viet Minh did not possess even a single aircraft, thereby giving the French complete control of the air (though not the jungle below).

Gen. Navarre therefore decided to establish a much larger airhead in the valley of Dien Bien Phu and to close both existing ones at Na San and Lai Chap. This *Operation Castor* would theoretically enable the French to open a military corridor between Hanoi and Vientiane in Laos. Soon afterwards, however, General Navarre retired to France and left General Cogny to take over the fight against the Viet Minh in Tonkin, using Dien Bien Phu as the strategic focal point.

The on-site commander selected for Dien Bien Phu operations was Colonel Christian de Castries, an elegant, adventurous aristocrat, who—disdaining the French academy at St. Cyr—had joined the army at age 20 as a private soldier, been promoted rapidly to sergeant, and then received a WWII field commission in North Africa.

Inside the valley were five fortified drop zones (each supposedly named after a former de Castries girlfriend), with the main one, *Natasha*, being where the initial drop would take place. The colonel's dour but highly professional assistant was Lt. Col. Pierre Langlais, commander of the airborne paras.

The drop began on Friday, 20 November 1953. It was theoretically the dry season, but for some reason Dien Bien Phu habitually received half again as much rain as any other valley in North Indochina. It began raining during the parachute exercise, making the old airstrip unusable for landings. Nevertheless, by the third day there were 4,500 sodden troops on the ground—a mixture of French paratroopers, loyal Vietnamese, and tough Foreign Legionnaires—plus Brigitte Friang, a reporter with five combat jumps already to her credit.

As tent camps were erected and firing positions dug, the paratroopers were in high spirits, feeling especially secure within the ring of hills that surrounded Dien Bien Phu like castle walls. Unfortunately, the excited combat troops in their exuberance neglected to plan for engineering defense works such as reinforced concrete bunkers to properly defend themselves against a determined enemy, and they were significantly under-supplied with heavy artillery, considering the size of the valley to be defended. Furthermore, such lightly protected artillery positions as they had, were in several cases poorly located and unable to provide mutual support from one to the other.

Meanwhile, protected from French aerial view by extensive jungle vegetation, a large Viet Minh force dragged its ample artillery up and over the surrounding hills of Dien Bien Phu by brute force and emplaced it—not on the reverse slopes in textbook fashion but well dug in and camouflaged on the forward slopes—overlooking French strongpoints and the crucial airfield.

In his book *Hell in a Very Small Place*, author Bernard Fall describes the Dien Bien Phu valley as it looked on the morning of 13 March 1954, before the battle erupted late that afternoon: *"As seen from the air or from the surrounding hills, Dien Bien Phu now looked like some gigantic primitive village whose population, not having mastered the art of building houses, had preferred to take shelter in holes in the ground. Inside the main center of resistance and on top of the main outlying positions, the last shreds of vegetation had completely disappeared."*

The assault began at 5 pm that day with a tremendous barrage of Viet Minh heavy artillery numbering some 200 guns. The late time of day was chosen to provide enough daylight for Viet Minh artillery to register on their French targets, but too late for the French to muster an air strike from Hanoi.

Fall goes on to say: *"The real surprise for the French was not that the Communists had that kind of artillery—in fact, its existence had been known for a year. What surprised the French completely was the Viet Minh's ability to transport a considerable mass of heavy artillery pieces across roadless mountains to Dien Bien Phu and to keep it supplied with enough ammunition to make the huge effort worthwhile."*

Throughout the ensuing lengthy battle of attrition over the next two months, the French were outmanned and outgunned while their fighter planes and bombers—deployed to interdict the swarms of Viet Minh coolies struggling through jungle trails on foot or bicycles to bring supplies to the front—suffered heavy losses from highly accurate Viet Minh anti-aircraft gunnery. A small 44-bed hospital located near the French command post at Dien Bien Phu was before long treating 3,000 wounded soldiers, most still scattered about on the ground outside awaiting their turn. With the airstrip becoming gradually useless, it was soon impossible to fly seriously wounded away from the battle zone.

The United Stated of America, still smarting from a 1953 armistice in Korea that left Communism undefeated, was unwilling to join the French in their battle against another Chinese client state in case that too might turn into a defeat. France was left to fight on alone, albeit with a US$300M contribution to their lonely war effort. Treating France as a surrogate force to continue the fight against communism, US leadership did not fully understand that they themselves would have to pick up the banner less than a decade later if the French were unsuccessful.

As Viet Minh assaults continued at Dien Bien Phu, with occasional setbacks offset by even more ferocious weaponry such as multiple rocket launchers supplied by China, most of the airfield was gradually captured from the French. The Chinese-trained Viet Minh then adopted First World War siege tactics by digging trenches closer and closer to the French strongpoints, overwhelming them one by one until the French periphery became too small even for accurate drops of desperately needed food, medical supplies and ammunition.

By 7 May at 5 pm, after numerous heroic deeds of self-sacrifice were unable to stem the flood of enemy troops, the French garrison declared a cease-fire, after which the battered and depleted remnants of the Dien Bien Phu fortress were marched into captivity by the Viet Minh.

The shock in Paris of this major defeat of around 14,000 men was profound: a solemn Requiem Mass was performed for the veterans, while almost all other public performances were cancelled for weeks, especially those by Russian artists. The defeat at Dien Bien Phu in May 1954 was a preamble to the complete French withdrawal from Indochina, which would transpire after negotiations at Geneva that June.

The shock was even more severe down south in Saigon, where many French nationals had become worried about their jobs and families as the battle news worsened day by day. The looming tragedy brought about a demand for psychological consulting to treat various sorts of anxieties.

*** DOCTOR MOON-SHE ***

Former Police Captain Séguin's home in Saigon was not well illuminated, but when the hesitant young couple drew near, they were certain it was the place they had been searching for. Next to the doorbell were two simple business cards one above the other in a little wooden frame. The top one read:

> Conseillère conjugale
> Docteur Lune-Elle
> Sur rendez-vous

The lower card was flipped over to reveal its English translation:

> Marriage Counsellor
> Doctor Moon-She
> By Appointment

The visitors both appeared to be French, or at least European. Shortly after ringing the bell, they were admitted by a young Vietnamese girl of perhaps fifteen, who led them into a parlor and invited them to be seated at a small circular table. From a nearby room came the buzzing sound of a small electric motor, which caused the man to glance in that direction.

"Madame Doctor will soon be here to welcome you," the receptionist said pleasantly. "I will bring you some tea. Please excuse me." The buzzing continued for a few more minutes, and about the time it ceased, the girl reappeared with two steaming cups.

"Doctor Moon-She suggests stirring the tea with these cinnamon sticks, to enhance the flavor," she smiled. "She will be with you shortly." The girl bowed and left the room.

The young couple, clearly nervous in each other's company, stirred and sipped the tea but avoided eye contact.

"I hope she knows what she's doing," the man grumbled. "This is all rather silly, if you ask me."

He took another gulp of cinnamon tea and stared at the slowly rotating ceiling fan. His companion mumbled assurances:

"It will be all right, my sweet. We must try something, you said so yourself."

Just then a door opened to admit an elegantly gowned slightly older woman with pleasant oriental features. She appeared to have been crying, however, for she fought to regain her composure as she slowly approached the table. The young man stood to meet her.

"Doctor Moon-She?" he asked, then quickly added: "Why, you're Madame Séguin! Do you remember? My wife and I met you at our wedding reception six months ago. Oh gosh, we were so distressed to learn of your husband's death." The young wife also rose to embrace their hostess.

"Oh, I am so terribly sorry to have intruded on your sorrow. We must leave at once. We got your name from a friend and didn't realize Doctor Moon-She was someone that we already knew."

"No, no, my dears, it is all right. Yes, I am Mey Séguin, and my professional name is Doctor Moon-She. I must work again, you know, now that André is gone. There is our three-year-old boy to care for, after all, and my two servants help a great deal but we all must eat. You met Tien just now. Her brother Huy works in the kitchen."

"What is your son's name, then?" the young wife asked.

"He is Thao. My husband named him for a boy he knew in Annam during the big war, who lost his life to the *Japoni*. You will meet little Thao later, but shall we get started now? I gather you have some marital problems, or you would not be here this evening. Please, let us sit down. Take off your shoes and be comfortable, like me."

Doctor Moon-She was back in control, as her two nervous clients plopped into chairs and stared glumly ahead while fumbling with their shoelaces. Then the doctor's next question stunned them both.

"From your demeanor, I think I see what the problem is. Tell me," she asked the pretty young wife, "would you mind if I seduced your husband—while you watch and learn? After that we can have some supper, and then it will be your turn."

SCENE EIGHT

Spanish-American Legacy – The Philippines

Although Manuel Quezon and Sergio Osmeña were successive Philippine presidents in exile during the Japanese occupation, and Osmeña even accompanied MacArthur in reoccupying the country, Manuel A. Roxas (photo) was the first president elected after the new nation's independence from the United States in 1946. Unfortunately for his party's liberal agenda, Roxas served just two years until a heart attack caused his death in 1948, while delivering a speech at Clark Air Force Base. Although he was succeeded by his vice president Elpidio Quirino, a fellow-liberal, Quirino's subsequent term was tainted by corruption and a rebellion by Communist-led Hukbalahap insurgents (the Huk Rebellion).

During his short tenure, Roxas had worked diligently to stabilize the country, which was severely damaged during the war and was facing near bankruptcy and serious criminal gang activity. For rebuilding the horribly devastated city of Manila, where Japanese naval infantry had opted to hold out to the end despite being ordered by General Yamashita to abandon the city, Roxas arranged for lend-lease funding from the US in return for which he granted the US the use of many military bases in the Philippines, with terms up to 99 years in some instances. Meanwhile

General Yamashita was hanged as a war criminal because of the naval infantry's refusal to evacuate and spare Manila from destruction.

*** *A MANILA ENCOUNTER* ***

President Roxas also became acquainted with an interesting individual who came over from China in 1947 to offer his services. The handsome middle-aged visitor's name was George Bolnar, who had served as Sergeant-Major of the Fourth Marine Regiment in Shanghai during the late 1930s, until his retirement in 1940. Since then, Bolnar had lived in Hong Kong until the Japanese invaded that British colony on 8 December 1941, barely managing to escape through Portuguese Macau to the interior of China.

All this he was relating to an attractive companion one afternoon, as they strolled about in the gardens of the famous Hotel Manila where General Douglas MacArthur had managed to persuade a former president of the Philippine Commonwealth to have the hotel build an entire sixth floor penthouse for him and his wife and son. The penthouse residence was part of MacArthur's compensation in his prestigious job as consultant to the Philippines with the glorious rank of Field Marshal, for the modernization of its creaky old military resources

"But how did you manage to reach Macau, Mr. Bolnar?" asked the pretty secretary, Angela Adonis, who had been assigned by President Roxas to accompany Bolnar at the re-dedication ceremony of the old Manila Hotel. Parts of the burned-out building were still a mess from the Battle of Manila two years before, but the lobby and two of six floors were once again open for business.

"Oh, I had a few friends with a small boat," the old Marine winked, "And after I reached Macau on the other side of the Pearl River Delta, I caught a ride to the Generalissimo's headquarters at Chungking. Figured he could use a little help, and he sure enough did put me to work."

"Gosh, Mr. Bolnar, is that why you're here in Manila now, to offer us some help? Gee, my boss will be glad of that, and me too." She fluttered her eyelids and smiled.

"Darn, Miss Angela, please don't call me 'Mister'. It makes me feel sort of ancient, whereas I am only fifty-two, just twenty years or so older than you, as a guess. I much prefer to be called George, OK? Say, did you see that big white heron flying past just now? At least I guess it was a heron."

"Oh, I'm so sorry, er, um, G .. George. I didn't see the bird because I was daydreaming, I think. But we don't have herons here; it was probably a white egret. Some people call them Chinese Egrets. They are really beautiful birds." She relaxed, in view of the small talk that was developing.

"Oh yes, it was a beautiful white bird all right, almost as beautiful as, well…I, um, I don't mean to be fresh or anything, but—Miss Angela—that bird was almost as beautiful as you are!"

"Oh George," she sighed and blushed, "just call me Angie, that's what my mom does … and my dad used to call me that too, before he…well, he was killed by the Japanese, sort of accidentally, they said, but we didn't believe it was an accident."

She paused, and gratefully accepted the cigarette that George was offering her with a sad expression on his face. They moved away from the hotel building and crossed the boulevard to sit on the sea wall that overlooked an apparently man-made, square-shaped marina at the edge of the bay. For some time, they sat silently, each lost in thoughts that the other had provoked. Eventually, Angie continued, somewhat bitterly:

"They killed my husband too, you know, back on Bataan. That was no accident, of course. He was a lieutenant with the PA troops that MacArthur was forced to surrender. Being a Filipino … they apparently just shot him. We don't really know much more than that. They were bad people, the Japanese, and look what happened to our beautiful Manila because of them. People say that Manila was almost as, what's the word? … almost as devastated as Stalinburg in Russia."

"Stalingrad, it was Stalingrad in Russia. I am really sorry to hear all this, Angie," George interrupted. "I never had a family to care about like you do, though I've made some good friends here and there. I guess my family was mostly the Marine Corps. I spent twenty years with them, a lot of it in Shanghai and other parts of China, but did you know that my entire former regiment disappeared trying to defend your island of Corregidor out there, not long after your husband died?" George was pointing out across Manila Bay at the little island where the Americans had surrendered in May of 1942 to the Japanese army. Angie listened to him in shock.

"The old Fourth Marines don't even exist anymore in the official Marine Corps records, can you imagine? Well, I guess we should be going back to the hotel for the ceremony, else you'll get in trouble with your boss. Maybe we can talk some other day about the war years."

"You're quite right," Angie agreed, still tearful. "Let's go back now so we don't remind each other of more sad memories."

Together they walked the short distance from the marina to the Manila Hotel lobby, where a considerable crowd had formed. Before reaching the entrance where security guards were busy checking all the visitors, they saw a pair of repainted US army jeeps draw up into the porte-cochère, followed by a long black Buick limousine and two more jeeps. Four smart-looking Filipino soldiers from each jeep jumped down and formed a large circle around the limousine, with the captain in charge opening the limousine's rear doors to let the Philippine president and his wife step out. As President Roxas nodded his thanks to the captain, he spotted George and Angela, who were by that time standing just outside the ring of soldiers. Touching the captain's shoulder to pause him, the president spoke quickly and softly to George:

"Tomorrow at ten, Mr. Bolnar, if you're not otherwise occupied. Miss Adonis will explain how to reach my offices."

With that, the president smiled and extended an arm to his fashionably dressed wife. They walked slowly through the crowd, alternately smiling or waving until they had disappeared into the lobby for the ribbon-cutting ceremony. The hotel's board of directors was quite pleased that the President had agreed to attend the event, but then, several board members were assumed to be his relatives.

"I think that sounded like good news," George remarked, cheerfully. "I do know where his office is; of course. Could you meet me at the entrance around 9:45? I have an earlier meeting on Escolta Street with my new bank manager."

As she nodded, he continued: "Say, Angie, are you his only secretary? And where did you get a name like Adonis? Was it your husband's? Doesn't sound very Spanish."

Angela smiled: "No, George, I am one of five secretaries for President Roxas, and you certainly do ask a lot of questions. We Filipina women keep our maiden names over here when we marry, and Adonis is a Greek name.

My Greek grandfather came to the Philippines around 1875 and liked what he saw. He was a sea captain, so he started a ferry service between the islands. After Grandpa passed on, my father kept it going until the war started. It was sort of like the Little White Fleet between Sarawak and Singapore, so they say. Most of our boats have been sunk by now, but a couple still exist. My brother Stefan is thinking of getting the service going again. Perhaps you could give him some suggestions. See you tomorrow."

Angie gave George a suggestion of a hug and a brief peck on the cheek. It was enough; Bolnar was hooked.

*** A LAND OF INTRIGUE ***

A week after meeting Angie at the Manila Hotel event, her new admirer George Bolnar was concluding a visit to the prestigious Jesuit institution of learning called the *Ateneo de Manila*, where many Filipino politicians and community leaders had been schooled. The Ateneo was a primary, secondary, and tertiary institution founded in 1909 during the American occupation. Although the Jesuits had come to the Philippines with the Spanish from Mexico in 1581, they were expelled in 1768 but allowed back once again in 1859.

Oddly enough, the Ateneo was proud to claim local Filipino hero José Rizal as an alumnus, even though Rizal's inflammatory writings against corrupt clergy and government leaders had led to his arrest, trial, and execution shortly before the Spanish-American War. George thought this dichotomy fit with his existing impression of the Jesuits being champions of the poor and oppressed on the one hand, and militant enforcers of Roman Catholic orthodoxy on the other. He had been asked by President Roxas to find out where they stood regarding the senseless Battle of Manila when Japanese naval infantry had provoked such heavy US artillery barrages that practically flattened the city.

That evening, after the Ateneo visit, he dined with Angie and her mother María at Angie's invitation.

"Momma, George here likes to be informal and call people by their first names. Is that all right with you?"

"Of course, my darling. Welcome, George, to our home in what's left of Manila. I am María Beltrán, the widow of Stéfano Adonis, as you probably know."

"Yes, ma'am…María. Angie told me that Adonis is a Greek name, and I was playing around with that in my old head one day and realized that Adonis spelled backwards is Sinoda, which is like Synod, the Greek word for a church convention."

"Well, aren't you the clever one, George," Angie chimed in, "and what is Ranlob supposed to mean then?"

"Ranlob? What the heck is that?" George asked.

"It's Bolnar spelled backwards, dummy!" Angie laughed.

"Well, Synod sounds a lot more interesting," George chuckled, "especially since I've been spending time with the Jesuits the last few days. They are quite an intriguing bunch, and their Synod is coming up in a few weeks, as a matter of fact. I've been invited to attend by Father José Ramos Padilla SJ, who is not only a retired Jesuit priest but a Spanish-American War veteran as well."

"My goodness," María said, "that sounds fascinating. I hope you will come by and tell us about it someday afterwards."

*** *A SPANISH AMERICAN WAR VETERAN* ***

After the 1947 Jesuit Synod in Manila, George Bolnar was mightily impressed by the old soldier-priest José Ramos, who looked to be around 75 or so. At George's invitation, they dined one evening at a quiet little restaurant in the old Spanish part of Manila known as Intramuro*s [Latin for 'inside the walls,' whence comes our word 'intramural' - Ed.].*

George learned from Fr. José that they were in the original walled city that had been so terribly damaged in February 1945 by the US Army because Japanese SNLF defenders under their Admiral Iwabuchi refused to surrender. Those Japanese troops just hunkered down inside the massive old Spanish fort and public buildings and took out their frustrations on the local Filipinos, while Americans rained artillery on their heads and blasted huge holes through the thick walls for USA vehicles to enter.

George knew that postwar reparations from Japan were unlikely to happen, and it would be decades before the Philippine government could afford to rebuild the old Spanish landmarks that had brought prewar tourists from all over the world, but some small businesses like their restaurant had managed to get going once more in the old part of the city.

"Are there still many Spanish veterans like yourself in the Philippines?" George asked as they munched on appetizers.

"Not so many now," the priest replied. "Most of them were repatriated to Spain after the US bought these islands as part of the war settlement in 1898. But Jesuits were able to remain, so I took my vows and gave up soldiering. Most of the war action had taken place in Cuba anyway, though of course there was a fairly large Spanish garrison here at the time as well, and therefore some fighting because no one in the Philippines realized that Spain and the US had already reached a final settlement."

"How did that war get started anyway? I don't really know much about it," George queried. "By the way, care for a local beer with the meal? I've already developed a fondness for the San Miguel dark."

"Yes, please. That is my favorite also." The two veterans of different eras munched on their *chicken adobo* and savored the cold beers. After the second bottles arrived, Father José began to reminisce.

"I was just sixteen when I joined the army in Spain, and eighteen when I went to Cuba. I remember well that the 'gringos,' as we called your people, were well established in Havana and even in the agricultural plantations. It often seemed like Cuba was both a Spanish and American shared colony, but I didn't really get to know any Americans. I just saw their ships coming and going and their people walking around."

"*Salud,*" George toasted when the third round of beer arrived. "Did you get to know any of the local Cubans?"

"Well, a few I guess. There was an active Cuban independence movement in those days, you know. The rebels knew what they were fighting <u>for</u> but apparently, they didn't understand who they were fighting <u>against</u>; first it was against us Spanish, so the rebels joined forces with the Americans, but later it was against the Americans themselves. When the Americans won the war, they promised to give Cuba its independence ten years later—and they were true to their word.

"The same thing was going on over here in the Philippines too," the priest continued. "There was a strong Filipino independence movement, whose leaders were in exile, then the Americans arrived and took over the islands from Spain and the Filipino independence leaders came back home and carried on their fight."

"But now the Filipinos have their independence and have elected President Roxas. So, what brought the Spanish-American War to a close?" George asked the priest, whom he had begun to call Padre.

"It was mainly the loss of our navy in the Caribbean," said Padre José. "Our fleet was bottled up in Havana Harbor while the gringos attacked our troops on land—including me; I fought in the Battle of San Juan Hill—then the navy decided to make a run for it, but your navy was waiting and sank enough of our ships that the governor of Cuba decided to surrender."

"That was it, then," George mused. "The *Treaty of Paris*, our payment of twenty million dollars for the Philippines and Guam, and the US Asiatic Fleet arriving in Manila Bay one day to sink some more of your fleet and take over our new colony in the Pacific. What happened to you after the war ended, anyway?"

"After being involved with that war, I decided that all war was immoral—still do, even more so after the war with Japan—so when the Americans let us go from Cuba I immediately joined the Jesuits, having heard about them helping the poor and educating people."

"Well, if you don't mind me saying this, Padre, you Jesuits also have a reputation for being the 'enforcers' for the Catholic Church. Is there any truth in that?"

The old priest smiled and extended his hand to George. "Thank you very much for the nice meal, sir, and the good company. I enjoyed getting to know another veteran. We must get together again and talk about your service days in China. I'm afraid I need to go now, as I must prepare for my class of young students in the morning."

*** *A CHANGING OF THE GUARD* ***

Lifelong bachelor George Bolnar, Sergeant Major USMC (Ret.), age 53, married the widowed Angela Adonis, age 35, on 15 March 1948. María Beltrán, the mother of the bride—who was roughly the same age as her son-in-law-to-be—gave away her daughter according to longstanding Filipino custom. The groom's best man was the Commanding Officer of Marines at the US Embassy whom George, as a frequent embassy guest in the company of Philippine President Roxas, had come to know. The wedding service was performed at the *Intramuros* Jesuit chapel by Father José Ramos Padilla SJ, from whom George had managed to extract some additional Jesuit secrets as their friendship grew.

Exactly a month later, on 15 April 1948, George and a few other staff accompanied President Roxas to Clark Air Force Base where the President gave a speech committing the Philippines to fully support US policies in the Cold War that was just beginning. Shortly after giving the speech, President Roxas became ill and died that very evening of a heart attack. Two days afterwards, Vice President Elpidio Quirino was sworn in as President, promising in public to continue the liberal reforms of his predecessor and close friend.

George lost his job at that point, since he was not on friendly terms with the former vice president. He and Angie therefore decided to move to Hong Kong, where George had spent several years after his retirement from the Fourth Marine Regiment that was based in Shanghai. They rented an apartment on the Kowloon side of the 'fragrant harbor,' and George began working as a consultant with the administration of Kai Tak International Airport. The following year, when Nationalist China's President Chiang Kai-Shek was ousted by Communist Chairman Mao Zedong, George— who had worked for the Generalissimo and his Wellesley College-educated wife Soong Mei-Ling during and after the Second World War—joined the Nationalist Party exodus to Taiwan, where he planned to start a company of some sort under his Bolnar name.

Scene Nine

Dutch Legacy – Indonesia

During the Japanese control of the Dutch East Indies, a bizarre relationship began to form between the Japanese leadership and a clever and charismatic Javanese politician named Achmed Sukarno (Soekarno in Dutch), who was around forty years old when the Japanese invaded Java. As a government functionary by then, Sukarno made the point of openly welcoming the Japanese conquerors to his country, which in turn made the Japanese eager to use Sukarno as their surrogate in dealings with the Dutch colonists that they were incarcerating as rapidly as possible.

Sukarno—actually Su Karno, 'Su' being an honorific much like 'Don' in the Spanish language—who like many Indonesians at the time went by only one name, was formally trained as a civil engineer, but his real talent lay in an amazing fluency with many languages that enabled him to interact with people easily and to become a charismatic politician.

During his youth he mastered Javanese, Sundanese, Balinese, and the simplified Malay that he later promoted as a national language, *Bahasa Melayu,* for Indonesia. He also learned Arabic during his Islamic studies and Dutch was the language of his schooling. After university he would master German, English and French, and finally Japanese during the war years. His love of languages seems to have mirrored a burning desire to converse with other people—for better or for worse—and he did indeed become a great orator.

While growing up, he spent considerable time in the village of his grandparents where he was exposed to the animism and mysticism of rural Java, thereby becoming a lifelong devotee of *Wayang*, the shadow-puppet plays based on Hindu epics, as narrated by master puppeteers who could hold an audience spellbound for an entire evening.

In his youth, Sukarno was also an active member of a secret society called Sarekat Islam, which was originally formed in 1912 as a cooperative of Javanese batik traders who later became clandestine supporters of Indonesian independence. Many of SI's members were active anti-colonists well before WWII.

Indeed, Sukarno ran afoul of Dutch authorities in the 1930s for his anti-colonial oratory and spent several years in jail and exile. Then, during the Japanese occupation, he persuaded Japan to declare Indonesia's independence on June 1, 1945, with himself as its first leader. In his acceptance speech he defined the Five Principles that are still the Indonesian government's doctrine today: nationalism, internationalism, democracy, social prosperity, and belief in God.

Two days after Japan's surrender to the Allies on 15 August 1945, Sukarno—prodded by young would-be revolutionaries known as the *Pemuda*—announced Indonesia's independence to the world from his revolutionary capital of Yogyakarta. This declaration unfortunately launched a series of bloodthirsty events by the *Pemuda* under its fiery leader Sutomo during a disgraceful period known as the *Bersiap*, which began during the insecurity vacuum when Japanese troops retired to the camps to protect their former POWs and civilian internees. The *Bersiap* chaos grew in intensity as British troops arrived to reestablish the colonial government until the Dutch were able to send their own troops to Java. During this chaotic period, thousands of Dutch, Indos, and Christians were tortured and murdered despite efforts by British and Japanese soldiers to protect them.

Later, Sukarno's neophyte Indonesian army successfully countered two Dutch attempts to retake the colonies by force. The Indonesians allowed 'pure' Dutch families to be repatriated to the Netherlands and elsewhere but rounded up many remaining Indos to hold as hostages and bargaining tools. On 27 December 1949, in exasperation (and under pressure by the United States of withholding Marshall Plan aid) the Netherlands formally transferred sovereignty to the Republic of Indonesia, and President Sukarno moved into the former Dutch governor's opulent palace in Jakarta.

From this period onwards, as the remaining Dutch and Indos were evacuated to Europe, Australia, Canada, and the US, Sukarno led his country through fantastic ups and downs, running the government as if it were a series of *Wayang* puppet plays of which he was so fond, and literally bankrupting the treasury from his personal and governmental excesses. To this flamboyant and erratic behavior, which spawned numerous political groups in favor or opposition to him, he added insults to the US and USSR, which had each provided Indonesia with a billion dollars or its equivalent in foreign aid, asking only for stability in return.

"To hell with your aid!" Sukarno shouted to the world, while driving inflation to fantastic heights at home and nationalizing all foreign-

owned assets (including P&T Lands, and even individual land holdings in Lembang such as Maggie's small plot). A casualty of all this theater and Sukarno's *Year of Living Dangerously* speech to the UN, was the replacement of democracy with dictatorship in 1964 under the guise of 'guided democracy.' In January 1965, Sukarno withdrew Indonesia from the United Nations because the UN supported the formation of Malaysia, which was considered by Sukarno to be "a neo-colonial encirclement of Indonesian territory" (referring primarily to Kalimantan on the island of Borneo).

The beginning of the end for Sukarno was a 1965 failed coup in which several senior military officers were assassinated, and after which another general, Hajji Suharto (photo), reversed the coup and sought vengeance. Assured that the Indonesian Communist Party (*Partai Komunis Indonesia*, or PKI) was behind the coup, the army went on to slaughter tens of thousands of Communist members and sympathizers, and gradually eroded Sukarno's power base.

The end itself for Sukarno arrived when Suharto (Su Harto) became acting president in 1967 and president in 1968, as Sukarno sank into disgrace and oblivion. However, upon Sukarno's death in 1970 from liver failure, an astonishing 500,000 people turned out to pay their last respects, including senior members of Suharto's government.

The Year of Living Dangerously was borrowed from Sukarno's 1964 UN speech as the title for a 1978 book by Australian writer Christopher Koch and a 1982 film by fellow countryman Peter Weir, depicting the turmoil of Indonesia during the 1965 attempted coup.

*** *MOHAMMED HATTA* ***

A key ally and supporter of Sukarno during his rise to power was Sumatra-born economist Mohammed Hatta, who served as Indonesia's Prime Minister (1948-50) and Vice President (1950-56). Hatta was also Indonesia's UN representative for the handover of sovereignty from Dutch rule in 1949.

After studying economics in the Netherlands for a decade, Hatta was arrested soon after his return to the Indies in 1932 because of his anti-colonial writings, and was imprisoned in West New Guinea, another Dutch colony. He stood shoulder to shoulder with Sukarno during and after the Japanese occupation, co-authoring Indonesia's Declaration of Independence in 1945, but in the 1950s when Sukarno's presidency became erratic and unpredictable, Hatta became alarmed at the country's mounting economic peril.

In December 1956, Hatta resigned his vice presidency over increasing disagreement with Sukarno's policy of 'guided democracy,' by which Sukarno gradually usurped the power of government for himself. Essentially a moderate, administratively oriented leader, Hatta felt that dealing with Indonesia's grave economic crises was of primary importance and feared that Sukarno's policies would bankrupt the nation. He was also consistently critical of Sukarno's anti-Western and anti-Malaysian foreign policy.

After Sukarno's downfall, Hatta came out of retirement to serve as special adviser to President Suharto on the problem of government corruption, which was an ironic assignment considering the massive cronyism and corruption that would develop during Suharto's lengthy rule of 31 years. That story, however, is beyond the scope of this book, which covers the postwar period until roughly 1965.

*** BEHIND THE SCENES IN JAKARTA ***

While the Year of Living Dangerously was being played out in 1964, confusion also reigned to a significant degree at the US Embassy in Jakarta where the US Ambassador to Indonesia, His Excellency Howard Palfrey Jones—himself a graduate of Columbia University School of Journalism and a former Army colonel—was a frequent host to the international press corps that was thirsting for truth about the famously-erratic President Sukarno. This was especially true after Sukarno delivered his dramatic speech to the United Nations the previous week. In that speech, the President had threatened to escalate a warlike confrontation (*Konfrontasi*) with the new nation of Malaysia that Britain had formed from its former colonies of Malaya, Singapore, Sarawak and Sabah. The world reaction to the speech had ranged from cheers (on the left) to groans (on the right), and there had already been a series of border skirmishes in Borneo, the large island where Indonesia and Malaysia were sharing a pre-WWII Dutch-English border.

In the course of his frequent press conferences, the ambassador was often questioned by a pair of American reporters from the Dallas Morning News and the Houston Chronicle, who were not only brother journalists but twin Texas siblings in the flesh, having been born some thirty years before in Waco, Texas, just a few minutes apart. One of the twins, the one from Dallas, was named Byron Spencer, whereas his brother who lived in Houston was Barron Spencer, their father having apparently been hard of hearing when his wife uttered her instructions during labor. In the maddening Texas drawl that each brother seemed to accentuate just to annoy everyone within hearing range, their names sounded exactly alike—particularly to the frustrated ambassador, who hailed from Maryland. To his ear, the name of each twin sounded exactly like 'Bahrn.'

Furthermore, both twins had the same slim build and were very close to an impressive height of six feet two inches. Each had wavy brown hair, and the only noticeable difference between them facially seemed to be the droopy mustache being cultivated by Byron. Barron, however, had somehow produced a clever replica of Byron's mustache, which he occasionally wore to press parties in a further attempt to confuse the twins' identities.

On Monday 24 August, a week after Sukarno's infamous UN speech, Ambassador Jones convened the regular daily press conference. There were at least two dozen accredited journalists present, including the Spencer twins, one of whom quickly held his hand in the air as the ambassador surveyed the room and gave him the nod.

"Mister Ambass'der," the Texan drawled, "Ah'm Bahrn Spencer fm th' Houston Chronicle. I wd lahk t'know ef there have been any fuhther battles in Borneo over th' weekend, and also what you personally feel will happen in th' near future regarding Malaysia. Thank you, Sir."

The Ambassador was no novice to Indonesian affairs, having gained a related education while serving in several posts before his current appointment, including the directorship of USAID for Indonesia. As the new US ambassador, he had expended significant effort toward earning President Sukarno's trust, even in the face of covert US activities over which he had no control, such as CIA efforts to undermine Sukarno, who—in the cold black and white assessment of the United States Congress—was considered to be a 'damned Commie.'

"Thank *you*, er, Bahrn, for the question," the ambassador replied. "I would like to say publicly that I sincerely hope President Sukarno will rethink his confrontive stance regarding Malaysia, and I have been told that Great Britain would like nothing better themselves. Nonetheless, Britain—as I understand it—is fully prepared to defend the border integrity of Malaysia with whatever means may be required. There has been no fighting over the weekend to our knowledge, so this gives me hope that the President has given the matter serious thought, in spite of the pressure that the Communists—that is to say the PKI—are applying to him."

In the embassy canteen that evening, the two Bahrns traded rumors with others of their brethren about the likelihood of a war erupting between Indonesia and Malaysia, and after a few beers jointly declared their unequivocal admiration of Ambassador Jones and his unflinching support for the nation of Indonesia, "warts and all." Eventually the talk turned to other regional turmoils. A highly respected reporter from New York, who looked to be in her mid-50s, told the group that she had just been ordered to pack up and leave Jakarta for Saigon, from where even more hot news was expected in the weeks to come.

"You boys be sure to cover Indonesia carefully," she told the group, "And maybe you'll have some big surprises here in a few months. Meanwhile if you get bored, come look me up in Saigon. My boss has a real nose for news, and he says Vietnam is where the action will be pretty soon, considering that one of our ships has been attacked by North Vietnam patrol boats. Cheerio!"

"Ah dunno, Margie," replied one of the Bahrns, "Ah reckon things'll get pretty darned excitin' 'round here soon, and you're gonna miss a lot of fun."

They were both right, as it turned out. A year later, on 30 September 1965, the PKI—with support from Indonesian Air Force leadership—assassinated 5 Army generals and others in an attempt to stage a coup and topple the Army-backed government. The coup failed, and General Suharto took charge of an ongoing bloody purge of PKI members, while President Sukarno gradually faded into obscurity.

Meanwhile in Vietnam, US Marines went ashore against the Viet Cong in August 1965, and President Johnson increased the draft to 35,000 per month. The 1960s had seemingly become the <u>Decade</u> of Living Dangerously.

*** TOTOKS AND INDOS ***

We have seen that the mixed-race Indos grew in numbers in the Dutch East Indies colony before WWII, taking on many of the civil service and military positions, but even though the Indos grew to some two hundred thousand by 1940, they were always less than one percent of the total Indonesian population. With their gene pool refreshed from time to time by the arrival of (mostly male) *Totoks* ('pure' Europeans), it was without a doubt the bilingual and bicultural Indos who kept the Dutch colonies running smoothly for such a long time, by helping new arrivals settle in and learn their way around. It was surely a great irony and waste of talent after the war, that newly independent Indonesians were persecuting talented Indos who might have helped the new nation get up on its feet faster. Even the roughly ten thousand Indos who elected to take Indonesian citizenship instead of repatriation found out later that they were still persecuted, and almost all of them petitioned to get their Dutch citizenship back.

The US granted 60,000 settlement visas to Indos, many of whom chose to live in Southern California. The author was honored to make the acquaintance of several US-resident Indos over the years, quite a few of whom had been in the Dutch Merchant Marine.

That the Dutch-speaking Indos were chased away from Indonesia, their birthplace, is hard to believe. Can the Dutch have been such strict colonists that even the sound of their language rankled the native populations?

One hears that it was somewhat the same situation in Vietnam. After the French were forced out in 1954, some say there was an effort to destroy all traces of their former presence, including the language.

It may be accidental, but somehow in both British and American versions of the English-speaking former colonies—Singapore, Malaysia, and the Philippines—English is still the common language of government and commerce. Perhaps that happened because independence for those former colonies was negotiated rather than fought for.

SCENE TEN

Japanese Legacies – Taiwan and Korea

We have not spoken much about two other Asian regions that ceased to exist as colonies after the Second World War ended. Both were former colonies of Japan in fact—Formosa for fifty years and Korea for thirty-five. Upon Japan's wartime defeat, the Allies made the following decisions:

The island colony of **Formosa** (a name bestowed by long-ago Portuguese explorers) would be returned to the Republic of China, the successor to the former Qing Dynasty of China from which Japan had acquired Formosa in 1895. It would thereafter be known in the west by its Chinese name of **Taiwan**.

The peninsular colony of **Korea**, which had been an independent kingdom when Japan seized it in 1910, would be restored to independence after several years of UN supervision and reconstruction.

There would be rocky roads and uncertain futures ahead in both cases. As Sir Winston Churchill once said: "However beautiful the strategy, you should occasionally look at the results."

The Republic of China on Taiwan

The large island of Taiwan, named *Ilha Formosa* (Beautiful Island) by Portuguese explorers who sailed by it in 1544 but did not settle, was colonized by the Dutch a century later, followed by an influx of immigrants from the Fujian and Guangdong areas of southern China. The Spanish even built a settlement in the north for a brief period to help protect their nearby Philippine colonies, but they were driven out by the Dutch in 1642.

In time, the island came under Chinese control during the waning years of the Ming Dynasty and the early years of the Manchu, or Qing Dynasty. A late-Ming hero named Koxinga (pron. Ko-hsinga), who expelled the Dutch colonists, is still revered by people in the south part of the island.

In 1895, after the defeat of its navy by Japan in the First Sino-Japanese War, the Qing Dynasty of China was forced to concede Taiwan to Japan in the *Treaty of Shimonoseki*. Taiwan was known to the Japanese as *Takasago Koku*, and its new capital Taipei, as *Taihoku*.

Initial attempts at colonization by Japan were fiercely resisted by both ethnic Han Chinese and aboriginal natives. By 1915 most Chinese had accepted the Japanese as rulers, but sporadic uprisings by aborigines continued into the late 1930s.

Japan was prompt with infrastructure development in Taiwan—hoping to develop it into a model colony and eventual Japanese province like Okinawa—building roads and railroads that are still in use today, and a large dam which created the lovely Sun-Moon Lake from a swampy valley in the mountains, as a steady source of hydroelectric power. Japan also dramatically improved healthcare and sanitation and introduced compulsory primary education to the island before that was even started in Japan.

By 1944 there were over 900 primary schools in Taiwan, including the aboriginal areas, plus several middle schools and a few universities in the larger cities. The Shinto religion was introduced, and some Shinto temples still exist there today. Limited self-rule was cautiously and gradually permitted as well. Parents were encouraged to give their children Japanese names, in return for which they received extra rations.

Although Japanese governance of Taiwan was at first paternalistic, there is no doubt that Taiwan eventually benefitted from the Japanese presence during its 50 years of existence (1895-1945). Several large Taiwan companies today, such as *Nan Ya* (Formosa Plastics) and others, got their start from Japanese technology transfer during the colonial period, and particularly in the war years.

*** *TAIWAN IN WORLD WAR II* ***

To the Han Taiwanese, who were primarily settled in the western plains and port cities of the islands, and the aboriginal tribes in the mountainous eastern regions (where they are still known today as the Mountain People), Japan decided to open its military academies and general recruitment shortly after the Second Sino-Japanese War began in 1937. Primarily the need was for translators at that time, for which Cantonese- or Hokkien-speaking men with Japanese language schooling were ideal candidates.

Eventually, the IJA and IJN began seeking regular army and navy officers and enlisted applicants. At first this was a selective process to obtain only the most qualified candidates, but by 1944 a mandatory draft was begun to help fill a desperate need for troops and officers. Over 200,000 men from Taiwan eventually served in the Japanese armed forces, with about 30,000 losing their lives during WWII.

A special commando group known as the Takasago Volunteers was formed from indigenous natives because of their skills in jungle survival, and it was in the indigenous region of Taiwan that the infamous Colonel Tsuji expanded the nascent IJA School of Jungle Warfare for the same reason.

Many Taiwanese women were conscripted too, as comfort women to perform sexual services for the army.

Taiwan airfields were used by Japan to launch the 9 December 1941 air attack on Manila that destroyed MacArthur's Army Air Corps planes on the ground, thereby denying air cover to Admiral Hart's Navy and General MacArthur's PA (Philippine-American) Army. Taiwan was sporadically bombed in retaliation over the next three years, but as the Pacific War grew steadily closer to Japan and its nearby islands, considerable Allied bombardment of Taiwan ports such as Keelung and Kaohsiung by US and British aircraft took place during the 1945 battles for the Philippines and Okinawa, with the result that Taiwan's postwar agricultural and industrial output was curtailed by roughly ninety percent.

After the Pacific war ended in August 1945, repatriation of Japanese civilians and military began in earnest, with some Taiwanese also going to Japan voluntarily. The Civil War on mainland China restarted immediately and lasted four more years until the armies of Chiang Kai-Shek (L) were defeated by the Communist armies of Mao Zedong (R). When Chiang's residual cadre fled to Taiwan in 1949, they first plundered gold bullion from the National Treasury and masses of art objects from the National Museum. The gold was used for backing the New Taiwan Dollar and various other purposes, and the art objects reside today in the fabulous National Palace Museum of Taipei.

*** *NEW HORIZONS* ***

One of several young men in Taiwan who had applied to join the Japanese army in the summer of 1936 was Hu An-Dong, whose parents were Hakka Chinese from the Fujian province across the Taiwan Strait on Mainland China. Even though they were newcomers among the existing Hakka population of Taiwan, the Hu family had nevertheless migrated to Taiwan before the Japanese arrived in 1895, and their son An-Dong was born on the island in 1910, the last of five children.

An-Dong—whose name means Eastern Peace—thought that he was probably given that name because by the time of his birth his parents and siblings were quite content with their lives in Taiwan, where they had managed to reach a satisfactory level of prosperity as rice farmers in the flatlands between the small but rapidly-growing city of Taipei and the important port of Keelung at the north end of the island. Rice was a cash crop that had been brought to Taiwan from Fujian Province centuries before, and Japan was a lucrative market for Taiwan rice providers like the Hu family.

[Prosperity is a state of achievement and well-being that most if not all Chinese seek throughout their lives. It drives them to take risks such as migrating to other lands for starting businesses or finding employment. SE Asia is teeming with Overseas Chinese, as the risk-takers are called after they arrive in places like Singapore, Penang, Java, Luzon, and Taiwan. Ed.]

Hakka Chinese were particularly adept at moving from place to place in search of prosperity, more so than other Han people, for the Hakka name means 'Guest People.' It is pronounced *Ke Jia Ren (客家人)* in the Mandarin dialect of Beijing in northern China near where they originated many centuries before, but the name probably morphed into Hakka from lengthy contacts with southern dialects like Cantonese or Hokkien. Most Chinese dialects are named after regions of China where speakers of those dialects have existed 'forever,' but the Hakka people are wanderers and wherever they migrate they consider themselves guests rather than locals.

There have been many famous Hakka people in recent history, such as Lee Kwan-Yew whom we read about in the chapter on Singapore, and Sun Yat-Sen, the founder of the Republic of China in 1911. Hakka men and women are typically quite resolute of character and of above average intelligence, and they pride themselves on coping with hardships. As such, they make excellent military, government, and business leaders. Hakka women are also renowned for not having had their feet bound and crippled during the long centuries when it was a custom for social advancement among other Han cultures.

Taiwan had a significant Hakka population when WWII began, possibly twenty percent of the total ethnic Han Chinese. Although the island's majority dialect was similar to Hokkien (also known as *Fujian hua,* the speech of Fujian Province across the Taiwan Strait), the Taiwan variant became known simply as Taiwanese. Hakka people could speak Taiwanese just as well as their own Hakka dialect, and spoke Japanese too.

An-Dong was very pleased when he arrived in Taipei—the bustling new Japanese capital of Taiwan—to receive his acceptance letter for training in the Imperial Japanese Army as an officer-translator candidate. In two more weeks he would be sent to the IJA junior academy at Asaka, Japan, for training in military discipline, customs, and weaponry, after which he would go to the senior academy at Sagamihara and then to a Tokyo language institute for advanced studies in the languages that he already spoke quite well—Japanese, Hakka, Taiwanese, and Cantonese—with an emphasis on technical vocabulary. The Japanese sergeant who gave him his acceptance letter had already told him to write his romanized name as Hu Andong, rather than Hu An-Dong the old-fashioned way. Of course, in Hanzi and Kanji it would always be 胡安東 no matter which way it was romanized. The sergeant also told him that Asaka was not the same place as Osaka.

Dodging through the hordes of motor scooters that had begun to choke the main Taipei avenues, Andong jumped onto a trolley that would take him to the Taipei Railroad Station for a train to the port of Keelung, where his parents were waiting to celebrate their son's new career. They were very proud of his recent achievement, they said on the telephone when he broke the good news. Not all Chinese in Taiwan were regarded so favorably by the Japanese colonists in 1936, even though the administration had announced that it was preparing Taiwan to become a province of Japan in a few more years. Every Taiwan citizen would then have equal rights with Japanese citizens in the home islands, so they said.

Andong went to Tokyo on a military flight, which thrilled him immensely. He had never known anyone personally who had been aloft in a plane of any sort, let alone an Army bomber. In his barracks at the academy, he made friends quickly with his Japanese classmates (who pronounced his name 胡安東 as *Haku Anto)* by teaching them how to play Mahjongg at high speed, which he had grown up with in Taiwan. He was able to make money off most of the cadets and even some of the Japanese and German instructors, which quickly built Andong's reputation as a clever professional gambler. The coursework and training pleased him a great deal also, and by the end of the first academic year he was 12th in a class of 186. Andong was the only one of that class whose specialty would be languages, although the class had three other Chinese members from Taiwan.

By the time his second year started in the autumn of 1937, two noteworthy events had recently transpired, that were making headlines in the world's newspapers. First was the mysterious disappearance of Amelia Earhart and her navigator Fred Noonan of Pan American Airways on a flight in Earhart's plane over the South Pacific on June 29. The other event was the commencement of hostilities between Japan and China on July 7, which quickly became known as the Second Sino-Japanese War.

Publications in the West caused suspicious readers to blame Japan for Amelia's disappearance, with wild tales being circulated that Japanese soldiers had captured and executed her and Fred for spying on Japan's Pacific islands. This was an unlikely event since the fliers were known to have been fairly close to the US Coast Guard cutter *Itasca* that was awaiting them at Howland Island in the Phoenix Group, far away from Japan's sphere of influence, when their plane apparently ran out of fuel and came down at sea.

It was the other event that had a big effect on Andong, for he was not even allowed to start his second year at the military academy before being pulled out and sent to an IJA garrison near Peking (Beijing), where Japanese and Chinese soldiers were heavily engaged in fighting after a skirmish outside the walled city of Wanping had rapidly escalated.

Andong had the temporary rank of technical sergeant for his questioning of captured Chinese soldiers, most of whom were scornful of being interrogated by a Chinese person wearing a Japanese uniform. To further complicate matters, Andong found that he could barely understand the speech of the northern Chinese prisoners and had to resort to writing notes back and forth with them, which greatly slowed the interrogation process. Eventually the colonel in charge ordered the prisoners to be shot without further questioning, and Andong was sent back to Asaka to finish his education.

Two years later, after catching up from a lost month but still graduating from the senior academy at Sagamihara with his original class, Andong finished 44th out of 112. He was commissioned as a second lieutenant and sent on to the language academy for a year, during which the Second World War began raging in Europe and North Africa. When he graduated in May 1940, he was meritoriously promoted to first lieutenant because of his exemplary academic performance.

When Japan invaded the neighboring US and European colonies on 7-8 December 1941, bringing WWII to the Pacific region, Andong served as an interrogator throughout the Japanese occupied territories, and managed to learn enough rudimentary English to question Allied naval and aviation prisoners. Although he tried to learn some Dutch, he was not successful. From his clear and detailed reports, the Japanese gleaned useful information concerning the deployment of Allied forces, and Andong held the rank of major by the end of the war in August 1945.

*** *CHANGING HORSES* ***

Major Hu Andong IJA was not repatriated with other Taiwan nationals who had been fighting in the service of Japan because of Allied doubts about his nationality and allegiance. The US Occupation Forces in Japan under General MacArthur eventually realized that Andong could be a very useful resource for interrogating Japanese and Communist Chinese captives, so in 1946 they offered him a different uniform and the rank of Lieutenant Colonel USA.

In 1949, when he was 39 years old, Andong—by then a Colonel and US citizen by dint of a field promotion and a Bronze Star award—was directed by US Army Intelligence to return to Taiwan with the Nationalist Chinese to keep an eye on Generalissimo Chiang Kai-Shek's entourage as they took over the government of Taiwan. The US badly wanted Taiwan as an ally after Chairman Mao and his Communists had triumphed in mainland China.

What better choice than multilingual Colonel Hu could there be to help the new US ambassador to the Republic of China on Taiwan—with its postwar mixture of Taiwanese, Chinese, Japanese, and even Communist sympathies—to develop the Republic of China in Taiwan into a loyal anti-communist partner for the United States of America?

When Lt. General Hu Andong retired in 1975 after thirty years in the US Army as an international troubleshooter, he and his Japanese wife Roko decided to remain in Taiwan with their adult children, all three of whom had been educated at the Taipei American School and 'Tai Da' (*Taiwan Daxüe*), the prestigious National University of Taiwan. One of the children's favorite professors at Tai Da had been Angela Adonis PhD, Professor of English Literature, with whom each of them had developed a long-term friendship after graduation. She was married to an elderly, balding American named George Bolnar, who often appeared at alumni-faculty reunions with his guitar and songbook.

In spite of the Communist takeover of mainland China in 1949, the Republic of China on Taiwan was still recognized by the US government as late as 1975—General Hu's retirement year—as the legal representative for all China, and the US Seventh Fleet still patrolled the Taiwan Strait.

The Koreas

In Korea's distant past, *The Three Kingdoms* of Baekje, Silla, and Goguryeo (later called Goryeo, from which the name Korea evolved) emerged during the period from 57 BC to 668 AD. These kingdoms, unified in 676 by the Kingdom of Silla during the Tang Dynasty in China, occupied not only the Korean Peninsula but much of what later became Manchuria. By the time of unification, the Baekje Kingdom—rather than China itself—had disseminated Buddhism and Chinese writing to the islands of Japan, where Chinese writing (known as Kanji) is still used in conjunction with Japan's Katakana and Hiragana phonetic scripts.

During the Joseong Dynasty (1392-1910), a Korean script known as *Hangul* was invented by by young King Sejong the Great (1418-1450). This clever new and accurate phonetic alphabet gradually replaced the Chinese pictographic writing (known in Korea as *Hanja* or *Hancha,* in Japan as *Kanji,* and in China as *Hanzi*), which was an amazing achievement. *[The Korean script Hangul is in use today in both North and South Korea despite their mutual animosity – Ed.].*

Now we'll have a little fun: To illustrate the complex differences among certain Oriental writing systems, below is the phrase 'Happy New Year' written in simplified Chinese *Hanzi,* informal phonetic Japanese *Katakana,* phonetic Korean *Hangul,* and *Akson* Thai, each followed by the author's very rough, home-made phonetic rendering and pronunciation guide for English speakers:

- Chinese: 新 年 快 乐
  (Sheen Nee-en <u>Kwai</u> Luh)

- Japanese: あけましておめでとう
  (Ah-kay <u>Mash</u>-tay Oh-may <u>Day</u>-tow)

- Korean: 새해 복 많이 받으세요
  (Say-yay <u>Poke</u> Mah-nay Pah-duh-<u>say</u>-oh)

- Thai: สวัสดีปีใหม่
  (Sah-<u>was</u>-dee <u>Pee</u> My)

You can both see and hear the great differences. Language being a reflection in many ways of a nation's culture, one could rightly conclude from the above that oriental cultures are not much alike, of which many a Western visitor to the Asia-Pacific region is blissfully unaware.

*** JAPAN TAKES OVER ***

During the lengthy golden age of the previously mentioned Joseong Dynasty, the Kingdom of Korea enjoyed several centuries of blissful peace but became more and more isolated from the rest of the world, earning for itself the international sobriquet 'Hermit Kingdom.' Japan was determined to break into that isolation and modernize Korea for its own benefit.

Korea had been under Chinese cultural influence up to that point, and Japan's determination to acquire Korea as an industrial and raw material satellite led to the First Sino-Japanese War, which Japan won after both China and Japan landed troops at Incheon, Korea, in 1894.

Korea's ongoing failure to keep abreast of defense technology resulted in a gradual encroachment by Japan that forced the Hermit Kingdom into a protectorate relationship by 1905, the same year that Japan defeated the Russian navy in the Battle of Tsushima when Russia attempted to intercede and help Korea rid itself of Japanese control. Then in 1910, Japan abruptly occupied Korea as a colony, as it had done with Formosa fifteen years before. The result for most Koreans was to be treated as virtual slaves in their own country.

*** KOREA IN WORLD WAR TWO ***

Before 1910, the number of Japanese settlers in Korea was already more than one-hundred-and-seventy thousand, as Japanese immigrants sought opportunities in trade and agriculture. After Japan's annexation of Korea, the number gradually climbed to over five hundred thousand by 1932, with landowners becoming mostly Japanese and tenants being all Korean.

In 1939 Japan embarked on cultural assimilation, and issued an edict requiring all Koreans to abandon their Korean surnames and adopt Japanese names instead. Many of the WWII commanders and guards in POW camps were Koreans—the Japanese apparently did not trust them as soldiers—and it is said that they were far crueler than the Japanese. *[This explains the confusion that existed among former Allied POWs after the war, where some Korean guards were identified in war trials or memorabilia as being Japanese —Ed.]*

Some Korean officer candidates had been attending the Japanese Military Academy even before 1910, and exceptional enlisted candidates were allowed into the Japanese Army from 1938. By 1944, however, the previously selective acceptance of Koreans into the IJA had changed to mandatory drafts as the war went steadily in favor of the Allies and more manpower was urgently needed.

By the time the war was over, the IJA included several ethnic Korean generals and numerous field grade officers. The highest-ranking Korean to be prosecuted after the war was Lt. General Hong Sa-Ik who had been in command of all Japanese POW camps in the Philippines.

On the civilian side of things, a combination of immigration and forced labor brought the total number of Korean emigrants to Japan to more than two million by the end of WWII, of which roughly two thirds were repatriated and one third chose to remain in Japan after the war.

After atomic bombs were dropped on Japan, and some Russian troops had stationed themselves at the northern part of the Korean Peninsula, US Army Colonel Dean Rusk proposed dividing the Korean administrative responsibilities between Russia and the US at the 38th Parallel (far enough north to include Korea's capital Seoul in the US zone), thereby creating a legacy that persists to this day.

In October 1946, the US Army Military Government issued an order allowing Koreans within the US zones of Japan and Korea who wished to do so, to restore their original Korean names. Many Koreans in Japan chose to retain their Japanese names, either to avoid discrimination or to meet later requirements for Japanese citizenship.

The war and its aftermath were times of great stress for the Korean population. Some who had been living in Japan during the Second World War and were repatriated afterwards, went back to Japan for the duration of the Korean War, leaving an elder child or parent behind as custodian for their Korean properties. For people of that generation, hearing a rendition of the national Korean folk song *Arirang* invariably brings tears to their eyes.

*** TOUGH SIBLINGS ***

By April 1945, twenty-seven-year-old twins Pak Him-Chan and his sister Pak Na-Yeong had managed to avoid the endless roundups of young people by the Imperial Japanese Army, because their village in the northern mountains was remote and difficult for IJA agents to access. From rumors that had reached their village, however, they knew what might happen to them if caught, so they were always on their guard as they tended the animals and crops on their parents' small farm. If any strangers were seen coming up the long winding dirt road from below, they would be warned to go into hiding, leaving their aged parents to deal with the visitors.

So far there had not been any strange visitors, thankfully, as everyone in their village had ignored the recent army order to select and register Japanese names for themselves, though they knew that more accessible villages down the mountain were under intense pressure to comply with that hateful order. It was yet another nasty scheme that the colonial authorities had dreamed up, so they could announce to the world one day that Korea was a Japanese province, rather than an occupied colony. Japan had already done this with Manchukuo that they had stolen from China—complete with the puppet emperor Pu Yi, and it was rumored that they were doing the same thing in Taiwan.

But punishment for the twins would be far worse than just being forced to change their names. They knew they would also be conscripted into active service with the army because of their relatively young ages. After a few weeks of indoctrination in military discipline and rifle practice at Busan, the Japanese staging port on the south coast, Him-Chan would likely go to Malaya or Singapore as a POW camp guard. Na-Yeong would almost certainly be sent overseas immediately as a comfort woman to perform sexual services for Japanese troops. The twins had made a vow to themselves and their parents that they would resist Japanese army service with their lives, if necessary.

Unfortunately, one rainy day in the spring of 1945 their luck ran out. Bae, the village headman, ran puffing to the Pak farmhouse: "Run quickly, friend Pak, and tell your children to hide. There are soldiers coming up the road in a big truck, many soldiers. We will all be questioned and perhaps worse!"

Panic set in when the younger Paks heard the news. It was still raining, and difficult for them to gather some outer clothes and food and run to the scraggly trees beyond the barn. Their footprints would be easy to follow, they realized, so they didn't stop at the trees but kept climbing higher into the rocky boulders where their tracks might be better hidden. Soon they heard the truck chug into the village and stop, with much shouting afterwards.

The twins hid behind some boulders and peered carefully back at the farm, which—from where they were hiding—looked about the size of a toy model. The sound carried quite clearly to their hiding place, however, and they could tell that the shouting was happening at several places along the village street.

Just then, Na-Yeong whispered to her brother: "Look, look, some soldiers come." The pair froze and watched carefully through the boulders to see if the two intruders that were approaching the barn would find their trail beyond. Perhaps they would still be safe, perhaps not.

Fearing for bad luck, Him-Chan drew a pig-carving knife from his jacket. When she saw it, Na-Yeong nodded, and reached for a broken shard from one of the boulders, which she held firmly in her gloved hand. Both twins were quite strong from their constant farm labors, and their squat physiques would give them an advantage over the skinny agents who stood near the barn, apparently wondering what to do next. From their awkward movements, those two appeared to be Korean civilians rather than Japanese soldiers, although they wore military rain jackets.

Finally, the agents turned back toward the road, having apparently worked out a plausible story between them to tell the officer in charge that there were no other people to be found in the farmyards, despite the muddy footprints that showed otherwise. The hidden twins relaxed but stayed where they were until the truck left the village a half hour later.

That night, the villagers held a council meeting. When they were all assembled, Headman Bae spoke first:

"This village is no longer safe for the Pak children. Those Japanese agents will be back soon, as they threatened, and next time they may bring dogs. I heard them say they should have done so today."

Pak the father spoke next: "You are right, friend Bae, our children being here are a threat to everyone else. My family is forever grateful that all of you have helped us hide them up to now, but it is surely time for them to leave. It will be arranged. If you will pray for their safety, we will forever be thankful."

Next morning the twins were given supplies and money by the elder Paks, but advice was not forthcoming. "We are sorry, dear children, but we do not know what to suggest for your safety. The Japanese and their Korean agents are everywhere. If you go north to Manchuria (using the correct name for the former Manchu province), although the border is close by it will be difficult to get through there to Russia, and if you stay in our own lands, there is hardly anywhere that they do not constantly search for young slaves. I wish you could contact the Americans, but they are far away. We do not know what to suggest but can only hope and pray that you will be safe whatever you decide to do."

When the twins were ready to start on their journey, their bundles carefully packed, and wearing several layers of clothing to ward off the cold, they bowed to their parents for what might be the last time. No one spoke but eyes glistened as the young pair left the farmhouse and started down the mountain, carefully avoiding the narrow dirt road.

*** RUSSIA BECKONS ***

The twins did decide to head for Russia, but along the East Sea coast rather than through Manchukuo across the Yalu River. Accordingly, they started northeast toward the small seaport of Hungnam, which was not very far away but could still take them a week or so of walking or borrowing rides from people they judged to be trustworthy. To help attract less attention, they were dressed identically as a pair of male laborers with dirty faces and worn clothing. Although it was early May, the weather was still cold at night, so they looked for some sort of shelter each afternoon, like an abandoned shed or a haystack.

Occasionally they had to cross small rivers or streams, in which case they would walk inland until they found some means to make the crossing, such as a footbridge or a kindly boatman. They were still some distance inland as they passed by Hungnam port and the nearby provincial capital of Hamhung, but they had to move back out towards the East Sea as they went further on, because the mountains seemed to push them that way.

Occasionally the young twins were able to find work to augment a small horde of coins but found it difficult to avoid questions about the coins not being the same as those in use locally. Because of working in a few places for a week or more, it was nearly two months from the day they left home until they arrived near another port city called Chongjin. Their goal of reaching Russia and its important southern seaport of Vladivostok seemed to be within their grasp at last—perhaps in another month, which would be August.

The Paks were cheered at the thought, but meanwhile needed new boots to replace the ones almost worn out from their long excursion. They carefully approached Chongjin by skirting a walled-off neighborhood signposted in both *Hangul* and *Hanja* with the name *Ranam*. They also observed several notices and signs in Japanese script, which probably meant that Ranam held a Japanese community or military garrison. Fearing for the latter, they slept away from the neighborhood until early morning, then moved quickly past it at the first light of day. One or two dogs barked at their passing, but not enough to alarm the dozing night-watchmen. Once into Chongjin itself, they followed a few early morning workers to a market area of small shops that seemed to serve working people like themselves. One shop that offered boots and shoes for sale had just opened its doors.

They were relieved to be welcomed inside by a Korean, rather than a Japanese owner, and to be offered a cup of green tea. The man politely suggested, after giving them several pairs of boots to try on, that they might enjoy using the public bath house nearby. Embarrassed at the stench that they must be exuding, Na-Yeong blushed and nodded, eyes averted. Him-Chan laughed out loud and thanked the fellow gratefully.

Feeling more human in view of their ablutions and improved footwear, the travelers treated themselves to a traditional Korean breakfast of dried fish and *kimchi* pickled cabbage at a little cafe near the bath house, after which they decided to cross Chongjin city along the waterfront, rather than returning inland to the rural foothills. They noticed a lot of busy construction and harbor expansion going on, apparently by the Japanese, and saw a few military vehicles among the busy morning traffic. All this made them glad to get beyond the frenetic activities of Chongjin port and back on their way toward Russia, which was probably going to take another week of walking.

A calendar in the cafe had shown the date to be 5 August 1945, and they learned in the cafe that the war in Europe had ended three months before, shortly after they had left home to begin their long escape from Japanese conscription. People told them that the war might end in Asia one day too, but there were no signs of it yet and the Japanese were firmly in control of Korea as usual.

"Dear brother of mine," Na-Yeong said when they were once again on their own, taking a break from their lonely trek, "When we get to the border, how will we cross into Russia? We have no visa and Korean or Japanese guards on this side will surely arrest us before we even see any Russians."

"Yes, my dearest sister," Him-Chan replied, smiling at the formality of her question, "I worry about that also, but I don't think we can plan anything until we see what the border facilities look like. Perhaps we will have to cross illegally somehow. In fact, it will almost certainly have to be an illegal crossing, so that we don't get arrested and turned over to the Japanese army."

Na-Yeong nodded her agreement, then picked up her bundle of clothes and food after seeing her brother closing his pack. The twins had been making rest stops several times a day for three months, and the routine was second nature. Together they bent under the loads and set off along the dirt path that followed the coastline toward the Russian border and Vladivostok. The August weather was fine, partly cloudy, and the air was nice and cool.

*** OUT OF THE FRYING PAN ***

Next morning, 6 August, the twins devoured their usual dried fruit breakfast and finished exercising to loosen stiff joints. They had already started along the path with their bundles when suddenly a strange white light filled the sky from the southeast direction of faraway Honshu, the main Japanese island. A strange wind soon followed, and then complete silence for a few moments. The birds fell silent too. It was an odd experience and Him-Chan supposed that it had something to do with the war. When the atmosphere became normal again, they resumed their trek.

The next couple of days were uneventful, but on 9 August another white flash was visible in the eastern sky close to mid-day, although not as dramatic as the previous one. They continued their onward trek more energetically, feeling that their arrival at the Russian border was somehow getting urgent. After walking for three more days, Him-Chan calculated that they should be able to see the frontier by the following afternoon.

They awoke on the 13th to the sound of many aircraft nearby. The dawning light revealed hundreds of men falling from the sky under what looked like big white balloons or sheets, something incredible that they had never seen before. Astonished, they crouched behind bushes and continued watching the descent of what they could soon clearly see were armed soldiers, not Japanese or Korean but from some other army.

"Russians! These must be Russians!" Him-Chan whispered excitedly, "Listen: they are shouting—and singing!"

It was true, the Russian parachutists were indeed singing as they approached the ground and rolled onto the rough hillside. Soon the Paks found themselves hidden in the center of a shouting, laughing, singing crowd of soldiers in camouflage.

"Well, we do not need to go to Russia after all, dear brother," laughed Na-Yeong. "Russia has come to us!"

An hour or so later, after they had been noticed coming out of the scrubby bushes with their hands in the air, they were taken by several friendly soldiers to their sergeant, and then to an officer who spoke a little Korean. Eventually they were interviewed by a Russian man who spoke Korean quite well. This more serious person said he was a civilian supporter, which the Paks assumed meant politician. They knew a little about Russian and Chinese Communists already, from the news that dribbled up to their village, but had never met one of either variety before.

"So, you are interested in going to Russia, eh?" the man said, smiling faintly. "Why is that exactly, please?"

The Paks told him their story, that they were trying to avoid Japanese capture for fear of harsh treatment, and that they had been walking toward Vladivostok for nearly five months, being reluctant to try crossing Manchuria to reach Russia.

"You need not worry about Manchuria any longer," the interviewer told them. "It belongs to us now; we invaded that puppet land on August 8, and now we are coming here to stop the Japanese from escaping Manchuria into Korea and onward by sea to Japan. You are with an advance element of the Red Army, you see. In a few more days our 25th Division will land at Chongjin, where you said you were recently, and at several other places along your coast."

"But what will happen to us?" Na-Yeong asked, nervously.

"You will be safe with our unit for the moment, then we will turn you over to a group of your fellow citizens who have been training in Russia. Tell me, do you know of Comrade Kim Il-Sung? No? Well, he will be delighted to welcome you both to his new organization, after he comes back to your country with our troops in a few more days. In our country, women are treated the same as men, and have the same opportunities," he said for Na-Yeong's benefit. "Comrade Kim will soon become head of the People's Republic of Korea! You are very lucky to be offered a chance to join his cadre!"

*** *THE KOREAN WAR* ***

On the heels of World War II, the Chinese civil war continued between Chiang Kai-Shek's Nationalist troops and those of Mao Zedong's Communist legions. In Manchuria, which Chinese Communists fought hard to occupy after Russia's capture of Japan's Kwantung Army, Kim Il-Sung's North Koreans gave significant assistance to Mao's forces in terms of food and information.

Chinese Communists eventually won the Manchurian territory then in 1949 they prevailed in all of China, forcing the residue of Chiang Kai-Shek's Nationalists to flee to Taiwan.

On 25 June 1950, when the army of North Korea, spearheaded by Russian T-34 tanks, crossed the 38th Parallel and invaded the South with brute strength and without warning, they were supported logistically by Communist China in gratitude for the help that North Korea had rendered to Mao in Manchuria.

Kim Il-Sung's army captured Seoul with ease and quickly pushed the fledgling South Korean army and its belated US reinforcements farther south until the invaders were finally stopped at a defensive perimeter around Busan, the former Japanese transit port at the very bottom of the Korean Peninsula. As the war went on, it became clear that the US predicament was mostly due to President Truman's aggressive downsizing of the defense budget after World War II ended.

General MacArthur in Tokyo and his few hundred occupation troops in South Korea had been caught completely off guard, but in September 1950 a clever UN counteroffensive was launched through the port of Incheon near Seoul by US Marines that liberated Seoul and cut off many North Korean troops from their supply lines. Those Communists who escaped capture were forced back north, hotly pursued by UN forces as far as the Yalu River border of North Korea and (Mao's reclaimed) Manchuria. This was MacArthur's attempt to unify the Koreas by force, just as Kim Il-Sung had attempted to do the previous June.

Then in October, China suddenly intervened to help North Korea by sending two hundred thousand or more Chinese troops across the Yalu, leading to a UN retreat southward while the First Marine Division fought its way out of encirclement at the Chosin Reservoir—remembered later by Marine survivors as The Frozen Chosin. The UN retreat continued until the summer of 1951, when Seoul was recaptured by the North. General MacArthur was relieved of command by President Truman, an event that unsettled the American public at first, but which no doubt enabled the Police Action (as Truman had named it) to be confined to Korea instead of all Asia. Eventually, as China took over command of the northern armies that had been bolstered to 700,000 mostly Chinese troops, the fighting changed to a war of attrition near the 38th Parallel, with Seoul once again in Allied hands. Twenty other UN member nations eventually participated in what became known as the Korean Conflict. Air battles and bombing raids continued for two more years until an armistice was signed on 27 July 1953. A demilitarized zone was established along the 38th Parallel, that exists to this day because a formal peace treaty was never signed.

The story of Korea is therefore incomplete, as is the story of Taiwan as it struggles to evade the grasp of mainland China. Consequently, so too is Scene Ten incomplete, and this book itself.

THE END

(but please read onward)

EPILOGUE

Centered around World War II in the Asia-Pacific region, this book has catalogued a fair amount of prewar and postwar history of the region's former colonies, interspersed here and there by fictional tales set in the historical ambience. If you have digested the entire work, you are to be congratulated! There was much to absorb, even though the material was just a summary of the many dramatic changes that took place in the Far East from, roughly, 1935 to 1965.

If you found some of the histories to be intriguing, the recommended reading in our bibliography could enhance your knowledge. Those works would also provide a heightened sense of the drama that affected people's lives in an important part of our planet that is once again coming back into focus for American and European observers.

More than 70 years have passed since the end of the Second World War, so perhaps we should review some of the major changes that have taken place in the Far East since then. Although there were certainly many changes in Europe after the war as well, those were not nearly as dramatic. Despite the ferocious land battles that took place in Europe, that continent remains much as it was before the war began there in 1939. Its modern populations for the most part occupy their historical homelands. Europe is a far nicer place to visit now, in fact, and more cohesive and internationally minded (despite Brexit) than it was before the war, but what can be said of the Asia Pacific countries today?

Well, the colonial governments are gone, and the local people are in charge— for the most part—which is the most obvious thing of all. Before summarizing some other ongoing changes in each of the countries that we wrote about, let's first jump back to the Late Middle Ages to compare what was then called The Old World and The New World, or more accurately Europe and The Rest of the World.

In Europe, following the decline of its first master-colonizer, the Roman Empire, and the subsequent long sleep that enveloped European lands from the 5th to the 15th centuries, advances in ship-building technology and the discovery of the compass (a Chinese invention) enabled wooden sailing craft to set forth from Portugal to begin exploring 'the rest of the world,' with the blessing of the Pope in Rome.

But a century before the Portuguese navigators and Spanish explorers had accomplished very much, China had already dispatched a substantial fleet under its Admiral Zheng He (the Chinese name He is pronounced like an Englishman saying "her," with the "r" being silent) to explore the Asian lands—and beyond—by sea. For reasons of Buddhist conservatism, however, China chose not to further pursue or publicize the admiral's amazing discoveries (he even brought back to China a live giraffe from Africa). Nonetheless, China's voyage of exploration was of a similar scale to those that European explorers were only able to accomplish a century or two further on.

When Europeans first visited China, they were surprised to learn that it was the original source of many remarkable innovations, scientific discoveries, and inventions that had somehow made their way into Europe, among them the 'four great inventions' of papermaking, the compass, gunpowder, and printing. From these early contacts by European colonizers, which China chose not to confront militarily, the West learned many new things about agriculture, science, medicine, ceramics, and so on.

In the more recent years of our own era—after recovering from the lengthy war with Japan followed by its own civil war and the costly support for North Korea and North Vietnam in their struggles with the United Nations—China in turn learned so much from the West that it has become the supply base for nearly everything that people in America and Europe consume in their daily lives. Clearly China's star is rising once again, as it did a thousand years before, and it may well become the major world power of the current century. It will certainly be one of them.

But what of the former European and American colonies in Asia, and their transformations after WWII, sitting as they do at China's door? Let's look at them briefly—in the order that they were introduced in this book—to see whether they have benefited from their colonial days, and how well they are likely to do in future as neighbors of the Great Chinese Dragon in an interconnected world.

There has been some mention in these pages of The Four Asian Tigers that emerged in the 1980s, while China was still primarily an agricultural nation. Those tigers were Taiwan, South Korea, Hong Kong and Singapore. Make of this what you will, but it is interesting that the first two on the list were prewar Japanese colonies, while the latter two were British colonial trading posts. For whatever reason, the former French, Dutch and American colonies did not develop the advanced technical knowhow and infrastructure to compete with the four Asian tigers when the US—and eventually Europe—began outsourcing their industrial manufacturing capacity as a cost-reduction strategy. Eventually, however, China took over much of that supply base with technology transfer that came from Taiwan and elsewhere, combined with China's lower cost infrastructure and vast manpower resources.

As Western clients pushed for more cost savings than even Taiwan could offer, Taiwan in turn set up subsidiary manufacturing in China, from which the knowhow rapidly spread as mainland Chinese entrepreneurs took up the outsourcing banner themselves. The rest is history; the ubiquitous Made in China label is found today on everything imaginable, from toys to clothing to appliances to computers and software.

Singapore

A tiny city-state on an island surrounded by Islamic nations, Singapore has been a remarkable success ever since its founding in the early 1800s. Its ethnic Chinese, Malay, and Tamil populations have adopted British forms of government, architecture, and culture, and its absorption of technology from the US and Europe has insured its future as a high-technology manufacturing center in a strategic maritime location.

Singapore has both an elected Prime Minister and an elected President, the former being Head of Government and the latter functioning as Head of State and government auditor. The prewar colonial governor's residence on a lovely 100-acre park-like property is today known as the *Istana* (a Malay word meaning 'Palace'), which is closed to the public except on a handful of holidays. It is the official residence of the President and houses the offices of both the President and Prime Minister.

Pragmatic Singapore looks to remaining prosperous in ages to come, being a friend to most other nations and a threat to none. Having leased out some of its former British Naval Base at Sembawang as a refueling station for the US Seventh Fleet is a good example of Singapore's pragmatism, gaining thereby the protection of a well-armed tenant. *[By contrast, the Philippines has kicked out the American army, navy, and air force - Ed.]*

The venerable Lee Kwan Yew, Singapore's modern-day founder, passed away in 2015 at age 91. He was a shining light of reassurance—although a fussy one at times—to skeptical Europeans and Americans that capable indigenous leadership was indeed possible in the former colonies of the Pacific Rim.

Malaysia

Malaysia has been slow to catch up with economic development in the Far East but is finally beginning to reach its stride. Its capital at Kuala Lumpur is a modern city with many conveniences, but Malaysia's economy still depends heavily on agriculture and mining, both having been developed during the period of British oversight. It was not sufficiently advanced to join the four Asian tigers when the US and Europe began outsourcing much of their high-tech manufacturing in the 1980s.

Malaysia's population remains mostly Islamic Malay, with a high percentage of assimilated Chinese, known as *Peranakans*. To its credit, Malaysia has forged bonds of friendship with Indonesia over their shared border in Borneo/Kalimantan, and with Singapore that it expelled from the Malaysian Federation after WWII. Given racial and religious stability in future, Malaysia should continue to do well in the 21st Century—although there are whiffs of corruption in high places that will hopefully be curtailed.

It is interesting that, in many nations where Christianity is the dominant religion, the separation of Church and State is earnestly sought after. In Islamic nations, by contrast, the integration of Church and State is more often the norm.

Vietnam

After a bitter insurgency against its former colonial overlord that ended with the expulsion of France in 1954, followed by a long and horrendous war between North Vietnam and its Viet Cong ally against South Vietnam and its main supporter, the United States, the country was eventually united in 1975 as a Communist nation. Some three million people died in the latter conflict, including 58,000 Americans, with over half the rest being local civilians.

It is a wonder that anything is left of the war-ravaged former French Indochina, but today it is welcoming Americans and Europeans as tourists and is steadily improving its economy. The chief obstacles that remain—the dismantling of a centralized economy, the elimination of rampant smuggling, and the growth of jobs outside the agricultural economy—are major tasks that may take considerable time, especially within the framework of a socialized state like China's successful but still-opaque model.

Cambodia

The trials and tribulations of Cambodia commenced in 1975, after Vietnam was unified. A member of the allied Khmer Viet Minh who became known as Pol Pot (real name Saloth Sâr), had become a Marxist-Leninist while in Paris during the early 1950s. Rejecting the Vietnamese Communist model of urban intelligentsia, Pol Pot instead strove to create a self-sufficient utopia based on communal agriculture. His political party, known as the Khmer Rouge, emptied the cities and forced millions of people into rural slave labor and eventual death by either starvation or execution, the latter being the fate of the educated classes and foreigners. It is estimated that some 2-3 million people—around 25 percent of Cambodia's population—died as a result of Pol Pot's gruesome policies. Piles of bleached skulls and mass graves in the killing fields became the hallmarks of Khmer Rouge excesses. Pol Pot is thought to have committed suicide in 1998.

As a result of the Khmer Rouge period, Cambodia's population is still 90 percent rural, but tourism now brings in some foreign exchange as the country strives to rebuild itself. Many people still live below the poverty line.

Indonesia

P&T Lands was nationalized under President Sukarno in 1957. The holding company, Anglo-Dutch Plantations Ltd, became Anglo-Indonesian Corporation PLC.

Because Indonesia has many regional languages, Bahasa Melayu (a simplified form of Malay) was adopted after independence as a sort of pidgin national language at the urging of President Sukarno. Many Indonesians are scornful of it.

After easing Sukarno out as president, General Suharto went on to serve as Indonesia's president for some 31 years (1967-1998) in a regime said to be tainted by cronyism and nepotism. Known in the press as The Smiling General, behind the smile was a person of inscrutable character.

The biggest challenge for Indonesia is to govern and manage its vast collection of islands large and small, while seeking to build a trustworthy identity on the international stage (and the same could be said for the Philippines).

A recent president of Indonesia was none other than a daughter of Indonesia's first president Sukarno, Ms Megawati Sukarnoputri.

Indonesia plans to construct a purpose-built national capital on Kalimantan in the island of Borneo, thereby abandoning the congested former Dutch capital of Batavia/Jakarta on Java.

The Philippines

Before WWII, the Philippines held the coveted position of the second highest per-capita income in East Asia, after Japan. The economy grew steadily through its Spanish colonial days and through the American occupation after the Spanish-American war. By 1935, Manila was one of the most-visited cities in the entire world.

When Japan occupied the Philippines from 1942-45, the economy took a steep dive and inflation was rampant, as happened in the other occupied former colonies, but the Philippines were further devastated by the month-long Japanese defense of Manila in early 1945 that practically destroyed the famous city, and by several postwar natural disasters. Nevertheless, other ex-colonies have somehow managed to deal with their recoveries more successfully than the Philippines, which in theory should have climbed back into a top tier because it no longer had to fight for its postwar independence, and because of the widely-spoken English language of its inhabitants at a time when English was becoming the dominant business language of the postwar era.

It has always been a mystery that this resurgence did not happen, but the main reason seems to have been an erratic pendulum-like succession of populist leadership, cronyism, dictatorship, and occasional martial law that tended to bankrupt the government, somewhat like the situation of Venezuela at the present time. In recent years, Filipino leadership has been more responsible—perhaps overly so on occasion—and we wish for the Republic a return to its bright future once again.

Taiwan

Facing an uncertain future because of China's determination to absorb it, and its own fervent desire for national independence, Taiwan is seen by some as a mere remnant of the Chinese civil war, but by others as a highly successful experiment in non-communist government. Its people are hard-working, creative, and quite well-off by regional standards.

Taiwan was the most successful of the four Asian tigers in the outsourcing days, before China stepped in and took over that role, and has spawned several world-class companies. Much of its admirable work ethic is perhaps the result of being occupied by Japan for 50 years. When it was handed over to Nationalist China at the end of WWII, Taiwan was far ahead of China in terms of economic development and public education. Arrival of the Nationalists rankled the local business community and spawned some serious attempts at independence from China by the populace, that were cruelly suppressed by the KMT.

The island of Taiwan—as the rump territory of the Republic of China (ROC) that lost the civil war to the Peoples' Republic of China (PRC) in 1949—was still recognized by the US until 1979 as the only legitimate government of all China, a rather preposterous viewpoint. But bowing finally to pragmatism at a quiet ceremony in Taipei on 1 January 1979, the US officially derecognized the ROC and established diplomatic relations with the PRC in Beijing. Former US consular duties in Taipei were taken over by a quasi-official entity called AIT (the American Institute in Taiwan), under an ambassador-level director.

Despite derecognition, business ties remain strong between the US and Taiwan, and the US has pledged military support to Taiwan in the event of a forced takeover by the PRC. It remains to be seen what the longer-term status of Taiwan will become—an alliance of some sort with the PRC or full and secure independence as a sovereign nation. Meanwhile its several world-class companies lead the way in bringing prosperity to its well-educated population.

The Koreas

It is sad to think of a country being angrily divided like North and South Korea, which share a common spoken and written language and many other hallmarks of their former centuries of shared culture. After 35 years as a Japanese colony, a divided Korea came about because of the Cold War that followed on the heels of WWII, which also brought about divisions in other countries, notably Germany. The other divisions have since been healed and there have been several attempts to reunite the Koreas, the most brutal being the Korean War of 1950-53 where each side's sponsor—the USSR and the US—strove unsuccessfully in turn for a military solution to unify the Peninsula.

The two halves have persisted in their mutual scorn and hatred of each other's ideology, with the North being ruled by the third generation of a Kim family originally trained in Russia, and the South by a conservative democracy carefully monitored by a rabidly anti-communist United States. Because the Korean war did not bring about a formal peace treaty, the ongoing relationship remains a suspended stalemate. The US has maintained a 30,000-strong garrison in South Korea ever since the 1953 armistice, to ensure that the stalemate does not erupt once again.

South Korea was sufficiently advanced technologically to become one of the four Asian tigers in the 1980s, and brought several world-class companies onto the international stage, such as Samsung and Hyundai, whereas North Korea, shrouded in secrecy, seems to have concentrated its technology into a quest for nuclear weapons, with which its neighbors remain threatened. Reconciliation seems farther off than ever, but the world lives in hope that it will one day happen by peaceful means. There were recent signs of this possibility at the 2018 Winter Olympics games in Pyeongchang, and perhaps even with the 2018 Trump-Kim summit.

END NOTES

Fictional Characters (in order of appearance)
Municipal Engineer in British Singapore Peter Perry, Wendy Perry his wife, and John Perry their son.

Former Singapore Engineer Alan Rees in Soebang, Java, and Margaret Rees, Alan's wife.

Singapore-trained Dutch water engineer Ronald van Noorden, his wife Corrie, and their son Bart.

RAF Squadron Leader JJ Howell and his wife Janice.

Cochinese schoolboy Thao in Annam, and his namesake Thao in Saigon.

French monks André and Georges in Annam.

Sr. IJA Lieutenant Tanamoto (Moto).

Jr. IJA Lieutenant Yamamura (Mura).

Jr. IJA Lieutenant Uekuchi (Kuchi).

French friar Bernard in Saigon, Cochin-China.

Vichy French representative in Saigon, François Bouvé.

Indo family Paul, Iris and Stephanie Meijer in Java.

Police Captain and former monk André Séguin and his Cambodian wife Duong Mey in Saigon.

Sister Tien and brother Huy, adopted Séguin servants in Saigon.

Police Lieutenant Louis de Lourier, assistant to Séguin.

Superintendent Perrier, head of the postwar French colonial police in Cochin-China.

George Bolnar, a retired US Marine from China.

Angela Adonis, a presidential secretary in Manila.

María Beltrán, Angela's widowed mother.

The Rev. José Ramos Padilla SJ, Jesuit priest and Spanish-American War veteran in Manila.

Byron and Barron Spencer, American journalists in Jakarta.

Hu An-Dong, a Hakka youth from Taiwan who became a Japanese major and an American major general.

Sister Pak Na-Yeong and brother Pak Him-Chan, rural Korean twins.

Verisimilitude

All other named characters are historical, to whom various words or actions may have been attributed by the author with the utmost respect, to enliven and dramatize their known public personae.

References

The more important historical people, ships, and events are listed alphabetically in the **End Notes**, which also contain a bibliography and other relevant information for those who might wish to explore the histories in greater detail.

Orthography

US spelling is used in these stories, for English text. Please see technical notes in the Postscript regarding such details.

Font Styles

The main body of text—including expressions of thought and speech—is printed in 12-point Times New Roman font. Thoughts expressed by individual persons are *italicized, without quotation marks*, whereas their spoken words are "printed with quotation marks" and not italicized.

Oriental Names

Romanized names of Japanese and Chinese individuals are written, like their *Kanji/Hanzi* equivalents, with surnames first. This is true of some Vietnamese and Korean names also.

ABBREVIATIONS

AVG–American Volunteer Group (Flying Tigers)

CIA–Central Intelligence Agency

HMS–His Majesty's Ship

HMAS–His Majesty's Australian Ship

HNLMS–Her Netherland Majesty's Ship

ICP–Indochina Communist Party

IJA–Imperial Japanese Army (a.k.a. IVA)

IJN–Imperial Japanese Navy

KMT–Kuomintang (Kuo Min Tang) Nationalist Party founded in China by Sun Yat-Sen in 1912 and led by Chiang Kai-Shek from 1925

KNIL–(*Koninklijk Nederlandsch Indisch Leger*) Royal Netherlands Indies Army

LST–Landing Ship, Tank

NEI–Netherlands East Indies (a.k.a. Dutch East Indies)

OSS–Office of Strategic Services, forerunner of the CIA (q.v.)

PA–Philippine-American (troops)

PKI– (*Partai Komunis Indonesia*) Indonesian Communist Party

POW–Prisoner of War (or perhaps HMS *Prince of Wales*)

PRC–The Peoples Republic of (Communist) China

ROC–The (Nationalist) Republic of China

SNLF–Special Naval Landing Forces (i.e. Japanese Marines)

UDT–Underwater Demolition Team

US–The United States of America

USA–United States Army

USAAC–United States Army Air Corps

USCG–United States Coast Guard

USMC–United States Marine Corps

USN–United States Navy

USS–United States Ship

USV–United Stated Volunteers (in the Philippines 1899-1901)

VOC– (*Vereenigde Oost-Indische Compagnie*) Privately-held Dutch East India Company

SOME OLD AND NEW NAMES

In Act One, the spelling of local place names follows the prewar system, shown below in the left-hand column and on a map in the beginning of the book. Modern equivalents are shown to the right, as used in Act Two, and on a map at the end of the book.

Acheh (Atjeh)	Aceh (all pron. "ah-cheh")
Bandoeng	Bandung
Batavia (Djakarta)	Jakarta
British North Borneo	Sabah, East Malaysia
Burma	Myanmar
Cambodia	Kampuchea
Celebes	Sulawesi
Djogdjakarta	Yogyakarta
Dutch East Indies	Indonesia
Dutch Borneo	Kalimantan
Dutch New Guinea	Papua
Formosa	Taiwan
Hollandia	Jaya Pura
Jesselton (N. Borneo)	Kota Kinabalu (Sabah, E. Malaysia)
Lourenço Marques	Maputo
Malaya	Malaysia
Malacca	Melaka
New Guinea	Irian Jaya
Pladjoe	Plaju, a suburb of Palembang, Sumatra
Siam	Thailand
Soebang	Subang

Soenda	Sunda
Soerabaja	Surabaya
Tjilatjap	Cilacap (both pron. "chill-a-chap")
Tjiater Pass	Ciater Pass ('Ci' as in Italian 'ciao')

GLOSSARY OF HISTORICAL PEOPLE, PLACES AND EVENTS

A

Aguinaldo, Emilio (1869-1964), Filipino revolutionary and self-declared first president

Anglo-Dutch Plantations, British holding company for P&T Lands

B

Bandoeng, important city in the mountains of Central Java

Bao Dai, puppet-Emperor of French Indochina

Batavia, Dutch East Indies colonial capital (see also Djakarta/Jakarta)

Bennett, Gordon, Lt-Gen Royal Australian Army in Singapore

Borobudur, large ancient Buddhist temple on Java, restored by Sir Stamford Raffles during his tenure as Lt Governor

Brooke-Popham, Robert, RAF Air Chief Marshal, Singapore

Buckner, Simon Bolivar, Lt. General USA, Okinawa Campaign

C

Camp O'Donnell, terminus of the Bataan Death March

Chennault, Claire, BG USAAC, founded the "Flying Tigers" in China

Chiang Kai-Shek (Jiang Jie-Shi in Mandarin - 蒋介石), President of Nationalist China in WWII, then solely on the island of Taiwan

Churchill, Sir Winston, British Prime Minister in WWII

Cogny, René. French Maj-General in charge of actions against the Viet Minh in Tonkin Province of postwar Indochina

D

De Castries, Christian, French Colonel captured by Viet Minh at Dien Bien Phu, bringing about the defeat of French forces

Decoux, Jean, Admiral of French Pacific fleet and Vichy French Governor-General of Indochina under Japanese supervision

Dewey, George, US 6-star 'Admiral of the Navy' after 59 years of service

Djakarta, Dutch spelling of Jakarta, capital of Indonesia

F

Fearey, Robert A., prewar secretary to US Ambassador Grew (q.v.)

Free French, the French government in exile and in opposition to the pro-German Vichy French government France

Friang, Brigitte, correspondent embedded at Dien Bien Phu

Force Z, RN designation for HMS *Prince of Wales* and *Repulse*

Funston, Frederick, MGEN USA, defeated Emilio Aguinaldo in the Philippines

G

Geiger, Roy, Maj. General USMC, Okinawa Campaign

Gibson, James Coe, member of the 20th Kansas Volunteers in the Philippines

Great War (The), later called World War One (WWI)

Greene, Francis, Brig. Gen. in the Philippine War

Grew, Joseph, prewar US ambassador to Japan

H

Halsey, William, Admiral USN, Third Fleet

Hanoi (Ha Noi), capital city of Tonkin Province, French Indochina

Hart, Thomas C., Admiral USN; Philippines and Java

Hatta, Mohammed, Indonesian Prime Minister and VP under Sukarno

Heenan, Patrick, alleged British turncoat in Singapore

Hirohito, *Showa* Emperor of Japan from 1926 to 1989

Ho Chi Minh (胡志明), Indochina's independence leader

Hofland, Peter William, Dutch developer of P&T Lands in Java

Homma, Masaharu (本間雅晴), Lt-General IJA Philippine campaign

Houston, USS, (CA-30) heavy cruiser sunk off Java

Hukbalahap (aka "Huks"), Filipino Communist Guerrillas

Hull, Cordell, US Secretary of State under FDR

I

Iida, Shojiro (飯田祥二郎), Lt-General IJA, 15th Army, Burma

Itagaki, Seishiro (板垣征四郎) General IJA, hanged for war crimes in 1948

Iwabuchi, Sanji (岩淵三次), Rear Admiral IJN, unauthorized defender
    of Manila against US troops in 1945, causing destruction of the city

J

Jackson, Charles, English pre-and post-war MD of P&T Lands

Jackson, Daphne, author-wife of Charles Jackson (*Java Nightmare*)

Jakarta, Indonesian port capital, located in West Java

Jansen, Sister Catharina, nurse at Soebang Hospital prior to her death at
    the hands of Japanese troops

Jones, Howard Palfrey, US Ambassador to Indonesia 1958-65.

K

Kalidjati Airfield near Soebang, strategic Dutch air base on Java

Kawaguchi, Kiyotake (川口清健) Major-General IJA 35th Infantry Brigade
    in British Borneo, Cebu and Guadalcanal

Kinkaid, Thomas, Admiral USN, Seventh Fleet (a.k.a. MacArthur's
    Admiral)

Kondo, Nobutake (近藤信竹), Admiral IJN, Solomon Islands

Konoye, Fumimaro (近衛 文麿), prewar Prime Minister of Japan

Kuching, capital city of Sarawak, Borneo

Kuribayashi, Tadamichi (栗林忠道), General IJA, Iwo Jima

Kurita, Takeo (栗田健男), Vice Admiral IJN, Battle of Leyte Gulf

L

Langlais, Pierre, Lt-Col. of French paratroops at Dien Bien Phu

Leach, John C., Captain of HMS *Prince of Wales*

Leach, Midshipman Henry, later Fleet Admiral Sir Henry Leach

Lee Kwan Yew (李光耀), first Prime Minister of Singapore.

Lembang, popular hill station in West Java, used by ABDA Command as temporary headquarters

Lourenço Marques, Mozambique. Southeast African city where diplomats and others were exchanged for repatriation in 1942

M

Mao Tse-Tung (Mao Zedong, 毛泽东), Chairman of the People's Republic of China that defeated the Nationalists in 1949

Matsui, Takuo (松井太久郎) IJA 5th Div. Malaya/Singapore

Miki, Kiyoshi (三木清) Japanese philosopher whose concept of *The Greater East Asian Co-Prosperity Sphere* was co-opted by militarists to justify their aggression in SE Asia

Minto, 1st Earl of, Governor-General of India (Sir Gilbert Elliot)

Mitscher, Marc, Admiral USN, TF58 Fast Carriers in the Pacific

McCain, John, Admiral USN, TF38 Fast Carriers in the Pacific

N

Navarre, Henri, French general in Indochina

NEI (Netherlands East Indies, aka Dutch East Indies), colonial government that replaced the VOC after Napoleon's defeat

Nomura, Kichisaburo (野村吉三郎), Japanese Admiral and prewar ambassador to the United States

Norodom Sihanouk, King of Cambodia 1941-55 and 1993-2004

O

Ozawa, Jisaburo (小沢 治三郎), Vice Admiral IJN, Leyte Gulf

P

P&T Lands (Dutch: *Pamanoekan en Tjassemlanden*), plantation holdings created by Stamford Raffles when Lt-Governor of Java

Palliser, Arthur, Rear Admiral RN, Chief of Staff to Admiral Phillips

Percival, Arthur E., Lt. Gen. surrendered Singapore in 1942

Phillips, Thomas, Vice Admiral RN, died aboard HMS *Prince of Wales*

Pol Pot (real name Saloth Sâr), Cambodian Communist revolutionary and politician who brutally decimated his country's population.

R

Raffles, Sir Stamford, founder of Singapore

Rawlings, Sir Bernard, Vice Admiral RN, TF78 at Okinawa

Rix Dollar, a pan-European currency used in Dutch colonies, similar idea as today's Euro currency (€)

Rooks, Albert H., Captain USN, awarded the Medal of Honor (post.) for actions with USS *Houston* in the Java Sea

Roosevelt, Franklin Delano, President of the United States during most of WWII, commonly referred to as FDR

Roxas, Manuel A., first Philippine president after independence

S

Saigon, capital city of Cochin-China Province, Indochina

Sakaguchi, Shizuo (坂口静夫), Maj. Gen. IJA, Dutch Borneo

SARFOR (Sarawak Forces) in British Borneo:

Second World War (The), also called World War Two or WWII

Shoji, Toshishige (東海林), Col. IJA 230th Reg. at Soebang, Java

Showa era, period of Japanese history corresponding to the reign of the Emperor Hirohito from December 25, 1926 until his death in 1989

Singapore, principal city of the Straits Settlements crown colony, later an independent republic

Singora, port city on the Kra Peninsula of Siam

Soerabaja (Surabaya), major Dutch naval base on NE Java

Soong Mei-Ling, Wellesley College-educated wife of Chiang Kai-Shek

Sprague, Clifton, Rear Admiral USN, Battle of Leyte Gulf

Spruance, Raymond, Admiral USN, Fifth Fleet

Subhas Chandra Bose, INA leader in opposition to the Allies

Suga, Tatsuji (菅辰次), Lt- Col. in charge of Borneo POW camps

Suharto, General, Indonesia's second president

Sukarno, Indonesia's independence leader and first president

T

Temasek, ancient name for Singapore

Thomas, Sir Shenton, prewar Governor of Singapore

Tojo, Hideki (東條英機), IJA General and Prime Minister of Japan through most of WWII

Tsuchihashi, Yuitsu (土橋勇逸), Lt. General commanding 48th Infantry Division's Eastern Invasion Force on Java

Tsuji, Masanobu (辻政信), Colonel IJA, elusive master planner for the Japanese conquest of SE Asia

Turner, Richmond Kelly, Vice Admiral USN, Amphibious Forces

Ushijima, Mitsuro (牛島満), General IJA, defender of Okinawa

V

Vichy, France. Seat of pro-German provincial government during most of WWII, headed by Marshal Phillipe Pétain

Vo Nguyen Giap, acclaimed Viet Minh military leader

W

Wainwright, Jonathan M., Lt. Gen. surrendered Philippines in 1942

Y

Yamamoto, Isoroku (山本五十六), IJN Marshal Admiral of the Japanese combined fleet

Yamashita, Tomoyuki (山下奉文), IJA Commanding General, Pacific Theater, known as "The Tiger of Malaya"

BIBLIOGRAPHY–
FURTHER READING

BORNEO–KALIMANTAN

The White Rajahs of Sarawak, Bob Reece, 2004: a history of the Brooke family in Borneo.

CHINA

Empire of the Sun, J. G. Ballard, 1984: memoir-novel about the fall of Shanghai.

China Calling, Alex MacKinnon & Barnaby Powell, 2008: Understanding China's worldwide strategic investments.

DUTCH EAST INDIES–INDONESIA

A Short History of Indonesia, Colin Brown, 2003: from an Australian textbook series.

Being "Dutch" in the Indies, U. Bosma & R. Raben, trans. by Wendie Shaffer, 2008: a history of creolisation and empire, 1500-1920.

Four Years till Tomorrow, Sheri Trompe, 1999: gruesome memoirs about wartime Dutch East Indies.

Indonesia: The Possible Dream; Howard Palfrey Jones, 1971: a US ambassador's view of the Sukarno-era turmoil.

Java Nightmare, Daphne Jackson, 1979: British and Dutch staff of P&T Lands interned in Japanese camps.

Subversion as a Foreign Policy, Audrey and George Kahin, 1995: the secret Eisenhower and Dulles debacle in Indonesia.

The End of an Era, Louis Pauselius, undated: self-published memoir-novel of the Japanese occupation and the Indonesian fight for independence.

The Loss of Java, P. C. Boer, 2011: final battles for the possession of Java.

The "P. & T." Lands, Wilfred Hicks Daukes, 1943: estates owned by the Anglo-Dutch Plantations of Java, Ltd. [and an early success with matrix management].

The Story of Dr. Wassell, James Hilton, 1943: Navy doctor saves the lives of wounded American sailors.

The Year of Living Dangerously, Christopher Koch, 1978: Turmoil in Indonesia during a 1965 attempted coup.

White Coolies, Betty Jeffrey, 1955: escaping Australian Army nurses murdered en route to Sumatra.

Women Beyond the Wire, Lavinia Warner & John Sandilands, 1982: British escapees from Malaya imprisoned in Sumatra.

INDOCHINA–VIETNAM

Bernard Fall, Dorothy Fall, 2006: a biography of Fall and his widow's memoir.

Hell in a Very Small Place, Bernard B. Fall, 1966: the siege of Dien Bien Phu.

The French Indochina War 1946-54, Martin Windrow, 1998: a pictorial overview.

Victory at Any Cost, Cecil B. Currey, 1997: the genius of Viet Nam's Gen. Vo Nguyen Giap.

INDOCHINA—CAMBODIA

Golden Bones, Sichan Siv, 2009: A Journey from Hell in Cambodia to New Life in America.

JAPAN

The Chrysanthemum Throne, Gary Van Haas, 2011: a novel depicting Emperor Hirohito's lifelong friendship with a fictional adopted companion.

The Tide at Sunrise, D&P Warner, 1974: a history of the Russo-Japanese War 1904-1905.

Accused American War Criminal, Fiske Hanley II, 2016: downed US aviator imprisoned in Tokyo by the Kempei Tai.

MALAYA—MALAYSIA

Moon Over Malaya, Jonathan Moffat and Audrey Holmes McCormick, 2014: British troops battle the Japanese invaders.

PHILIPPINES

A Different Kind of Victory, James Leutze, 1981: a biography of Admiral Thomas C. Hart.

As Good as Dead, Stephen L. Moore, 2016: the daring escape of American POWs from a Japanese death camp.

Indestructible, John R. Bruning, 2017, the amazing "Pappy" Gunn helps turn the tide against Japan.

SINGAPORE

From Third World to First, Lee Kwan Yew, 2000: the Singapore Story 1965-2000.

Hostages to Fortune, Arthur Nicholson, 2005: the loss of HMS *Prince of Wales* and *Repulse.*

Merdeka and Much More, K. G. Tregonning, 2010: reminiscences of a Raffles professor 1953-67.

Odd Man Out, Peter Elphick and Michael Smith, 1994: the story of Singapore traitor Patrick Heenan.

Singapore to Freedom, Oswald W. Gilmour, 1943: an engineer's last-minute escape from the Japanese invaders.

Singapore's Dunkirk, Geoffrey Brooke, 1989: a collection of escapee stories, mostly tragic.

Spotlight on Singapore, Denis Russell-Roberts, 1965: a senior British officer's tribute to the men and women who were there.

The Art of Charlie Chan Hock Chye, compiled by Sonny Liew, 2016: amusing comic strip account Singapore's independence struggle.

The Heroes, Ronald McKie, 1960: daring Australian commandos captured and executed in Singapore.

The Singapore Grip, J. G. Farrell, 1978: historical novel describing life in Singapore, and the reasons for its loss to the Japanese.

To the Kwai—and Back, Ronald Searle, 1986: a POW's war drawings 1939-1945.

Tōbō - One Woman's Escape, Jane Tierney, 1985, an escape from the Japanese in Singapore, Sumatra, and Java.

With Freedom to Singapore, Oswald W. Gilmour, 1950: the belated post-war reoccupation of Singapore.

GENERAL

Dornier Wal—a Light Coming over the Sea, Michiel van der Mey, 2005: European seaplanes of the 1920s.

Heritage and Memory of War, Gilly Carr and Keir Reeves, 2015: a study of lingering war memories on small islands.

Paradise in Ruins, Antwyn Price, 2019: A Novel (view) of the Pacific War.

The 40s, The New Yorker, 2014: the story of a decade.

The Rising Sun, John Toland, 1970 (2 volumes): the decline and fall of the Japanese Empire 1936-1945.

Pan Am at War, Mark Cotta Vaz and John H. Hill, 2019: how the airline secretly helped America fight WWII.

SOME MOVIES WITH COLONIAL VENUES

INDOCHINA–VIETNAM

Indochine, 1992 for 1930, Catherine Deneuve, French with English subtitles.

The Quiet American, 2002 for 1952, Michael Caine, English.

JAVA–INDONESIA

The Year of Living Dangerously, 1982 for 1965, Mel Gibson, English.

MALAYA–MALAYSIA

A Town Like Alice, 1956 for 1942, Virginia McKenna, English.

SIAM–THAILAND

The Bridge on the River Kwai, 1957 for 1944, William Holden, Alec Guinness, English.

SINGAPORE

Tenko, 1984 for 1942, Ann Bell et al, English.

The Virgin Soldiers, 1969 for 1950, Lynn Redgrave, English.

A HISTORICAL REFERENCE

Overview of the Pacific War Battles

When Japan surprised the world with its audacious attack upon **Pearl Harbor** in Hawaii, the Allied Nations that would oppose and eventually defeat Japan were almost completely unprepared to wage a massive conflict in the Pacific Theater, struggling as they had already been in Europe and Africa against the professional armies of Nazi Germany and its ally Italy for the prior two years.

Concurrent with the Pearl Harbor attack in December 1941 Japan assaulted **Wake Island**, a former Pan Am refueling stopover west of Hawaii that was in the process of being provided with defenses by a civilian engineering group, guarded by a party of Marines. The first Japanese attempt to invade Wake was successfully repulsed by Marine aircraft and gunnery but a second invasion succeeded three weeks later, and the surviving US personnel were taken into captivity.

Following the further loss of British, Dutch, and American colonies **Singapore, Malaya, Java, and the Philippines** in February and March— as described in the first half of this book—the US carried out a surprise raid on Tokyo in April 1942 by launching 16 bombers from aircraft carrier USS *Hornet*, demonstrating to Japan that its home islands were vulnerable to US retaliation. This **Doolittle Raid** (named for its leader Lt. Colonel James "Jimmy" Doolittle USAAF) was a much-needed morale-booster for the US and Allies, and the alarm that it generated in Japan led to Admiral Yamamoto's hasty decision to engage the US fleet, which eventually resulted in a serious loss for Japan.

Meanwhile in May 1942 Japan attempted to invade Port Moresby in southern New Guinea, but its invasion fleet was intercepted by US carriers *Lexington* and *Yorktown*, resulting in the **Battle of the Coral Sea**, a tactical win for Japan but a strategic win for the US despite the loss of *Lexington* and heavy damage to *Yorktown*. This battle marked the first time that US forces had been able to check a major Japanese advance, and heavy damage to Japanese fleet carriers *Shokaku* and *Zuikaku* meant that they would be unable to participate in the crucial Battle of Midway, soon to follow.

The **Battle of Midway** in June 1942, just a month later and six months after Pearl Harbor, finally marked a turning point in the Pacific War. Midway Atoll (another former Pan Am refueling base) was selected by Admiral Yamamoto for what he hoped would be a trap to destroy the US fleet carriers *Hornet* and *Enterprise*. He therefore committed his four remaining fleet carriers from the Pearl Harbor raid—*Kaga, Akagi, Hiryu* and *Soryu*—under Vice Admiral Nagumo to lead an attack on Midway, which Yamamoto would follow some 250 miles behind in his flagship *Yamato,* with a fleet of battleships to mop up US defenses after Japanese planes had put the remaining American carriers out of action.

Unbeknownst to Yamamoto, however, the Americans had managed to repair USS *Yorktown* in Hawaii—barely in time for the battle to come—and had also broken the main Japanese naval code, being aware thereby of most Japanese plans, which included a simultaneous invasion of the western Aleutian Islands off Alaska intended to keep Tokyo out of US bomber range. In the aerial battles that erupted when the fleets contacted each other near Midway, Japan lost all four fleet carriers and several other warships, while the US lost only the hastily refurbished *Yorktown* and a single destroyer.

Upon receiving the disastrous news, Admiral Yamamoto hastily withdrew his battleship fleet, and the carrier loss at Midway was kept secret from the Japanese public for the rest of the war. Midway Atoll itself was subsequently turned into a useful US submarine repair and refueling base.

In August 1942, the **Battle of Guadalcanal** began with an invasion by US Marines in the Solomon Islands to impede enemy advances toward Australia, and to capture a useful Japanese airfield under construction. In an extensive six-month land war of attrition that the First Marine Division and the Army's American Division eventually won by February 1943, both the US and Japan lost considerable naval and air resources in hellacious battles trying to reinforce and defend their troops. In fact, the US Navy lost more personnel in those peripheral naval battles than the Marines did ashore.

Guadalcanal was the other turning point in the Pacific War after Midway, becoming a springboard for further advances up the Solomon chain, leading to the eventual capture of **Bougainville** and the isolation of **Rabaul**, which was the regional Japanese command center.

The Gilbert and Marshall Island Campaign from November 1943 through February 1944 included the capture of **Makin** and **Tarawa** in the Gilbert Islands—where the Second Marine Division got stuck on Tarawa's shallow reef at neap tide and was mauled by Japanese artillery—plus **Majuro**, **Kwajalein**, and **Eniwetok** in the Marshalls. The latter campaign's purpose was to provide staging bases and large fleet anchorages in the Central Pacific for capturing the Marianas, which would put Japan within B-29 bombing range.

In February 1944 the Japanese fleet anchorage at **Truk** (Chuuk) was heavily bombed and then isolated like Rabaul, leaving many warships and cargo vessels on the bottom of the lagoon and its marooned former defenders facing starvation. *[The shallow lagoon at Truk is a favorite diving site today, with its many Japanese wrecks to explore. Ed.]*

In June 1944 the hard-fought **Mariana** and **Palau** Campaigns began, which lasted until September, a mere four months that reflected the vast improvements in Allied logistics and mobility. During this time the large islands of **Saipan**, **Guam**, and **Tinian** in the Marianas, then **Peleliu** and **Anguar** in the Palaus, were captured by Allied forces. On Saipan, Navajo Code Talkers were successful in directing naval gunnery onto Japanese positions, but a sad occurrence was the mass suicide of over a thousand Chamorro civilians, urged on by Japanese propaganda.

The **Battle of the Philippine Sea** occurred while the US Fifth Fleet was still near Saipan. A large Japanese fleet under Vice Admiral Ozawa, including three fleet carriers, sailed eastward from the Philippines intending to engage the Americans in an all-out naval battle, a recurring fantasy of the IJN. Admiral Raymond Spruance, the Fifth Fleet commander, dispatched his Fast Carrier Task Force (TF58) under Vice Admiral Marc Mitscher to engage the Japanese, whose carrier planes were augmented by land-based aircraft from Guam and Saipan. The resulting two-day engagement—the largest naval battle of WWII up to that point—became known in the press as the **Marianas Turkey Shoot** because of the disproportionately high losses suffered by Japan, amounting to over 600 carrier and land-based planes. In addition, two Japanese carriers were sunk by US submarines.

After capturing Saipan in June 1944, US Marines recovered former US possession Guam a month later, followed by Tinian. From these islands in the Mariana chain a new phase of the Pacific War would soon begin, with constant B-29 bombing raids on the Japanese homelands. That phase would eventually lead to atomic bombs and the end of the war, but the endpoint was still over a year away.

One of the bloodiest protracted island battles of this campaign, which was also a prelude to the recapture of the Philippines, was the Marine Corps attack on **Peleliu** in the Palau Islands. Japan had held those former German islands since the end of the First World War and had ample time to (illegally) fortify them with networks of caves, tunnels and underground bunkers. It took over a month and very heavy losses to secure Peleliu, a rugged natural fortress that Admiral Halsey had recommended to be bypassed.

The Battle of Leyte was the next big Allied invasion, directed impatiently by General MacArthur who had vowed to return to his beloved Philippines, to recover that US colony and liberate the prisoners that Japan had taken on Bataan and Corregidor. In late October 1944, MacArthur's Sixth Army began landing on the island of Leyte. A much-heralded press photo showed the general himself coming ashore from a landing craft with Allied staff members and Philippine President Sergio Osmeña (L, in pith helmet).

The Sixth Army made steady progress inland over the next few days, securing the provincial capital Tacloban on 21 October and some days later securing all the ports but one on Leyte's west coast. Ormoc Bay and City were still in Japanese hands, though, and it was there that General Yamashita—the "Tiger of Malaya" who had led the conquest of Malaya and Singapore—decided to bolster Leyte's defenses by bringing the 30th Infantry Division from Mindanao ashore at Ormoc Bay.

As the US Sixth Army pushed deeper into Leyte, the Japanese struck back by sea and air. After losing forty percent of their aircraft to advanced US defenses, they resorted to deadly *Kamikaze* suicide attacks on US shipping patrolling or anchored in Leyte Gulf to the east side of the island. In the first day of this gruesome new tactic, a corps of suicide pilots crashed their bomb-laden planes directly into US ships, sinking an escort carrier and damaging many other vessels.

In the complex **Naval Battle of Leyte Gulf**, the IJN had once again—as in the Philippine Sea—decided to seek a decisive encounter to destroy the US fleets that were defending the Sixth Army landings on Leyte. Their plan was to attack with three major task forces, one of which included four aircraft carriers (with very few aircraft aboard) that was to act as a decoy by drawing Admiral Halsey's Third Fleet northward, away from Leyte Gulf. Hoping the ruse would be successful, two other groups of heavy surface ships would enter the gulf from the west—both north and south of Leyte—to destroy the transports and supply vessels, and Admiral Thomas Kinkaid's Seventh Fleet that was protecting them.

The more powerful Japanese naval force of the latter two—the Central Force under Admiral Kurita—contained the largest battleships in the world, *Yamato* and a sister ship *Musashi* that had been built under tight secrecy between the world wars, featuring 18-inch guns and enormous tonnage and speed, in clear violation of international treaty agreements, but which were yet untested in battle.

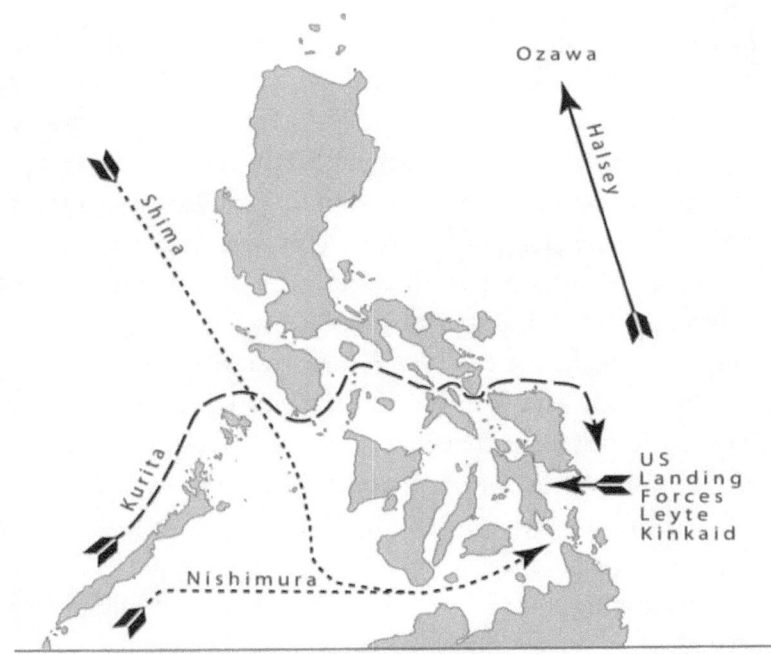

The Philippines
The Japanese plan to repel the American invasion at Leyte--Oct. 1944.

The Central Force sailed from Brunei to proceed through the San Bernardino Strait north of Leyte, intending to join the Southern Group in attacking the landing force and the US Seventh Fleet in a north-south pincer movement. What was to become the largest naval battle of World War II (and perhaps the largest in the history of mankind) opened in the **Palawan Passage** on 23 October 1944 with an attack on the Central Force by submarines USS *Darter* and *Dace*, which sank two of Kurita's heavy cruisers and crippled a third. As the remaining Central Force proceeded into the **Sibuyan Sea** it was attacked on the 24th by planes from Halsey's Third Fleet, before Halsey became aware of Ozawa's decoy Northern Force that was trying hard to attract his attention.

Halsey's carrier planes were focused on battleship *Musashi*, forcing the great ship to retire and eventually sink that evening after being struck by 17 bombs and 19 torpedoes. Although some hits were also scored on *Yamato* and others, the bulk of Kurita's force continued intact through the **San Bernardino Strait** during the night, to appear suddenly off the Island of Samar north of the US invasion force where Halsey's Third Fleet had only recently been stationed until being lured away by Ozawa's successful decoy ruse.

The Japanese Southern Force—uncoordinated due to an IJN ban on radio communication during the operation—consisted of two separate groups under Admirals Nishimura and Shima that sailed independently towards Leyte Gulf through the **Surigao Strait**. Nishimura's group was far in the lead, unbeknownst to him. Awaiting the Japanese ships was a deadly Allied blocking force of PT boats, destroyers, cruisers, and refitted battleships from Pearl Harbor, that had been sequentially positioned during the night to trap the approaching enemy.

Close to midnight the PT Boat flotilla attacked Nishimura's "First Striking Force" and gave warning to the main US defenders awaiting beyond the Surigao Strait. Although the Japanese ships successfully dodged all the PT Boat torpedoes, they suffered severe torpedo damage further on from US destroyers, which sank one of Nishimura's two battleships and three of his four destroyers.

Perhaps thinking that Shima's group was ahead and might need his assistance, Nishimura continued to press onward with his remaining battleship *Yamashiro*, cruiser *Mogami,* and destroyer *Shigure*, of which only *Shigure* would survive to retreat to Brunei (and be sunk later by an American submarine). Unlucky Admiral Nishimura succumbed to the Seventh Fleet and went to his watery grave with battleship *Yamashiro*.

Vice Admiral Shima's "Second Striking Force," trailing 35 miles behind the unfortunate Nishimura, lost a light cruiser to the PT squadron and then, upon encountering the tattered remains of Nishimura's force, Shima ordered a retreat. Although spared for the moment, his escaping ships would all be sunk in later engagements around Leyte.

The Southern Force pincer movement therefore failed, but Kurita's Central Force was moving well into position during the early morning hours, thanks to Ozawa's Northern Force—the decoy force of four carriers and their escorts—having finally been noticed by US Third Fleet scout planes. Halsey had taken the bait and charged northward with the entire Third Fleet to engage what he presumed to be the main Japanese force with its four large carriers. In so doing he consciously left the San Bernardino Strait unguarded, having decided there was no need to even order his battleship group TF-34 to remain behind. After his planes sank *Musashi* the previous day, Halsey perhaps assumed that Kurita's Central Force had turned back or was no longer a threat, but this controversial decision was to dog him for the rest of his career.

Admiral Kurita with his Central Force was consequently able to surprise elements of the Seventh Fleet south of Samar, proceeding to do battle before dawn on the 25th in what became known as **The Battle off Samar**. Despite losses in the Palawan Passage and Sibuyan Sea actions, the Japanese Central Force was still very powerful, consisting of the giant *Yamato* and three other battleships, six heavy cruisers, two light cruisers, and eleven destroyers.

Never imagining that Halsey would take his six battleships and their escorts along with him to attack Ozawa's carriers and expose the Seventh Fleet's flank, Admiral Kinkaid continued to focus his main battle strength south of Leyte Gulf to block the Japanese Southern Force, which he was doing admirably. Thus, in the path of the Central Force that steamed southward towards Leyte Gulf from Samar, were only the Seventh Fleet's collection of sixteen slow, unarmored escort carriers (CVE) and a few lightly-armed destroyers (DD) and destroyer escorts (DE), organized into three Task Units for protecting the landing craft from air and submarine attack, not for doing battle with capital ships.

The nearest of those Task Units to Kurita's looming Central Force was Rear Admiral Clifton Sprague's TF77.4.4, with six escort carriers and a few DDs and DEs. Upon sighting the enemy fleet on radar, Sprague coolly directed the little carriers to launch their planes and then run for the cover of a rain squall to the east and had his DDs and DEs make a smokescreen to conceal the retreating carriers. While responding with smoke, the destroyers, on their own initiative, charged into the enemy fleet to launch a spread of torpedoes, which caused the Japanese fleet to break formation to avoid the torps. Meanwhile each US escort carrier gamely fired its sole 5-inch gun at Kurita's ships while launching their planes.

In the darkness with poor-quality radar, and unaware—because of the IJN radio silence edict—that Ozawa had succeeded in drawing Halsey's carriers away, Kurita assumed he had encountered a powerful Third Fleet carrier group, and abruptly ordered his ships to take independent action in combatting the presumed threat.

During the ensuing chaos as the heroic US destroyers attacked aggressively with torpedoes, 5-inch 'popguns,' and fanatical determination, they were inevitably sunk one by one by Kurita's heavier guns, but soon the other two US Task Units dispatched their aircraft to attack the Central Force with whatever weapons they had available, and collectively the sixteen escort carriers managed to get 450 planes into the air. Being without air cover itself, the Central Fleet was highly vulnerable to American planes, having only antiaircraft fire for protection. The ferocity of the US defense seemingly confirmed to Kurita that he was engaging major fleet units instead of mere escorts, so he ordered his ships to regroup and withdraw, thereby losing the opportunity to destroy the shipping in Leyte Gulf.

Being still unaware of the **Battle off Samar**, Halsey—who had finally managed to catch up with Ozawa's decoy fleet and was engaging it off **Cape Engaño**—suddenly received an emergency message from the Seventh Fleet asking for urgent and immediate help for its escort carriers. He also received a terse inquiry from Admiral Nimitz in Hawaii, who had been monitoring the radio traffic during the various phases of the Leyte Gulf actions. Enraged by the supposed criticism, Halsey seemed to lose his self-control before finally turning his Third Fleet around to the south. His aircraft and battleships arrived too late to engage the retreating Central Force, catching only a rear-guard destroyer as the rest of Kurita's fleet disappeared back through the San Bernardino Strait to Brunei, thereby ending the **Battle of Leyte Gulf**. Having failed to stop the Allied invasion by naval action, the Japanese then launched their 'Special Attack Force' of *kamikaze* suicide attacks by land-based planes against the Allied troop transports in Leyte Gulf and the escort carrier units off Samar, sinking several ships.

The Battle of Iwo Jima was the next major event in the Pacific Theater, taking place in February and March 1945 while MacArthur's Sixth Army liberated other islands of the Philippines, and Army Rangers made lightning raids upon known Japanese POW camps to free emaciated US prisoners before they were summarily executed.

Iwo Jima is part of a volcanic island chain roughly halfway between the Marianas and the Japanese home islands. B-29 Super Fortresses flying unescorted over Japan from Saipan and Tinian in the Marianas were sustaining high rates of damage from antiaircraft and fighter defenses as they bombed the major Japanese cities. These long-range planes needed a support base within fighter escort range of Japan, that could also be used by any damaged bombers unable to reach the Marianas on their return. Iwo Jima, with its three airfields (from which Japanese planes had been continuously attacking the Marianas), provided a possible solution but it would require considerable effort to take it away from Japan.

Code-named *Operation Detachment*, the battle for Iwo Jima by 110,000 'Leathernecks' of the 3rd, 4th, and 5th Marine Divisions was supported by the US Fifth Fleet. Expected by Nimitz to require only five days to subdue it, bleak and dusty Iwo Jima had been well fortified with thousands of bunkers and caves and 11 miles of interconnecting tunnels. The battle became instead a brutal campaign of attrition, lasting over a month despite the nearly 6-to-1 numerical superiority of attackers to defenders.

Japanese defenders were skillfully commanded by IJA General Kuribayashi Tadamichi, who told his men that the battle would doubtless be fought mostly underground. He urged soldiers to each kill ten of the enemy before they died. Of some 21,000 Japanese defenders, only 213 were captured alive by the end of the campaign, and General Kuribayashi's body was never identified. There were more American casualties (killed or wounded) on Iwo Jima than Japanese, a unique circumstance in the Pacific War.

The raising of "Old Glory" on Mount Suribachi, photographed by Joe Rosenthal early in the battle, became an iconic image the world over, an inspiration for the Marine Corps War Memorial at Arlington Virginia, a tribute to the heroic Japanese defenders, and the inspiration for several highly-rated movies, especially *Flags or Our Fathers* and *Letters from Iwo Jima* by Clint Eastwood.

One other huge remaining task before the planned invasion of Japan was to capture the large island of **Okinawa** and its satellites in the Ryukyu chain, a mere 340 miles from Tokyo. Okinawa would provide the Allies with a suitable fleet anchorage, staging area, and air base for the eventual conquest of Japan. The ensuing 82-day **Battle of Okinawa** that began on 1 April and ended on 22 June 1945 was so stupendously costly and complex that war planners realized a million men would be needed for invading the home islands.

For the Okinawa invasion a special 10th Army was created, consisting of four Army and three Marine infantry divisions and a joint Army-Marine tactical air force. Referred to as 'the typhoon of steel' because of the sheer numbers of Allied ships and armored vehicles that assaulted the island, the battle was one of the bloodiest in the Pacific, with roughly 76,000 Allied and 117,000 Japanese combatants killed or wounded, including drafted Okinawans in Japanese uniforms. Nearly 150,000 Okinawan civilians were killed in addition, amounting to nearly half of the prewar population.

The supporting Central Pacific Task Forces consisted of the Fifth Fleet under Admiral Raymond Spruance, with the Fast Carrier Force TF58 under Vice Admiral Marc Mitscher and British Carrier Force TF57 under Vice Admiral Sir Bernard Rawlings.

To execute the landings at various locations around the island cluster, the Joint Expeditionary Force TF51 under Vice Admiral Richmond Kelly Turner included a plethora of landing craft and other ships such as escort carriers, UTD flotillas, gunfire support groups, fire support landing craft, and of course the attack transports, LSTs, and numerous other specialty vessels for bringing the infantry and armor ashore. There were well over a thousand ships, large and small, the biggest group being TF56 with the Tenth Army aboard under General Simon Bolivar Buckner USA. In all, the Army had over 102,000 soldiers, and there were 88,000 Marines and 18,000 Navy and Coast Guard personnel.

Japan had used *Kamikaze* suicide tactics since the Battle of Leyte Gulf but for the first time they became a major part of the defense. During the Okinawa landings of April and May there were seven major *Kamikaze* attacks on the Allied fleet, involving over 1500 planes.

The British carrier fleet TF57 was initially tasked with neutralizing airfields at other Japanese islands such as the Sakishima Islands and Formosa that might otherwise provide air support to Okinawa. Upon joining the bombardment of Okinawa afterwards, one of TF57's fleet carriers HMS *Formidable* was struck by *Kamikaze* planes, but because British carriers had armored flight decks she was out of action for less than an hour.

Japanese ground forces on Okinawa were under the command of General Ushijima Mitsuru, who directed the two and a half divisions of his 32nd Army with skill even though heavily outnumbered by Allied ground forces.

On 18 June the US Tenth Army's Commanding General Buckner was killed while monitoring the forward progress of his troops. He was temporarily replaced by Major General Roy Geiger USMC, the only Marine to ever command a numbered US Army (and the only Marine to later witness the Japanese surrender aboard USS *Missouri* in Tokyo Bay from the front-row). After the Okinawa Campaign, Geiger was replaced by Army General Joseph "Vinegar Joe" Stillwell who had been in the Burma Theater following his staff assignment with Chiang Kai-Shek in China.

Extensive use was made of civilians by the Japanese Army on Okinawa, including middle school children for front-line service, about half of whom were killed on suicide missions.

Operation *Ten-Go* was the attempted attack by a strike force of ten Japanese surface vessels led by the super battleship *Yamato*. The small task force had been ordered to fight its way through the Allied naval forces and then beach *Yamato* to use her guns as coastal artillery and her crew as naval infantry. The Japanese ships were spotted by a US submarine shortly after leaving home waters on 7 April and intercepted by more than 300 US carrier aircraft over two hours, during which *Yamato*—the world's largest battleship—exploded and sank. *Yamato* thereby followed her sister ships *Musashi* lost in the Battle of Leyte Gulf, and *Shinano* torpedoed by US submarine *Archerfish* during her conversion into the world's largest aircraft carrier in November 1944, while proceeding unescorted down the Japanese coast.

Before the Battle of Okinawa ended in late June 1945, Nazi Germany had surrendered to the Allies in May, thereby ending the war in Europe. Only brief celebrations were held by Allied forces on Okinawa, who were still battling the Japanese.

After the capture of Okinawa, the Allies continued planning **Operation Downfall**, a massive invasion of the Japanese home islands, but before that operation took place two major events rendered it unnecessary: Russia's declaration of war on Japan of 8 August with their liberation of North Korea and Manchukuo; and the US atomic bombings of Hiroshima and Nagasaki on 6 and 9 August.

Emperor Hirohito announced his country's unconditional surrender on 15 August 1945. (Above) General MacArthur signs for the United States on September 2 aboard USS *Missouri* in Tokyo Bay, witnessed by US and Allied brass. Behind him stand Lt. Generals Wainwright (foreground) and Percival, recently liberated from a Japanese POW camp in Manchuria.

EAST ASIA WIT

CHINA

MYANMAR

LAOS

HAINAN

THAILAND

VIETNAM

KAMPUCHEA

*ANDAMAN
SEA*

*GULF OF
THAILAND*

Aceh

MALAYSIA

Melaka

Sarawak

Singapore

K

SUMATRA

Plaju

INDONESIA

Sunda
Jakarta
Bandung
Cilacap

Subang
Ciater Pass
JAVA

NORTH KOREA
SOUTH KOREA
JAPAN

MAP AREA

Maputo

ODERN NAMES

TAIWAN

PHILIPPINES

Kinabalu
abah
○

CELEBES
SEA

tan

○ *Sulawesi*

Jaya Pura ○
PAPUA
○ *Irian Jaya*

ya

0	500 Miles
0	500 KM

www.ingramcontent.com/pod-product-compliance
Lightning Source LLC
Chambersburg PA
CBHW020443130626
46549CB00001B/273